INDIANAPOLIS

CROSSROADS OF THE AMERICAN DREAM

INDIANAPOLIS

CROSSROADS

OF

THE

AMERICAN

DREAM

By Senator Richard G. Lugar

Photography Editing by Craig Arive

Profiles in Excellence by Diane Raflo

Art Direction by Brian Groppe

URBAN TAPESTRY SERIES
TOWERY PUBLISHING, INC.

Sponsored by the Indianapolis Chamber of Commerce

The Capital Commons foun-
tain in Indianapolis gleefully
greets visitors to the Crossroads of America and the
heart of Indiana.

Pan American Plaza is
home to the capital city's
tourism center. Visitors to
Greater Indianapolis can
count on a refreshing welcome to this dynamic, diverse
regional community (opposite).

Library of Congress Cataloging-in-Publication Data

Lugar, Richard.

    Indianapolis: crossroads of the American dream / by Richard G.
Lugar ; photo editing by Craig Arive ; Profiles in excellence by
Diane Raflo ; art direction by Brian Groppe.

        p.   cm. — (Urban tapestry series)

    "Sponsored by the Indianapolis Chamber of Commerce."

    Includes index.

    ISBN 1-881096-27-0

    1. Indianapolis (Ind.)—Description and travel.   2. Indianapolis
(Ind.)—Pictorial works. 3. Indianapolis (Ind.)—Economic
conditions. 4. Business enterprises—Indiana—Indianapolis.
5. Industries—Indiana—Indianapolis.   I. Raflo, Diane, 1947-
II. Indianapolis Chamber of Commerce.   III. Title.   IV. Series.

F534.I34L84   1996

977.2'52—dc20   96-4853
                                                                                       CIP

Towery Publishing, Inc., 1835 Union Avenue, Memphis, TN 38104

Publisher: J. Robert Towery
Executive Publisher: Jenny McDowell
National Sales Manager: Stephen Hung
National Marketing Director: Eleanor D. Carey
Marketing Coordinator: Carol Culpepper
Project Directors: Harry Nelson, Dawn Park, Jim Tomlinson
Editorial Development: David Dawson
Senior Editor: Michael C. James
Associate Editors: Mary Jane Adams, Lori Bond, Lynn Conlee, Carlisle Hacker, Jason Vest
Editorial Intern: Jennifer Larson
Editorial Consultant: Marilyn Shank / Shank Public Relations Counselors, Inc.
Editorial Contributor: Kathleen Prata
Captions: Kim LaSalle
Profile Designer: Laurie Lewis
Technical Director: William H. Towery
Production Manager: Brenda Pattat
Production Assistant: Jeff McDonald

INDIANAPOLIS

N THE CENTER OF AN OTHERWISE BLANK SHEET OF PAPER stood a neat round dot with a meandering line running to its left. I was instructed that the dot represented Indianapolis' Monument Circle and the bending line traced the path of the south-flowing White River. My task as a Boy Scout was to locate a long list of parks, cemeteries, buildings, streets, and landmarks, making a map of the city. As a boy who seldom wandered far from his Washington Boulevard home on the north side or the family farm in Decatur Township, creating this map was my first real introduction to Indianapolis.

A PROUD HISTORY

INDIANAPOLIS HAS BEEN ADDING TO ITS PLACE ON THE MAP EVER SINCE IT abruptly became Indiana's political and geographical center in the 1820s. Within 30 years of its beginnings, the city developed a large manufacturing base and emerged as a major stockyard and railroad hub, earning the first of its many distinguished nicknames, "Crossroads of America." With visionary leadership, talented artists, and such nationally known writers as poet James Whitcomb Riley and novelist Booth Tarkington, Indianapolis closed the 19th century as a city known for progressive thinking.

Early in the 20th century, the growing city established itself as a motor capital, producing such automobiles as the Marmon, Stutz, and Duesenberg. The year 1911 marked the first Indianapolis 500, which was to become the largest single-day sporting event in the world. By World War II Indianapolis was also known as a major toolmaking capital, earning yet another moniker, "Toolmaker to the Nation."

THE SOLDIERS' AND SAILORS' MONUMENT STANDS IN THE CENTER OF MONUMENT CIRCLE IN DOWNTOWN INDIANAPOLIS.

A SPECTACULAR FIREWORKS DISPLAY PAYS HOMAGE TO THE COUNTRY'S LARGEST CIVIL WAR MONUMENT, DEDICATED TO THE COMMON SOLDIER (OPPOSITE).

INDIANAPOLIS LOVES A PARADE (PAGES 6 AND 7), AND HAS GOOD REASON TO CELEBRATE. IN ITS 1995 ECONOMIC REPORT, THE CORPORATION FOR ENTERPRISE DEVELOPMENT RANKED INDIANA FOURTH IN THE NATION IN ECONOMIC PERFORMANCE.

While I was mostly unaware of this proud history as a boy, I sensed that Indianapolis was a great metropolitan area. Then, like now, the city had wonderful performing arts, attracting many of the great names in entertainment and politics. My brother Tom and I would spend Saturdays at the Indianapolis Symphony Orchestra's concerts for children and, on many Fridays, my mother would take us to the intimate Murat Temple or the extravagant English Opera House to see such legendary performers as Jascha Heifetz, Arthur Rubinstein, Fritz Kreisler, and Sergey Rachmaninoff. When Wendell Willkie delivered his 1940 campaign speech from the balcony of the old English Hotel on Monument Circle, I was still small enough to nestle my way through the crowd to a position just below this great Hoosier presidential candidate.

Through my youthful eyes, Indianapolis and all its amenities appeared wondrous. Yet it was when I returned from Oxford University and the navy and became a member of the school board that I began to develop a sense of how unique and blessed this city is, both in its natural resources and those of the extraordinary people who have lived and served here. ➢

In the Heart of the Heartland

As the city most centrally located to the nation's top 100 markets, Indianapolis has a natural function as a transportation hub. This capacity proved crucial in the early days of the city's development and became increasingly important as new modes of transportation evolved. Today Indianapolis is intersected by seven interstate highways—more than any other city in America—and five major railroads have interconnecting routes out of the city. The bustling Indianapolis International Airport has grown into one of the busier cargo and passenger carriers in the nation.

Indianapolis is not only located in the heart of the nation, it is located in the heart of Indiana as well. This central location makes for an ideal capitol site and a natural focal point for leadership within our state. In an age when communication is increasingly important, television and radio stations broadcasting from Indianapolis reach nearly half the population of the entire state, unifying many Hoosiers in terms of the messages we hear and eventually share.

LOCATED IN THE GEOGRAPHIC CENTER OF INDIANA, INDIANAPOLIS IS THE NATION'S 12TH-LARGEST CITY AND AN ECONOMIC HUB THAT MANUFACTURES MORE THAN 1,200 PRODUCTS IN THE PHARMACEUTICAL, ELECTRONICS, METAL FABRICATION, AND TRANSPORTATION INDUSTRIES.

THE STATE CAPITOL IS THE EYE OF THE CULTURAL, ECONOMIC, AND ARTISTIC HURRICANE THAT IS INDIANAPOLIS (OPPOSITE).

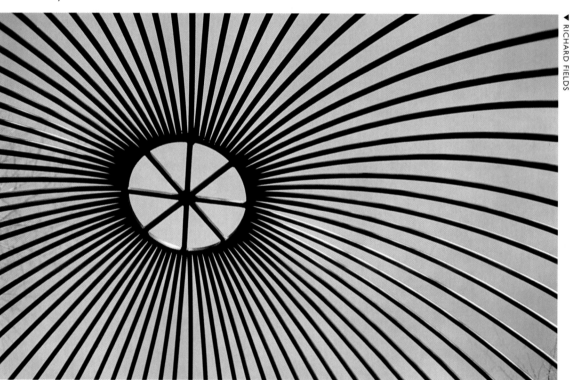

Challenging and Rewarding Times

While Indianapolis has naturally been favored with central geography, rich soil, an excellent climate, and four distinct seasons that continually bring a sense of renewal to our lives, it is a city that has had to struggle to attain its present-day status as one of the most livable places in America.

Like many other cities throughout the nation during the 1950s and 1960s, Indianapolis witnessed a decline in its industrial manufacturing base and a residential exodus to the suburbs. While the city began to battle back with economic diversification led by insurance, pharmaceuticals, and sports, many of our own citizens continued to espouse derogatory names for our city, such as "Naptown" or "Indy-No-Place." This underlying

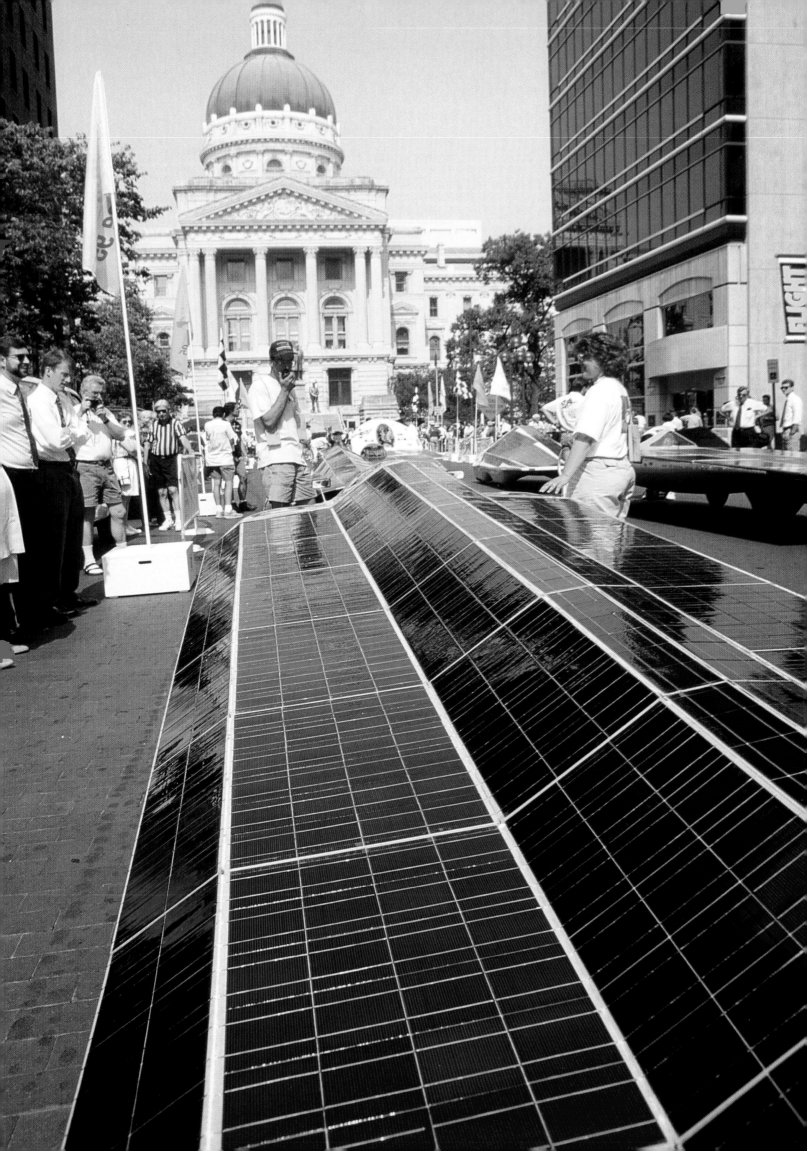

feeling of antipathy was a sign of the times in the 1960s, when great civil strife consumed the attention of many cities.

It was during this period, after having served on the school board for three years, that I decided to run for mayor in 1967. I ran on the idea that Indianapolis should be a great city and that the basic elements, under the right conditions, could be put in place to achieve this goal.

When I became mayor in 1968, I explored the concept of consolidating many of the functions of our city and county governments. The Greater Indianapolis Progress Committee produced essential studies and eventually drafted the legislation known as Unigov, short for "unified government."

Unigov required repealing all laws pertaining to Indianapolis and Marion County, and formulating an entirely new set to institute a new city. Just as I had done as a Boy Scout, a group of concerned individuals began with a blank sheet of paper and set out to chart a new map of Indianapolis, hewing a new physical landscape and a new strategic outline for our city's future.

A SUNRAYCE DRIVER CAPTURES THE SPIRIT OF A CITY KNOWN FOR ITS ABILITY TO ENGINEER PROSPERITY.

THE INDIANA STATE HOUSE (OPPOSITE) NODS ITS APPROVAL TO INDIANAPOLIS ON PARADE—A STRIKING PARTNERSHIP BETWEEN PUBLIC AND PRIVATE SECTORS.

The timing of this movement toward consolidation was particularly important, as many cities were faced with a grave danger to people and property as a result of the social upheaval in 1968. Yet, in Indianapolis, a great number of individuals with compelling vision and idealism pushed forward, determined not to live in constant civic turmoil. Civil rights groups and the League of Women Voters worked with our administration to bring about greater harmony and the possibility of social justice, while at the same time creating a powerful city, economically and governmentally.

Unigov legislation was passed by the Indiana General Assembly in 1969 and implemented in 1970. Overnight, Indianapolis leaped onto the map, growing from 84 to 388 square miles, increasing its population from 485,000 to 745,000, and nearly doubling its tax base. ➤

Unigov was to be the last great consolidation of county and large city government in the nation. The process created what is today the 12th-largest city in the United States. Unigov remains one of our city's best reasons for economic growth, continually earning Indianapolis national recognition as one of the best municipal governments in the country.

PUBLIC/PRIVATE PARTNERSHIPS

ALSO EARNING NATIONAL RECOGNITION ARE THE INNOVATIVE APPROACHES TO public/private-sector management born from the process of Unigov. These coveted public/private partnerships literally changed—and continue to change—the face of Indianapolis through sweeping renovation, building, and future planning projects.

One of the first of these revitalization and expansion projects was the creation of a dynamic urban university in the heart of an expanding city.

Butler University, with its beautiful campus nestled along the east bank of the White River and the Central Canal, had played an important role in our city since 1850. On the

▼ RICHARD FIELDS

city's south side, Indiana Central University—what is now the University of Indianapolis—had yet to grow into the comprehensive university it is today. Indianapolis was also only a short drive away from other major universities such as Indiana, Purdue, Ball State, and Indiana State. Yet there was a growing need for a major university that was not only close to downtown Indianapolis, but also an integral part of the city.

By combining the strengths of Indiana and Purdue universities, and consolidating many smaller schools scattered around the city, Indiana University-Purdue University Indianapolis (IUPUI) was created, forming what is now the third-largest institution of higher learning in Indiana, with nearly 28,000 students and 170 degree programs. The remarkable health and medical facilities, the law school, and the sports complex—which includes the world-class Indiana University Natatorium and Track and Field Stadium—

that are now part of the school are tremendous assets to Indianapolis. In a time when we understand that everyone will need several educations in life, IUPUI plays an active role in educating traditional and nontraditional students. By the 1990s almost half of IUPUI's student body was more than 25 years of age.

Public/private partnerships also were engaged to erect the $23.5 million Market Square Arena, home of the resurgent Indiana Pacers, and to revitalize the historic City Market, now a popular lunchtime destination for downtown visitors and workers. Since the 1970s nearly $4 billion in public and private funds have been invested in downtown Indianapolis, producing one of the most vibrant central business districts in the country. Citizens now enjoy the RCA Dome and Indiana Convention Center, the renovated Union Station, the Indianapolis Zoo, the Eiteljorg Museum, and several new hotels and office buildings. Another $168 million has been invested in building and renovating amateur and professional sports facilities, earning Indianapolis yet another exciting name, "Amateur Sports Capital of the World."

THE INDIANA CONVENTION CENTER AND RCA DOME, A MULTIPURPOSE SPORTS AND CONVENTION FACILITY, OFFERS A STUNNING SETTING FOR CONCERTS, CULTURAL EVENTS, AND CONVENTIONS. THE DOME HOSTS MORE THAN 2 MILLION PEOPLE EACH YEAR AND IS HOME TO THE NFL's INDIANAPOLIS COLTS (LEFT AND OPPOSITE).

EXCEPTIONAL CIVIC LEADERSHIP

EVERY CITY NEEDS SOMEONE OR SOME GROUP WHO WILL TAKE HOLD WITH A VISION for the future. Simply hoping for a better day does not produce this kind of leadership. From early in our city's history, Indianapolis has been blessed with a continuity of very strong civic institutions and generations of leaders—industrial, corporate, citizen, and elected.

Other cities have had great benefactors, but on a per capita basis, perhaps Indianapolis has been the most blessed, with great families that have taken profound pleasure in developing this city. The family responsible for starting what is now a world leader in the pharmaceutical industry—Eli Lilly and Company—also initiated a legacy of philanthropy with the Lilly Endowment Inc. The Lilly family and the endowment have supported the city and people of Indianapolis in countless ways with gifts totaling more than $1.46 billion since 1937. The Krannert Charitable Trust, established by Ellnora and Herman Krannert, paid out more than $200 million in grants during its 27-year existence, contributing not only to our skyline, but also to the arts, medicine, and education.

With other institutions such as the Indianapolis Foundation, our city's largest and oldest community foundation in which smaller gifts are pooled to bring about great change, Indianapolis will continue its long and productive philanthropic tradition.

INDIANAPOLIS TODAY

IT IS WITH GREAT PRIDE TODAY THAT I DESCRIBE INDIANAPOLIS IN DETAIL TO THOSE who have never ventured to our city. It is with even greater pride that my wife, Char, and I bring newcomers to our state and hometown.

Many of our visitors enter through the Indianapolis International Airport, a facility that has made Indianapolis a giant in the transportation and distribution industries. The

INDY'S REVITALIZED DOWNTOWN IS A BREATHTAKING BLEND OF OLD AND NEW. A MODERN SCULPTURE GRACES THE COURTYARD OF THIS HARDEE'S BUSINESS COMPLEX.

THE CANAL WALK OFFERS YESTERYEAR CHARM IN THE HEART OF DOWNTOWN'S BUSINESS DISTRICT (OPPOSITE).

airport's success can be directly attributed to the insightful, long-range planning of the Indianapolis Airport Authority, which purchased thousands of acres more than a quarter century ago for future growth and developed the facility's expansive infrastructure. Over a 15-year period, more than $1 billion was invested in the airport, which now carries some 6.5 million passengers and 596 tons of cargo annually, making it the 12th-busiest cargo airport in the United States.

I am quick to point out to my visitors the vitality of the industrial parks and aviation industry of the airport complex, which is arguably one of the greatest job generators in our state. I have to be quick, though, for as soon as we drive over the hill the eye is privy to our city's striking skyline marked by the American United Life Building, Bank One Tower, RCA Dome, and Market Square Arena—all only 12 minutes from the airport. Indianapo-

lis has outstanding architecture, and what is beautiful from a distance is even more beautiful when you are in its midst. The revitalization of the city that began in the 1970s has continued through the 1990s with one of the largest construction projects in the state's history, the spectacular new Circle Centre Mall. Opened in September 1995, Circle Centre treats visitors, convention delegates, and residents to a vast, three-city-block shopping, dining, and entertainment complex in the heart of downtown. Costing more than $300 million, the 800,000 square feet of retail space includes two anchor department stores, approximately 100 specialty shops, a multiscreen cinema, restaurants, and an eight-story glass rotunda dedicated to fine arts exhibits and performances.

Of course, Indianapolis offers more than just a dynamic downtown. There are the charming shops and restaurants of Broad Ripple Village, and the historic neighborhoods of Irvington, Fountain Square, Chatham Arch, and Lockerbie Square. Or the privacy of Eagle Creek Park, one of the largest municipally owned and operated parks in the nation, offering 4,000 acres filled with sycamore, maple, and oak trees on a reservoir. Or the Children's Museum, the world's largest museum of its kind, attracting more than 1 million

AN INTRICATE SCULPTURE WELCOMES VISITORS TO THE ATHENAEUM, HOME OF THE AMERICAN CABARET THEATER AND THE CITY'S OLDEST RESTAURANT, WHICH IS LISTED ON THE NATIONAL REGISTER OF HISTORIC PLACES.

THE ROMANESQUE ARCHITECTURE OF UNION STATION OFFERS A ROMANTIC SETTING FOR SOME OF THE CITY'S HOTTEST NIGHTCLUBS AND MORE THAN 45 SPECIALTY SHOPS (OPPOSITE).

visitors each year to exhibits that engage both the young and the young at heart.

Indianapolis is also home to many historic landmarks. Visitors enjoy touring the home of America's 23rd president, Benjamin Harrison, or taking in the 284-foot Indiana limestone Soldiers' and Sailors' Monument on Monument Circle, which doubles each December as the world's largest Christmas tree. The Madame C.J. Walker Urban Life Center, built as a tribute to America's first self-made African-American millionaire, includes an attached theater where such greats as Louis Armstrong and Lena Horne have played to thundering crowds. And of course there is the world-famous 2.5-mile track, home of the Indianapolis 500, the Brickyard 400, and the Hall of Fame Museum. ➤

On the Cusp of a New Millennium

INDIANAPOLIS' ABUNDANT NATURAL RESOURCES, EXCELLENT LOCATION, RICH tradition of service, vibrant business climate, sound government, and intangible, but real quality of Hoosier hospitality give me great confidence in saying that our city has the best potential for growth of any city in America. We have a successful track record of achievement now and great promise for the future.

As we sit on the cusp of a new millennium, this promise lies in the solid foundation that has been laid since the city's beginnings in the 1820s. Indianapolis is an ideal city for the 21st century and beyond. Unlike other cities, there is no need to keep ripping out this foundation and rebuilding, for our ways of living, investing, and managing our city have a sound and true aspect that carries with it a sense of history, tradition, and longevity.

Indianapolis has also become a mecca for young people who come here to find excellent jobs, establish careers, meet other young people, get married, and have children. They have planted roots, and that bodes well for the future of Indianapolis.

The future will surely present Indianapolis with difficult challenges along the path to

more achievements. In our increasingly shrinking world, the people of Indianapolis may be required to expand their thinking and entertain a broader, more regional type of governance that works toward the goals and dreams of all of central Indiana. We need to see a common destiny with neighboring cities and towns. If we do, I think Indianapolis is positioned to be a juggernaut of growth and optimism.

Things do change. Over the years, midcourse corrections are important. My confidence in Indianapolis is based on certainty that its citizens and leaders will have the vision to embrace our rich heritage and history, and the wisdom to create future plans vital for continuing success.

Were I again a Boy Scout starting with that blank sheet of paper with a dot in the center and the meandering line running to its left, I cannot imagine constructing a more well-balanced city than present-day Indianapolis, a city as vibrant as any in the nation.

Through my travels in the navy and as a United States senator, I have come to know this: It is neither buildings nor mountains, neither commerce nor oceans that make a city great. It is the spirit and determination of its people, who enjoy living together and who utilize the natural elements at hand to build the buildings and initiate the commerce that shapes a great city of tradition, opportunity, and hope. Such is Indianapolis. ◆

SENATOR RICHARD G. LUGAR OF INDIANA, FORMER MAYOR OF INDIANAPOLIS, DRAFTED LEGISLATION FOR UNIGOV, CONSOLIDATING THE CITY AND COUNTY GOVERNMENTS.

THE UNIGOV INITIATIVE THRUST THE CITY INTO THE FOREFRONT OF MIDWESTERN BUSINESS CENTERS (OPPOSITE).

WITH A GOOD ATTITUDE AND GREAT DEDICATION, INDIANAPOLIS' POLICE OFFICERS KEEP THE CITY SAFE AND SMILING (PAGE 24).

A PHOTOGRAPHER CAPTURES THE MOMENT AT THE START/FINISH LINE OF INDIANAPOLIS MOTOR SPEEDWAY, HOME OF THE INDIANAPOLIS 500 (PAGE 25).

PAGE 24: HAROLD LEE MILLER
PAGE 25: STEVE BAKER / HIGHLIGHT PHOTOGRAPHY

A tepee graces the grounds of the Eiteljorg Museum of American Indian and Western Art (TOP). The Festival of Turning Leaves at Old Indiana Fun Park, just outside Indianapolis, celebrates central Indiana's Native American heritage (BOTTOM).

The Eiteljorg, an unusual adobe-style museum of southwestern art, features artists such as Frederic Remington and Georgia O'Keeffe (OPPOSITE).

The Indianapolis Motor Speedway—home of the Brickyard 400 and Indianapolis 500—offers the most famous stretch of road in Indianapolis (PAGES 26 AND 27).

The Indianapolis skyline is deceptively serene (PAGES 28 AND 29). Top-ranked sports arenas, striking downtown monuments, hotels and convention facilities, and attractive economic development initiatives for expanding businesses make Indianapolis a city on the move.

PAGES 26 AND 27: STEVE BAKER / HIGHLIGHT
  PHOTOGRAPHY
PAGES 28 AND 29: RICHARD FIELDS

T HE INDIANA WAR MEMORIAL
Plaza sprawls across five
blocks, honoring soldiers killed
during World Wars I and II, as
well as the Korean and Vietnam
wars (OPPOSITE, TOP).

The beautiful ruins at Holliday
Park whisper secrets from an ancient past (OPPOSITE, BOTTOM).

THE COLUMNS THAT SOLEMNLY guard the grounds of Holliday Park are a surprise to unsuspecting visitors. Not visible from the park entrance, they offer old-world splendor and mystery to this family recreation area.

Stunningly beautiful and remarkable in detail, the Soldiers' and Sailors' Monument is the only Civil War monument in the nation dedicated to the common soldier.

The Indiana War Memorial is home to a 450-seat auditorium; a military museum containing weapons, uniforms, flags, jeeps, and a helicopter; and 24 antique stained glass windows (PAGES 36 AND 37).

An impressive array of businesses thrive in Indianapolis, supported by a skilled workforce drawn from all regions of the metropolitan area. The Pyramids, an office complex and well-known northwest landmark, attest to the progressive economic climate.

Indianapolis has roared into the '90s with development initiatives for expanding companies. Low living costs, respected colleges and universities, and ample cultural and recreational amenities strengthen the city's appeal.

BOLD AND MAGNIFICENT, MODERN Indianapolis architecture is a study in glass and steel. The Capitol Center Atrium in Circle Centre Mall nurtures nature in the heart of the city.

THE EXPANSIVE EXTERIORS OF Merchants Plaza (TOP) and the Indiana Government Center (BOTTOM) are impressive reminders of the city's determination to stride into the future.

A PATCH OF BLUE PEEKS OVER
the shoulders of Indianapolis' newest downtown shopping
venue, Circle Centre Mall.

Sᴜɴ, ꜱᴛᴇᴇʟ, ᴀɴᴅ ꜱʜᴀᴅᴏᴡ ᴄᴏᴍ-bine exquisitely beneath the Mall's glass domes.

Downtown Indianapolis is an architectural wonder that draws businesspeople, shoppers, and tourists to enjoy the urban scenery.

V ISUALLY DRAMATIC AND INNO-
vative, the glass-enclosed
rotunda of the 12,500-square-
foot Artsgarden offers a broad
range of art exhibits, concerts,
and lectures.

GIANTS
FROM THE
BONE ZONE

THE INDIANA STATE MUSEUM, which once served as Indianapolis' City Hall, features marble columns and a Tiffany-style stained glass dome (LEFT).

The museum includes five floors of exhibits and is home to a Foucault pendulum similar to the Smithsonian Institution's (RIGHT).

Tʜᴇ ᴇɴᴛʀᴀɴᴄᴇ ᴏғ Cʜɪʟᴅʀᴇɴ's Museum features a fascinating timepiece that literally tallies the minutes in the fluid movements of its pendulum (ʟᴇFᴛ).

The museum is the largest facility of its kind in the world, offering five stories of interactive exhibits (ʀɪɢʜᴛ).

THE INDIANAPOLIS-MARION
County Public Library operates more than 20 branches throughout the county. The Children's Learning Center in Speedway extends a cheerful invitation to explore the stacks.

H ISTORIC GOVERNMENT LEGISLA-
tion, passed in the dignified
chamber of the Indiana State
House, has propelled the state to
a position of strong economic
leadership.

THE FOUR-STORY, LIMESTONE Indiana State House features regal columns, a huge dome, and breathtaking marble interiors. No visit to Indianapolis is complete without a tour of the facility.

FROM THE SPLENDID ARCHES OF the Illinois Building (PAGE 52) and historic Crown Hill Cemetery (PAGE 53) to the old-world romance of Union Station (RIGHT), Indianapolis is one of the most attractive cities in America.

U NION STATION, AN 1888
Romanesque Revival rail-
way depot, houses beautiful plas-
ter moldings, wrought iron, and
stained glass windows, as well as
some of the city's hottest night-
clubs, specialty shops, and
eateries (ABOVE AND OPPOSITE).

CIRCLE CENTRE MALL repre-
sents a $314.5 million
investment in downtown revitalization. Leading retailers such as
Nordstrom and FAO Schwarz
reside in the four-level retail and
entertainment complex of shops,
restaurants, and nightclubs.

▲ TIM BICKEL / HILLSTROM STOCK

THE INDIANA CITY MARKET HAS been in continuous operation since it opened in 1886. Fresh meat and produce, baked goods, and a wide variety of deli items stock the shelves of this unique downtown attraction.

RICHARD FIELDS

WITHIN THE WALLS OF INDIA-napolis' older properties you find dazzling designs, such as this spiral staircase located on the Alverna Estate.

EXTERIOR DESIGN IS NO LESS dazzling. Here, nature and humanity sculpt a small masterpiece from sun and snow.

Indianapolis really heats up in the summer when the Kroger Circle Fest kicks off Brickyard 400 festivities. The family festival features exhibits of all kinds, nearly 30 bands, and appetizing specialties from some of Indy's best restaurants (ABOVE, TOP AND BOTTOM).

An embroidery machine is one of the many fascinating attractions at Circle Fest (OPPOSITE).

Every Memorial Day weekend, thousands of visitors speed into town for the Indianapolis 500, which draws the largest crowd of any sporting event in the world. "The Greatest Spectacle in Racing" begins off the track, where the city starts its engines with the 500 Parade.

One of many galas offered throughout race weekend, the 500 Parade features floats, marching bands from around the state, and some of the finest precision drill teams in the country.

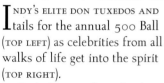

Indy's elite don tuxedos and tails for the annual 500 Ball (TOP LEFT) as celebrities from all walks of life get into the spirit (TOP RIGHT).

Dick Simon offers play-by-play commentary from the track (BOTTOM LEFT), while Tom Carnegie shows nothing can dampen the enthusiasm of avid IndyCar fans (BOTTOM CENTER).

Former Indianapolis 500 winner Mario Andretti waves the checkered flag as grand marshall of the 1994 500 Parade (BOTTOM RIGHT).

THE INDIANA BUCKLE UP FLOAT reminds visitors that no matter what vehicle they choose, it's best to play it safe behind the wheel.

T HE FINAL HOURS BEFORE THE Indy 500 are electrifying, with celebrities and former winners circling the track. Jacques Villeneuve, the 1995 winner, was the first Canadian and the youngest driver to win the race (TOP RIGHT). Willie T. Ribbs also made history as the first African-American to drive in the Indy 500 (BOTTOM LEFT).

Jim Nabors, shown here with Florence Henderson, is a familiar race face (BOTTOM RIGHT). No race begins before he's sung "Back Home Again in Indiana."

For around six hours each May, the Indianapolis Motor Speedway becomes the 24th-largest "city" in the United States, ranking between Cleveland and Seattle. Close to half a million people attend the race.

W HILE THE CROWD PREPARES
in the stands, the crews
prepare in the pits.

THE ACTION IN THE PITS IS AS riveting as that on the track. Good timing and teamwork during pit stops are essential elements to winning.

T HE START OF THE RACE MAY well be the most exciting time at the Indianapolis Motor Speedway (TOP).

Corporate sponsors are enthusiastic participants in the Speedway's events, whether displaying their support on automobiles or on less mechanical places (BOTTOM LEFT AND RIGHT).

The Indianapolis Motor Speedway has a 79-year history as the venue for one of America's premier sporting events. The Brickyard 400 has a circuit length of 2.5 miles and offers 200 laps of blistering speed (PAGES 72 AND 73).

PAGES 72 AND 73: RICHARD FIELDS

STEVE BAKER / HIGHLIGHT PHOTOGRAPHY

For those who prefer to travel on two legs instead of four wheels, ample parking available outside the Speedway allows visitors to migrate to the track without getting stopped in traffic (TOP).

Fans and drivers alike get caught up in the excitement of the race (BOTTOM LEFT AND RIGHT).

N͟OT FAR FROM THE M͟OTOR Speedway is the Indianapolis Hall of Fame Museum. The museum contains one of the world's largest and most varied collections of racing memorabilia, including the Borg Warner Trophy (ABOVE LEFT).

More than 30 past Indy 500 winners are featured in the museum's Hall of Fame (TOP AND BOTTOM RIGHT; OPPOSITE, TOP AND BOTTOM LEFT).

Classic and antique cars are among the museum's exhibits (ABOVE RIGHT). Visitors will find a half-hour film on the history of the track and race highlights in the Tony Hulman Theatre. A gift shop, photo shop, and 18-hole PGA golf course are also located on this historic site.

COMPLETELY RESTORED, OWNED, and operated by the Indiana Dinner Train Company, this red engine transports travelers into the past in a time-honored Hoosier tradition of train travel.

Ample municipal resources, like the city's fire department, recently earned Indianapolis recognition as one of the best places to live in North America out of the 343 metropolitan areas rated by *Places Rated Almanac.*

INDIANAPOLIS' AMPLE MEDICAL
facilities and services ensure
that quality health care is only
moments away.

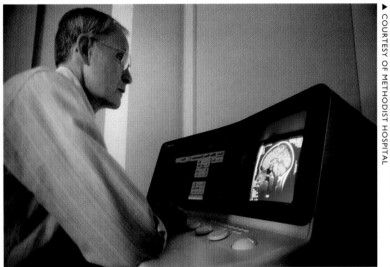

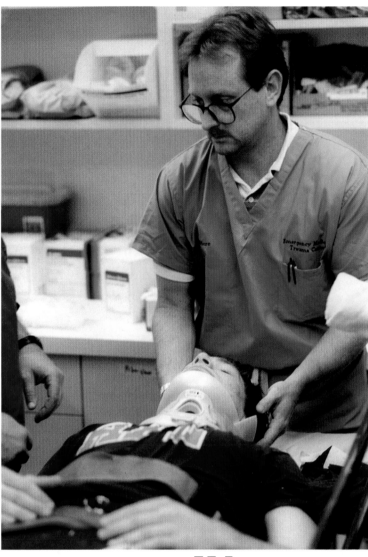

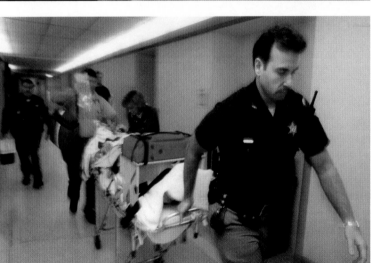

WITH A GENEROUS DOSE OF humanity and expertise, all segments of the local health care community mesh together to form a well-trained whole.

Indianapolis has cleaned up its act in the last decade and earned an outstanding reputation as one of America's cleanest cities. Celebrating life and nature on Earth Day, one veteran takes a stand against war (TOP LEFT).

A vivid demonstration against toxic waste illustrates Indianapolis' "think green" attitude (BOTTOM LEFT).

In other Earth Day activities, the local airport does its share by using soybean fuel to power its "biodiesel" shuttle (TOP RIGHT). Local citizens tend to a park, sending recyclables to local waste facilities (BOTTOM RIGHT).

Careful attention to the environment offers beautiful results. Nature returns the compliment with an uncanny pattern in the Indiana frost (OPPOSITE).

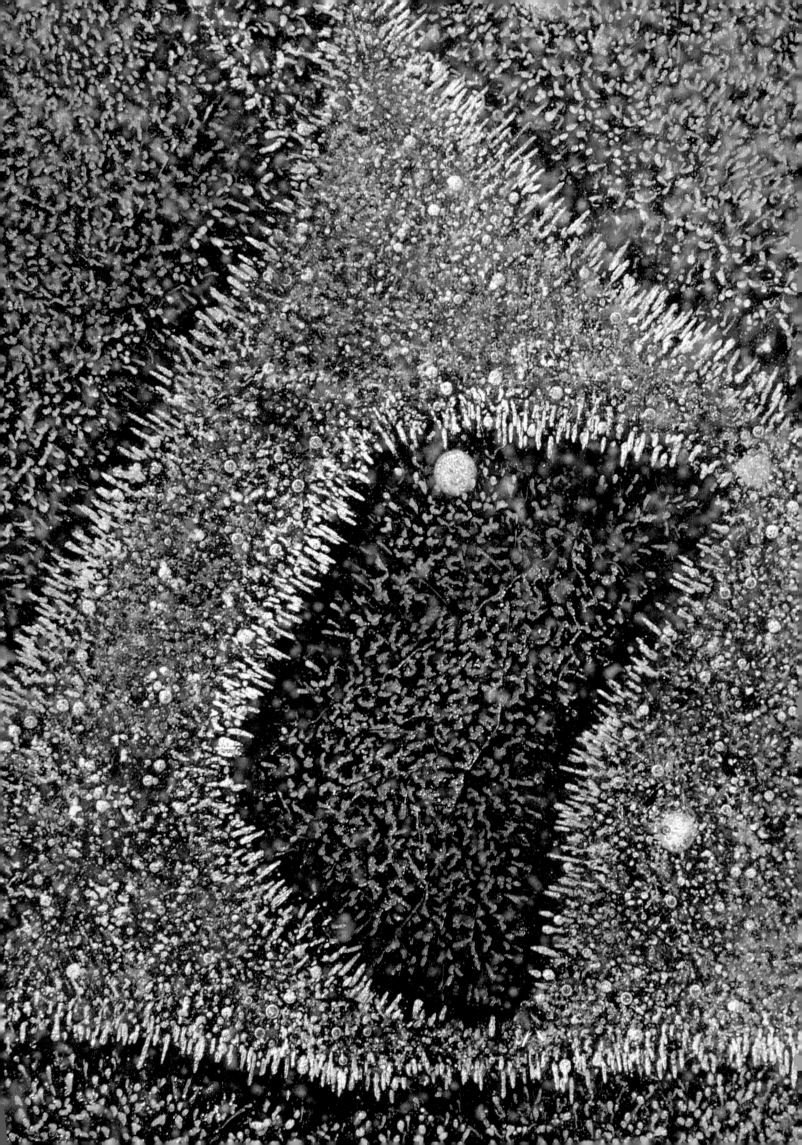

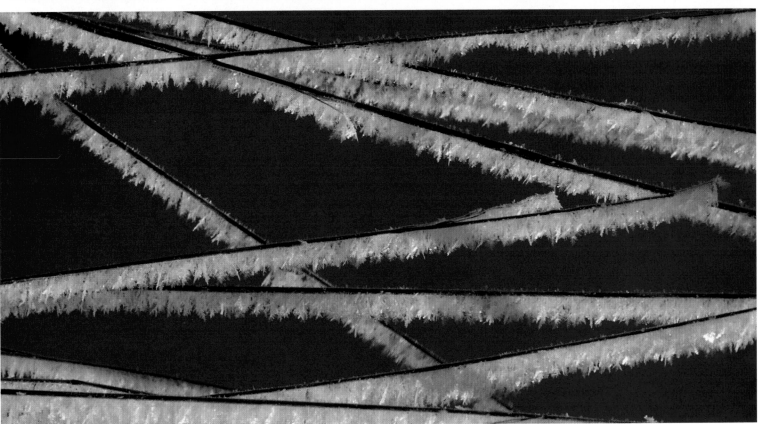

INDIANA IS TRULY A WONDERLAND in winter, offering charming, snow-covered woodlands and crisp, cloudless days.

Indiana is a treasure trove of spring beauties. Graceful tulips, wild lilies, and dainty daffodils dress the opulent countryside (ABOVE, PAGES 86-89).

PAGES 86-89: RICHARD FIELDS

Lᴜsᴄɪᴏᴜs ꜰᴇʀɴs ᴀɴᴅ ʟᴇᴀᴠᴇs ᴀʀᴇ the canvas upon which visitors paint summer dreams.

Eagle Creek Reservoir and Park, the nation's largest city park, is home to an impressive nature preserve. Here, a biologist surveys a wetlands area connected to the park.

Furry but friendly, a few of Indiana's hairier citizens peek out to extend a warm Hoosier welcome to passersby.

The Indianapolis Zoo is short on cages and long on providing natural settings for birds of all feathers.

A YOUNG VISITOR TO THE renovated zoo listens to the chatter of a conspicuously comfortable ostrich.

THE DESERT BIOME AT THE Indianapolis Zoo replicates the arid environment of the western states, warming the hearts of some cool-looking characters.

Tʜᴇsᴇ ꜱɴᴏᴡ ʟᴇᴏᴘᴀʀᴅꜱ ʜᴀᴠᴇ plenty of room to roam at a comfortable distance from zoo fanciers.

ONE OF THE MORE POPULAR attractions at the Indianapolis Zoo is the Whale and Dolphin Pavilion. The 74,000-square-foot facility is the world's second-largest totally enclosed, environmentally controlled dolphin exhibit. The pool holds more than 2.3 million gallons of water (TOP).

The shark tank always draws fascinated onlookers from both sides of the glass (BOTTOM).

Fish aren't the only water lovers at the zoo (OPPOSITE).

THE WATERS BUILDING AT THE
zoo features more than 200
species of aquatic life. Approximately 18,000 square feet of
space is devoted to visitors. Most
of the facility is occupied by
animal holding areas and 32 life-
support systems.

▲ TIM BICKEL / HILLSTROM STOCK

THROUGH REALISTIC EXHIBITS, the zoo strives to foster the desire to preserve earth's plants and animals as well as educate visitors on important elements of nature.

$\mathbb{W}$ ITH 4,000 ACRES OF FOREST
and a 1,300-acre reser-
voir, Eagle Creek Reservoir and
Park is an ideal setting for boat-
ing, swimming, fishing, and other
family fun.

B ASS, CATFISH, AND BLUEGILL ARE favorites among locals and visitors who come for sun and fun at Eagle Creek.

Located on the northeast side of Indianapolis, Geist Reservoir is a breathtakingly beautiful recreation and residential area that offers waterskiing and other high-energy water sports.

T HE FALLS AT GEIST ARE AMONG the most spectacular in the Midwest.

Nestled in the nooks and crannies of Indianapolis are numerous oases where nature enthusiasts can enjoy an afternoon of fishing at one of the city's many lakes, rivers, and ponds.

H UNTING IS A FAVORITE PASTIME for many Indianapolis residents.

A rainbow places a healing hand on the countryside after a summer thunderstorm (PAGES 108 AND 109).

PAGES 108 AND 109: RICHARD FIELDS

M ORE THAN 15 MILLION ACRES of land in Indiana are devoted to farming. Staple crops include corn, which is used for grain, green chop, silage, and seed.

W HEAT, ANOTHER INDIANA
CASH crop, is destined for
bread, oatmeal, and pizza crust.
A young boy stops along the
fence at the edge of his family's
farm to drink in the late afternoon
sun (PAGES 112 AND 113).

PAGES 112 AND 113: RICHARD FIELDS

INDEPENDENT, FAMILY-OWNED
farms are common in America's
heartland, where the size of most
farms ranges between 50 and
179 acres. Beef and dairy cows,
as well as hogs and sows, are the
principal livestock.

W HILE THE SMALL FARMER IS becoming as hard to find as these wooden rail fences, farming remains a strong Hoosier tradition. It's the principal occupation for more than 30,000 individuals in the state.

TIM BICKEL / HILLSTROM STOCK

Conner Prairie, an open-air living history museum accredited by the American Association of Museums, sits on 210 acres and offers a firsthand look at early 19th-century settlers in the Old Northwest Territory.

LAMBS FORM A GENTLE PART
of Conner Prairie's appeal.
Fall oak leaves trace an en-
chanting pattern on a barbed wire
fence that is echoed in the ceiling
of a woodland Native American
wigwam (PAGES 118 AND 119).

PAGES 118 AND 119: RICHARD FIELDS

FREETOWN VILLAGE IS A MUST-
see for anyone interested in
African-American lives and culture in post-Civil War Indiana.
The village offers living history
performances, such as a Civil
War reenactment, to promote the
importance of African-American
culture in society (RIGHT; OPPOSITE,
BOTTOM).

INDIANA IS FAMOUS FOR ITS FALL foliage. These sumacs and other bushes and trees reach their peak about the second week of October (LEFT; PAGES 122 AND 123).

PAGES 122 AND 123: RICHARD FIELDS

A GLORIOUS INDIAN SUMMER
greets visitors to Indiana in
autumn. Bestowing a bountiful
harvest, the sugar maples burst
into flame and issue drops of
sweet sap from their trunks.

A Brown County farm bustles during fall harvesttime, preparing grain for the marketplace.

THE RUSTIC APPEAL OF A FARM, right down to the pumpkins, is a reality in Indiana.

Rusty relics of the past, an old farming combine and a toy tractor offer quaint visions of farm life to passersby (PAGES 128 AND 129).

PAGE 128: STEVE BAKER / HIGHLIGHT
    PHOTOGRAPHY
PAGE 129: TIM BICKEL / HILLSTROM STOCK

A DECIDEDLY HOOSIER LOVE
of tradition keeps beloved
historic sites and artifacts in mint
condition. Stouts Shoes, which
opened in 1888 on Massachu-
setts Avenue, is none the worse
for wear today (TOP).

Perfectly preserved, antique
toy fire engines invite children of
all ages to play (BOTTOM).

J UST 20 MINUTES FROM DOWN-
town Indy, Zionsville has preserved its original brick Main
Street (TOP).

Northeast of the tranquil village, sister suburb Carmel keeps
its own tradition, bringing an old
warrior out for show (BOTTOM).

Signs of the times give a nod to nostalgia in many Indianapolis business establishments. Bill's Fabulous 50's Drive-In still offers scrumptous dishes at reasonable prices (TOP LEFT).

Betty Boop welcomes all comers to her own tavern (BOTTOM LEFT).

A McDonald's Restaurant in Lebanon has one of only two original signs still in use in the country (TOP RIGHT).

Each year, Broad Ripple Park hosts the Oldies Car Show, where classics like this '57 Chevy enjoy another day in the sun (BOTTOM RIGHT).

Though it may not be as wild as it once was, Red Key Tavern still swings with the best of them (OPPOSITE).

Taking pride in its past, Indianapolis is a mosaic of preserved and renovated historical homes, some dating back to the 19th century.

A Victorian house and its accompanying classic car are as much a part of Zionsville's landscape today as they were in years past (TOP).

In the heart of urban Indianapolis, the peaceful tree-lined streets of Lockerbie Square, the oldest Indianapolis neighborhood listed on the National Register of Historic Places, are a reminder of simpler times (BOTTOM).

WOODRUFF PLACE HAS ITS own historic charm (TOP). Poet James Whitcomb Riley spent the final 23 years of his life as a paying guest at 528 Lockerbie Street, now the James Whitcomb Riley Museum. His belongings are showcased in the romantic Victorian home (BOTTOM).

B ED-AND-BREAKFASTS LIKE THE Rock House in Morgantown beckon visitors for an overnight stay (TOP).

Originally Clark's Opera House, where Sarah Bernhardt appeared, Gisela's Kaffeekränzchen in Zionsville offers authentic German food and a harmonious atmosphere (BOTTOM).

A SUNDIAL TELLS TIME WHILE providing a window into history (TOP).

This three-story Italianate mansion at 1230 North Delaware Street was home to Benjamin Harrison, the 23rd president of the United States (BOTTOM).

Solemn stone architecture, like the entrance to the Pennsylvania Lines station, etches silhouettes in the Indianapolis landscape (TOP).

The Art Deco detailing of the Coca-Cola Bottling Company in downtown Indianapolis is a monument to an earlier time (BOTTOM).

THE AWE-INSPIRING ENTRANCE OF Crown Hill Cemetery, the second-largest cemetery in the nation, provides a gateway to the burial sites of President Benjamin Harrison, the notorious John Dillinger, 10 governors, 14 Civil War generals, and three vice presidents (TOP).

A lamb at the Immaculate Heart of Mary church and school bids a gentle welcome to all visitors (BOTTOM).

A statue of the Virgin Mary graces the grounds of Crown Hill Cemetery (PAGE 140).

Stephen Baker's acclaimed bronze bust of a jazzman pays homage to local musicians (PAGE 141).

Broad Ripple Village welcomes all comers in a time-honored tradition (PAGE 142).

The creaking of an old door is half the fun of going from room to room in many of Indianapolis' historic homes (PAGE 143).

PAGES 140, 141, AND 142: STEVEN BAKER / HIGHLIGHT PHOTOGRAPHY

PAGE 143: TIM BICKEL / HILLSTROM STOCK

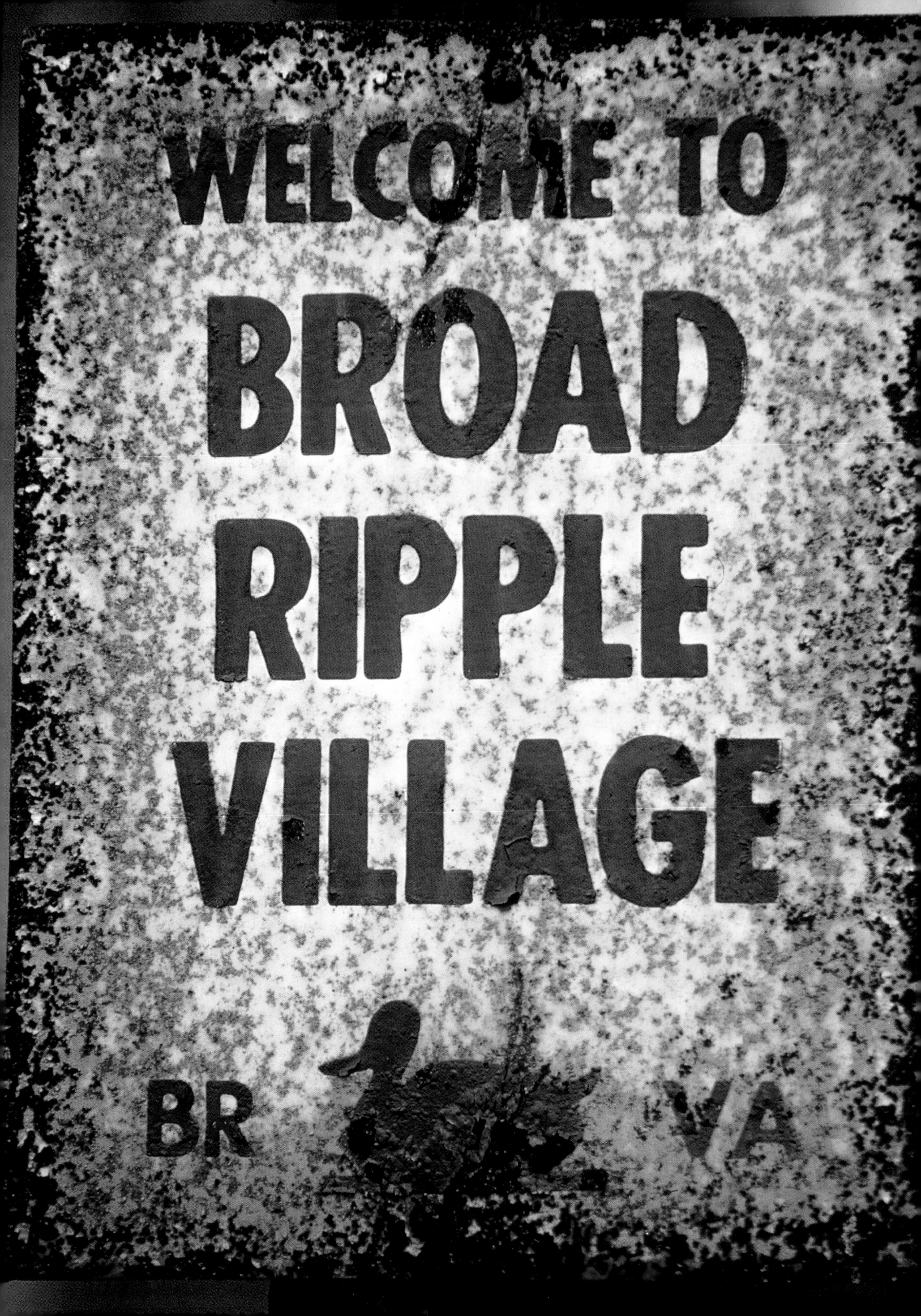
WELCOME TO
BROAD
RIPPLE
VILLAGE
BR
VA

From rock to reggae to jazz to rave, Broad Ripple Village delivers some of the best music and nightlife in Indianapolis.

Among Indy's hottest night-clubs are Route 66 (TOP LEFT), the Vogue (BOTTOM LEFT), Broad Ripple Comedy Club (TOP RIGHT), and the Butler Area Reggae Bar (BOTTOM RIGHT). Live rock, blues, jazz, and comedy are served up in a confluence of popular culture.

T HE INDIANAPOLIS SYMPHONY
Orchestra performs under a
canopy of blue and the baton of
renowned Maestro Raymond
Leppard.

THE ATHENAEUM BEERGARTEN IS an elegant setting for an evening's entertainment. Built in the 19th century, the Athenaeum features the American Cabaret Theater and the charming Rathskeller Restaurant.

A DAZZLING FIREWORKS DISPLAY lights up the vibrant India-napolis skyline (ABOVE LEFT).

The Indiana State Fairgrounds comes ablaze every August with the brilliant lights of the midway (TOP RIGHT) and the sparkling smiles of children of all ages (BOTTOM RIGHT).

THE CHURNING OF COTTON candy and the Ferris wheel; the smell of corn dogs, popcorn, and elephant ears; and screams from the thrilling amusement park rides fill the night air at the State Fair.

A SPECTACULAR LIGHT SHOW
flashes across the sultry
summer sky.

THE LINK OBSERVATORY IN
Mooresville offers the curious a closer look at unearthly
mysteries.

CHRISTMAS GLOWS IN THE HEART-
land on houses and in sacred
stained glass portraits.

L EAFLESS TREES RAISE THEIR
arms to rescue a falling cres-
cent moon from the crisp winter
dawn (TOP).

A stained glass window at
St. Paul's Episcopal Church offers
solace to its admirers (BOTTOM).

The Indiana State Museum decks its halls with Christmas ornaments during the busy holiday season (TOP).

While the Indiana State House serves up a yuletide celebration (BOTTOM), Indianapolis trims the largest Christmas tree in the world (OPPOSITE).

THE INSTRUMENTS OF A MARIACHI band stand at attention, ready to be played in a Mexican fiesta celebrating Indianapolis' cultural diversity.

Sᴘᴀɴɪsʜ ᴅᴀɴᴄᴇʀs ᴛᴀᴘ ᴏᴜᴛ ᴛʜᴇ rhythm, color, and joy that is part of their heritage.

S T. PATRICK'S DAY BRINGS OUT
the Irish in Indianapolis
(ABOVE AND OPPOSITE).

▲ STEVE BAKER / HIGHLIGHT PHOTOGRAPHY

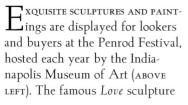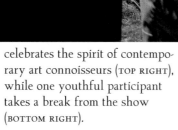

Exquisite sculptures and paintings are displayed for lookers and buyers at the Penrod Festival, hosted each year by the Indianapolis Museum of Art (ABOVE LEFT). The famous *Love* sculpture celebrates the spirit of contemporary art connoisseurs (TOP RIGHT), while one youthful participant takes a break from the show (BOTTOM RIGHT).

The Indianapolis Museum of Art has acquired more than 600 contemporary artworks since 1963, including pieces by Robert Irwin, James Turrell, and Sol Lewitt. A number of outdoor sculptures are displayed on the museum grounds.

COUNTRY CRAFTSMANSHIP AND music are part of the fabric of midwestern life. Indiana artisans make music in a variety of ways.

Hoosiers are found kicking up their heels in country dance clubs (BOTTOM LEFT) and pricking up their ears to music legends like Dolly Parton (TOP) and folk musician Mitch Rice (BOTTOM RIGHT).

▲ RICHARD FIELDS

FROM ELEMENTARY SCHOOL TO college, marching bands are a favorite of Hoosier audiences, especially when the Indiana State Fair hosts its marching band competition.

WORLD'S LARGEST DRUM

Purdue

THE STATE FAIR MARCHING band competition draws out the brassy best (TOP LEFT); ball boys stand ready to retrieve balls at a tennis tournament (BOTTOM LEFT); and cheerleaders prepare to whoop it up for the home team (BOTTOM RIGHT).

The World's Largest Drum, a feature of the Purdue University marching band, is always a huge hit at the 500 Day Parade (TOP RIGHT).

W HEN YOU START RUNNING basketball fever, you know you have "Hoosier Hysteria." Statewide, basketball is beloved, revered, and played wherever you can hang a hoop.

AN AMERICAN PLAZA, SITE OF
the 1987 Pan Am Games, is
not immune to Indiana's basketball obsession.

Since the mid-1970s, Indianapolis has hosted more than 330 national and international sporting events. Hoosiers begin sports at a young age: Students at St. Bridget's prepare for a game of softball (top), while a Christamore House boxer wears a different kind of glove (bottom).

ARGER THAN LIFE, INDIANA
Pacer star Reggie Miller looks
down from a giant mural on the
exterior of Market Square Arena.

K ITE-FLYING COMPETITIONS, the Indiana State Fair Balloon Race, and the International World Rowing Championships are all a part of Indy's colorful sports scene (LEFT AND OPPOSITE).

Swimming is always a popular sport in Indianapolis, although the Indiana University Natatorium really gets into the swing of things by hosting the U.S. Olympic swimming and diving trials.

Rowing is also a splash in Indy, as the 1994 World Rowing Championships at Eagle Creek Reservoir and Park demonstrate.

Among the top sporting events in Indianapolis is the Senior PGA golf tournament (top right). The Major Taylor Velodrome is a world-class bicycle racetrack and the site of numerous national competitions (bottom right).

Tʜᴇ Iɴᴅɪᴀɴᴀᴘᴏʟɪs Iɴᴅɪᴀɴs called Bush Stadium home in the summertime until 1995. Now housed in a brand-new downtown ballpark, the team draws cheers from hometown fans.

THE INDIANS' MASCOT GIVES small fans a high five at the crack of the Indian bat (TOP AND BOTTOM LEFT). The Class AAA team is the farm club of the Cincinnati Reds (ABOVE RIGHT).

HOME TO THE NFL's Indianapolis Colts, the RCA Dome draws more than 2 million people annually. Completed in 1984, the sports and convention facility hosts year-round special events (TOP). The Colts face off against the Cleveland Browns in the RCA Dome (BOTTOM LEFT).

The Indianapolis Ice hockey team, a Chicago Blackhawks affiliate, calls Market Square Arena home (BOTTOM RIGHT).

T HE RCA DOME HAS AN Astroturf playing surface and a seating capacity of 60,129. This playground for the Indianapolis Colts opened May 3, 1984 (TOP).

Jim Harbaugh, the Colts' quarterback, maintains a steady vigil over his team's offense (BOTTOM LEFT).

One of the most exciting games in recent history sent the Pittsburgh Steelers to Super Bowl XXX, while the Colts returned home to end their 1995 season. It was the team's first play-off berth since 1987 (BOTTOM CENTER).

Buoyed by a tremendous up-turn in the 1995 season, Colts fans have contracted an incurable case of "horse fever," enthusiastically supporting the team (BOTTOM RIGHT).

FOOTBALL PLAYERS DON'T DO ALL the fancy footwork at the RCA Dome. More than 30,000 people turn out for the annual Bands of America Grand National Championships. Seventy-five of the nation's top high school marching bands compete in the event.

Voted Tournament of the Year for the past seven years, the RCA Championships are held each August at the Indianapolis Tennis Center. The center has 18 outdoor courts, an 8,000-seat stadium court, and a 2,000-seat grandstand court.

I NDY RACERS AREN'T ALWAYS found in cars. More than 12,000 people race on foot in the Indianapolis 500 Mini Marathon.

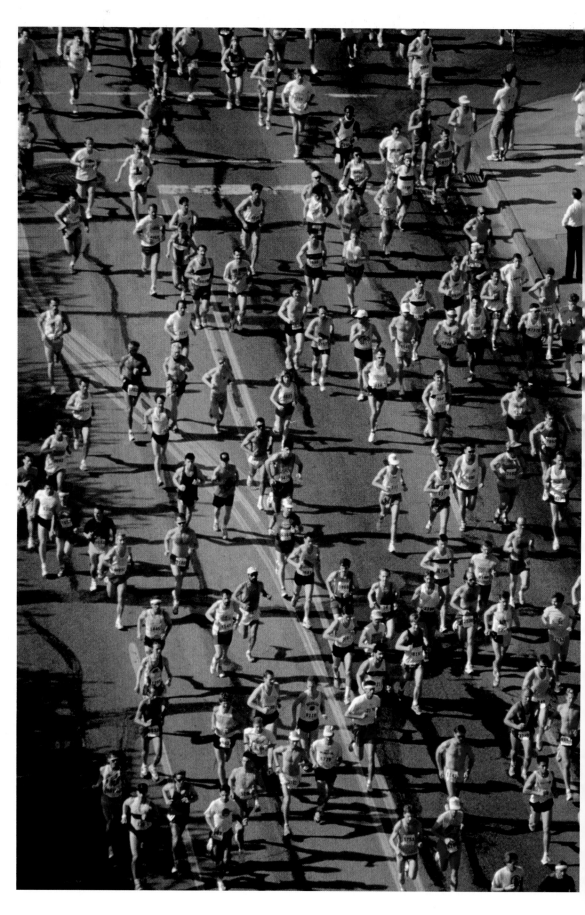

A FALCON SOARS INTO THE clouds above the Indianapolis Market Tower, an inspiring metaphor for the progress made by the city below (TOP).

Indianapolis greets visitors with a beautiful cityscape that attests to the community's progressive attitude (BOTTOM AND OPPOSITE).

Profiles in Excellence

A look at the corporations, businesses, professional groups, and community service organizations that have made this book possible. Their stories—offering an informal chronicle of the local business community—are arranged according to the date they were established in Indianapolis.

◆ Alexander & Alexander of Indiana Inc. ❧ American United Life Insurance Company® ❧ Ameritech ❧ R.W. Armstrong Associates ❧ Bank One, Indianapolis, NA ❧ Bates USA/Midwest ❧ Best Lock Corporation ❧ Blaising St. Claire Associates ❧ Boehringer Mannheim Corporation ❧ Brightpoint, Inc. ❧ Browning-Ferris Industries of Indiana, Inc. ❧ BSA Design ❧ Business Furniture Corporation ❧ Butler University ❧ Canterbury Hotel ❧ Carrier Corporation ❧ Chautauqua Airlines, Inc./USAir Express ❧ Chrysler Corporation Indianapolis Foundry ❧ Citizens Gas & Coke Utility ❧ Community Hospitals Indianapolis ❧ Conseco, Inc. ❧ Crossmann Communities, Inc. ❧ Crowe Chizek ❧ CSO Architects Engineers & Interiors ❧ DowElanco and DowBrands ❧ Farm Bureau Insurance ❧ FedEx® ❧ First Indiana Corporation ❧ General Motors ❧ Guidant Corporation ❧ Hamilton Displays, Inc. ❧ The Heritage Group ❧ Hoosier Orthopaedics and Sports Medicine, P.C. ❧ IBJ Corporation ❧ The Indiana Hand Center ❧ Indiana University Medical Center ❧ Indiana University-Purdue University Indianapolis ❧ Indianapolis Chamber of Commerce ❧ Indianapolis Museum of Art ❧ Indianapolis Symphony Orchestra ❧ Inland Mortgage Corporation ❧ IPALCO Enterprises, Inc. ❧ ITT Educational Services, Inc. ❧ Ivy Tech State College, Central Indiana Region ❧ IWC Resources Corporation ❧ The Justus Companies ❧ KeyBank National Association ❧ Lacy Diversified Industries, Ltd. ❧ Eli Lilly and Company ❧ Lilly Industries, Inc. ❧ Macmillan Publishing USA ❧ Mansur Group ❧ Marsh Supermarkets, Inc. ❧ Martin University ❧ Mayflower Transit, Inc. ❧ Mays Chemical Company, Inc. ❧ Merrill Lynch ❧ Methodist Health Group ❧ The Morley Group Inc. ❧ MSE Corporation ❧ MyStar Communications Corporation ❧ NatCity Investments, Inc. ❧ National City Bank, Indiana ❧ National Wine & Spirits Corporation ❧ NBD Bank, N.A. ❧ Northside Cardiology, P.C. ❧ Omni Severin Hotel ❧ Quantum Health Resources, Inc. ❧ REI Investments, Inc. ❧ RE/MAX of Indiana ❧ Roman Catholic Archdiocese of Indianapolis ❧ St. Elmo Steak House ❧ St. Vincent Hospitals and Health Services ❧ Service Graphics Inc. ❧ Software Synergy, Inc. ❧ The State Life Insurance Company ❧ Telamon Corporation ❧ Thomson Consumer Electronics ❧ Union Federal Savings Bank ❧ University of Indianapolis ❧ VASA Brougher, Inc. ❧ WTHR, Channel 13 ❧ Young & Laramore ❧ Zimmer Paper Products Incorporated ❧

1834-1929

1834	NBD Bank, N.A.
1834	Roman Catholic Archdiocese of Indianapolis
1839	Bank One, Indianapolis, NA
1855	Butler University
1865	Lilly Industries, Inc.
1865	National City Bank, Indiana
1871	IWC Resources Corporation
1876	Eli Lilly and Company
1877	American United Life Insurance Company®
1877	Citizens Gas & Coke Utility
1881	St. Vincent Hospitals and Health Services
1883	Ameritech
1883	Indianapolis Museum of Art
1887	Union Federal Savings Bank
1890	Indianapolis Chamber of Commerce
1894	The State Life Insurance Company
1896	Alexander & Alexander of Indiana Inc.
1902	St. Elmo Steak House
1902	University of Indianapolis
1908	Methodist Health Group
1910	The Justus Companies
1912	Lacy Diversified Industries, Ltd.
1913	Omni Severin Hotel
1914	Indiana University Medical Center
1915	First Indiana Corporation
1915	Merrill Lynch
1922	Business Furniture Corporation
1926	IPALCO Enterprises, Inc.
1927	Mayflower Transit, Inc.
1928	Canterbury Hotel
1929	General Motors

HE GENESIS OF THE ARCHDIOCESE OF INDIANAPOLIS, HEADQUARtered in the O'Meara Catholic Center on North Meridian Street, dates back to May 6, 1834, when the Diocese of Vincennes was founded. The territory of this early diocese covered the entire state of Indiana as well as the eastern portion of Illinois. In 1857 the territory was divided, leaving the southern half of Indiana under its tutelage.

SAINT JOHN THE EVANGELIST CHURCH, POPULARLY KNOWN AS OLD SAINT JOHN'S, WAS FOUNDED IN 1837 AND IS THE OLDEST CATHOLIC CHURCH IN MARION COUNTY. LOCATED ACROSS THE STREET FROM THE RCA DOME AND THE INDIANA CONVENTION CENTER AND WITHIN A BLOCK OF THE NEW CIRCLE CENTRE MALL, THE CHURCH SERVES HUNDREDS OF DOWNTOWN OFFICE WORKERS EACH DAY; FANS DURING FOOTBALL SEASON; AND TOURISTS, CONVENTION GOERS, AND OTHER VISITORS YEAR-ROUND (RIGHT).

On March 28, 1898, the title of the diocese was changed to the Diocese of Indianapolis, after the fifth bishop moved his residence from Vincennes to Indianapolis. In 1944 Pope Pius XII called for the creation of the Archdiocese of Indianapolis, as well as the creation of the Diocese of Evansville and the Diocese of Lafayette. Throughout these years of change, the goal of the church of central and southern Indiana has always been to serve God and the community.

A MISSION OF EDUCATION

Aside from meeting the spiritual needs of its parishioners, the Archdiocese of Indianapolis is committed to educating the youth of the community who will one day become its leaders.

In Indianapolis, the archdiocese operates eight center-city Catholic schools, with a total of 33 elementary and four high schools throughout the area. Enrollment is continually on the rise. At the beginning of the 1994-95 school year, there were more than 21,000 students enrolled in kindergarten through 12th grade, with almost 1,400 in preschool programs. In January 1994 Archbishop Daniel M. Buechlein unveiled Center City Commitment 2000, a plan that outlines six strategies to ensure vibrant parishes and to strengthen Catholic schools in the urban neighborhoods of Indianapolis.

SISTER OF PROVIDENCE SUSAN DINNIN ASSISTS A PARTICIPANT IN A CARING PLACE, AN ADULT DAY CARE PROGRAM OF CATHOLIC SOCIAL SERVICES. HOUSED IN FAIRVIEW PRESBYTERIAN CHURCH IN INDIANAPOLIS, THE CENTER SERVES 38 SENIORS (BELOW).

RICHARD W. CLARK

For the first time in its history, the archdiocese is looking beyond its 211,000 members to gain support for its efforts. "There's been a major effort to reach out for the first time to the corporate community and the foundations in the city," says Daniel J. Elsener, executive director of Catholic education.

He adds, "There's an image in everyone's mind—including those who are Catholic—that the kids in our center-city schools are white, middle-class, Catholic children, when, in fact, they are nonwhite, they are poor, they are below the poverty level, and they are not even Catholic, by and large." For instance, Elsener points out that about 75 percent of the students at St. Rita Elementary School are non-Catholic.

Addressing the business community, Elsener states, "Since these children are being educated to be good workers—good citizens of this community—our rationale for going to the business community is that we're educating their future employees. Statistics seem to show that we're doing a pretty good job of it, and we need their help. We're educating the citizenry of this area."

CHARITABLE EFFORTS FOR THE COMMUNITY

Aside from the educational goals of the archdiocese, charitable endeavors play an important part in its role within the community. There are considerable efforts to improve the quality of life for those Indianapolis residents who are struck by hardship.

The vast local network of Catholic charities includes everything from counseling, pre- and postnatal care, adoption services, refugee resettlement and immigration services, youth programs, health services, housing, and social support services. "There's also the Birthline program that offers alternatives to abortion," says Thomas Gaybrick, who oversees eight Catholic Charities agencies.

"Through the family and children's services provided, we seek to hold troubled families together and to help individuals achieve their potential," adds Gaybrick. This resource offers services to persons of all ages, from the very young to the elderly. Two adult day care centers offer an alternative to institutionalization for the frail elderly. Diagnostic services and treatment are provided to at-risk or learning-disabled preschool-aged children and are designed to ensure better learning and social experiences once these children enter elementary education.

Another extremely successful venture for the archdiocese has been the Senior Companion program. This initiative matches seniors who are alone with a companion who can stop by or call on the senior to reduce a sense of isolation. Many delightful friendships have developed through Senior Companion. The Neighborhood Youth Outreach Program at Saint Joan of Arc Parish has also been a success.

Through this program, the church gym is open nightly for recreational activities—such as African dance classes—that are designed to keep area youth off the streets. None of these services are restricted to Catholics, but are offered to anyone who needs assistance.

SHELTER FOR THOSE IN NEED

The archdiocese also maintains a crisis office in the Xavier Building, which is located next door to the O'Meara Catholic Center. Here, those in need can receive emergency food and clothing. The Holy Family Shelter on the city's south side houses homeless families for up to three months. During their stay, these temporary residents work with paid staff and volunteers who assist with job training and finding permanent housing.

In September 1995 a transitional housing facility at St. Patrick's Parish was dedicated on the near south side of Indianapolis. Here, troubled families are able to stay for two years while they get back on their feet.

The Archdiocese of Indianapolis has undergone many transitions since its founding, but it has always maintained a dedication to its original mission: to serve God and the community. "We find that people

need help, and we're trying to provide it," says Gaybrick. "We're more deeply involved in the life of Indianapolis than most people tend to think."

▶ THE INDIANAPOLIS STAR / KELLY WILKINSON

▶ RICHARD W. CLARK

CLOCKWISE FROM TOP: SISTER NANCY CROWDER, A DAUGHTER OF CHARITY OF SAINT VINCENT DE PAUL, IS DIRECTOR OF HOLY FAMILY SHELTER, A CATHOLIC SOCIAL SERVICES FACILITY THAT OFFERS SHORT-TERM HOUSING, MEALS, COUNSELING, CHILD CARE, AND JOB ASSISTANCE TO HOMELESS FAMILIES. SISTER NANCY WAS CHOSEN AS WOMAN OF THE YEAR IN 1995 BY READERS OF THE INDIANAPOLIS STAR.

BEV BALASH, A MIDDLE SCHOOL SCIENCE TEACHER, MAKES A POINT WITH SOME OF HER PUPILS AT SAINT JOAN OF ARC SCHOOL, ONE OF EIGHT CENTER-CITY CATHOLIC SCHOOLS THAT ARE RECEIVING RENEWED COMMITMENT FROM THE ARCHDIOCESE AND THE COMMUNITY.

ADMINISTRATION OF THE ARCHDIOCESE IS LED BY ARCHBISHOP DANIEL M. BUECHLEIN, O.S.B. (CENTER), WHO IS ASSISTED BY A NINE-MEMBER MANAGEMENT COUNCIL, INCLUDING FATHER JOSEPH F. SCHAEDEL (LEFT), VICAR GENERAL AND MODERATOR OF THE CURIA, AND SUZANNE MAGNANT, CHANCELLOR OF THE ARCHDIOCESE AND HEAD OF THE SECRETARIAT FOR LEADERSHIP, PASTORAL FORMATION, AND SERVICES.

HE SLOGAN FOR NBD BANK, "THE RIGHT BANK CAN MAKE a Difference," accurately portrays this organization's philosophy and mission. ♦ Founded locally in 1834 as the State Bank of Indiana, the organization became Indiana National Bank, later INB National Bank, and now NBD Bank, N.A. The bank continues to have a strong commitment to supporting community needs and services. With assets of more than $10 billion, NBD Bank is the state's largest banking operation.

The bank's parent company, NBD Bancorp, Inc., and First Chicago Corporation entered into a merger agreement effective November 30, 1995. This "merger of equals" has created the Midwest's leading provider of financial services to both consumers and corporate customers. NBD Bank, N.A. is a wholly owned subsidiary of First Chicago NBD Corp., which has approximately $125 billion in assets.

NBD Bank provides a full range of deposit, loan, investment, and transaction services through its 66 banking centers and 90 automatic teller machines in the Indianapolis metropolitan area. NBD Bank offers statewide banking as well, allowing customers to transact business at any of its 235 banking centers in Indiana. Through these locations, the bank offers not only convenience and a full range of services, but also a spirit of goodwill that reaches into the very fabric of the communities it serves.

COMMITMENT TO THE COMMUNITY

NBD Bank is involved in all aspects of our community," says Andrew J. Paine Jr., president. "This commitment comes from the minds and hearts of our directors and senior management, who set the tone. Banks are historically key players in their communities. We've simply taken that to a higher level."

Through the Indianapolis Chamber of Commerce, NBD Bank has participated in the Two Percent/Five Percent Club since the program's inception in 1986. Members set aside 2 percent of their corporate pretax income for philanthropic needs in the community. NBD Bank has also earned high marks for its CRA (Community Reinvestment Act) activities.

NBD Bank has forged strong alliances with neighborhood churches, bringing the bank to the neighborhoods in a grassroots outreach effort. "Some people are intimidated by banks," says Michael W. Rodman, vice president. "Rather than ask people to come to us, we go to their neighborhoods and churches, places where they feel most comfortable."

COMMUNITY ACTIVITY

In 1995 NBD Bank celebrated its silver anniversary as sponsor of Indianapolis' preeminent Fourth of July fireworks show. State-of-the-art fireworks are launched from high atop the bank's 36-story downtown tower. This pyrotechnic tradition, begun in 1970 as a gift to the community, continues to be a festive holiday celebration, received more enthusiastically every year.

Another highlight for NBD Bank each year is its sponsorship of the Indianapolis 500 Leaders Circle Club, which recognizes all drivers who have led a lap in the 500. In 1995 Jacques Villeneuve was inducted into the club.

EMPLOYEE VOLUNTARISM

Recognizing the volunteer spirit of its employees, NBD Bank encourages and supports those individuals within the bank who offer their time and talent to organizations such as the American Cancer Society, Big Brothers, Big Sisters, and the United Way. Employees participate on the board of the Indianapolis Public Schools as well as in the city's youth projects, fund-raisers, citizens' groups, and arts organizations. Some of NBD Bank's most notable volunteers are recognized each year as Bankers HOURS (Honoring OURS) recipients. This prestigious distinction is paired with a $1,000 check, to be awarded to the charity of the honoree's choice.

NBD Bank also makes significant financial investments in such organizations as the Circle Centre Development Corporation, a lending consortium of approximately 12 partners that was established to

IN 1995 NBD BANK CELEBRATED ITS SILVER ANNIVERSARY AS SPONSOR OF INDIANAPOLIS' PREEMINENT FOURTH OF JULY FIREWORKS SHOW.

GRAYDON PHOTOGRAPHY

provide funding for downtown's new Circle Centre Mall.

Informal groups of NBD Bank employees also rehabilitate houses at the request of various neighborhood associations. "Ten years ago, 20 of our employees painted a house in a northwest neighborhood at 30th Street and Rader. This house was owned by an elderly, retired woman. Ever since then, I've been keeping an eye on the house," notes Rodman. "This year, while the owner was in the hospital, flowers were stolen from the window boxes. One of our employees just went to a garden shop and replaced all the flowers for her."

In 1995 bank employees decided to create a community garden. A plot of land was purchased by the Concord Community Development Corporation. At one time ravaged by urban blight, this abandoned lot was transformed into a thriving garden filled with giant sunflowers, rosebushes, white and blue irises, and a variety of vegetables. Neighborhood children, guided by local volunteers, constructed a large scarecrow and helped plant and maintain the garden.

Making a difference in the lives of Indianapolis residents has been an essential part of the mission of NBD Bank. And as the state's largest banking organization, NBD Bank will continue to play an important role in the communities it serves throughout Indiana.

▶ GRAYDON PHOTOGRAPHY

As part of the bank's commitment to the community it serves, informal groups of NBD Bank employees rehabilitate houses at the request of various neighborhood associations.

▼ GRAYDON PHOTOGRAPHY

▶▼ GRAYDON PHOTOGRAPHY

EMBRACING CHANGE COURAGEOUSLY WHILE SEIZING OPPORTU-
nities for continuous improvement, Bank One, Indianapolis, NA
looks to the future optimistically, convinced that it will be one of
the emerging megabanks in the next 10 years. ♦ President J. Albert
Smith Jr., a third-generation banker, surveys national and global
trends from his 48th-floor suite in the Bank One Tower—right in

the heart of the city's financial district. His all-encompassing view of the city parallels his comprehensive view of the banking industry.

A dynamic leader, Smith knows change well, as today's Bank One, Indianapolis is the result of 34 mergers. "This bank was at the forefront of the consolidation movement," says Smith. "It's a trend that will continue. In 10 years, 50 banks that are national in scope will control two-thirds of the country's assets. This trend is being driven by productivity pressures and competition in a global marketplace. Ten years from now, there will be financial powerhouses. We plan to be there."

Smith sees the future of banking on a spectrum with a few large national banks at one end and small community banks at the other. The megabanks will attract significant capital, offer a varied menu of services, and invest heavily in technology. Small community banks will be geographically limited, will offer relatively little in the way of

technological services, and will not have significant availability to customers. These banks will be able to maintain highly personal customer relationships, but with a higher delivery cost. Smith predicts banks somewhere in the middle will be squeezed out of their market position as their niche becomes increasingly undefinable.

Smith adds that U.S. bank mergers offer geographical advantages nationally and improvements

in competition internationally. "Our industry will become much more competitive internationally," he says.

A CENTURY AND A HALF OF CHANGE

The history of Bank One, Indianapolis spans more than 150 years and has included a number of mergers and many name changes. In 1839 Stoughton A. Fletcher started a bank

BANK ONE HOUSES MORE THAN 1,000 OF ITS EMPLOYEES IN THE BANK ONE TOWER—A PART OF BANK ONE CENTER, A TWO-BUILDING COMPLEX LOCATED IN THE HEART OF DOWNTOWN INDIANAPOLIS (RIGHT).

BANK ONE HAS MORE THAN 65 FULL-SERVICE BANKING CENTERS CONVENIENTLY LOCATED THROUGH-OUT THE INDIANAPOLIS METRO-POLITAN AREA (BELOW).

called S.A. Fletcher Company with a capital investment of $3,000. By 1872 the privately owned institution had acquired deposits of $643,541. The bank's original charter was changed in 1898, and the organization was renamed Fletcher National Bank. Twelve years later, Fletcher National and American National Bank merged to form Fletcher American National Bank. In 1924 the bank merged with National City Bank, and in 1931 its name was shortened to Fletcher Trust Company.

Fletcher Trust Company and the American National Bank of Indianapolis consolidated in 1954 as the American Fletcher National Bank and Trust Company. American Fletcher National Bank and Fidelity Bank & Trust, owned by Frank E. McKinney Sr., merged in 1959. On December 31, 1968, under the Bank Holding Company Act of 1956, American Fletcher National Bank became one of three financial institutions in the country to be part of a one-bank holding structure, with its parent company being named American Fletcher Corporation. Under the leadership of McKinney, the organization grew to become the largest bank in Indiana by 1972. At year-end 1986, the bank had recorded $4 billion in assets.

On January 26, 1987, American Fletcher Corporation was acquired by Banc One Corporation, a multibank holding company based in Columbus, Ohio. The name of the Indiana bank was changed to Bank One, Indianapolis, NA. Today, it enjoys the unique atmosphere of cooperation and communication among financial institutions throughout the city. "In a lot of communities, banks don't cooperate. It's a win-lose situation. That's not true in Indianapolis. The corporate community wrote checks for $71 million to provide equity for the downtown mall project. That's unheard-of. We have a strong commitment to lending and to giving," says Smith. "Banks have an obligation to make loans to benefit their community. Small-business lending and consumer lending will fuel the economic growth of the community."

A National Company

Bank One, Indianapolis is an affiliate of Banc One Indiana Corporation, a subsidiary of BANC ONE CORPORATION. As of June 30, 1995, BANC ONE CORPORATION had assets of $86.8 billion and common equity of $7.6 billion, and now operates 65 banks with 1,408 offices in Arizona, Colorado, Illinois, Indiana, Kentucky, Ohio, Oklahoma, Texas, Utah, West Virginia, and Wisconsin. BANC ONE CORPORATION also operates several additional corporations that engage in data processing, venture capital, investment and merchant banking, trust brokerage, investment management, equipment leasing, mortgage banking, consumer finance, and insurance.

Bank One, Indianapolis, NA continues to build on its historic success and the success of its parent company by monitoring the quality of its credit, technology, people, earnings, and service.

Customers and investors measure that success favorably, while Bank One consistently strives to exceed their expectations.

A COUPLE ENJOYS AN EVENING CARRIAGE RIDE AROUND DOWNTOWN'S MONUMENT CIRCLE WITH THE INDIANAPOLIS SKYLINE HIGHLIGHTED BY THE BANK ONE TOWER.

UTLER UNIVERSITY'S GROWTH REFLECTS THE GROWTH OF ITS hometown. "The better Indianapolis does, the better we do," says President Geoffrey Bannister, Ph.D. "We can help the city by being a point of pride, and that's our objective." ♦ As Indiana's second-largest independent college, Butler has an enrollment of more than 4,000 students, two-thirds of whom are state

BUTLER HAS NEARLY 30,000 ALUMNI IN 50 STATES AND 37 FOREIGN COUNTRIES (BELOW).

AN INDIANAPOLIS FAVORITE, THE UNIVERSITY'S HOLCOMB GARDENS IS HOME TO THE CARILLON BELL TOWER (BOTTOM LEFT). ITS AMERICANA BELLS PRODUCE 366 DIFFERENT TONES.

BUTLER OFFERS 60 MAJOR FIELDS, PLUS SPECIAL MAJORS AND CONCENTRATION AREAS (BOTTOM RIGHT).

residents. "We actually serve more Indiana students than any other private institution," says Bannister.

SERVING A GROWING STUDENT BODY

In the fall of 1995, Butler welcomed more than 850 freshmen, a number that has been growing in recent years. But the university's mission is not just to cater to the 18- to 22-year-old student; it also serves a sizable graduate student population.

To that end, Butler offers a full range of academic programs through University College; the colleges of Liberal Arts and Sciences, Business Administration, Education, and Pharmacy and Health Sciences; and Jordan College of Fine Arts. According to Bannister, Butler's professional programs set it apart from the 32 other independent universities in Indiana that mostly focus on liberal arts.

"Probably the most unique is the College of Pharmacy and Health Sciences. There are only 50 in the country. And it's an appropriate specialization for us in a state with companies such as Eli Lilly," he says. "We're also offering the first program in Indiana for physicians' assistants, in association with Methodist Hospital."

Internships are required in most departments to strengthen the bond between the city and the university. "That helps to keep us closely tied to what's happening in the community and allows us to draw upon the resources of Indianapolis," says Bannister.

Nationally, Butler has earned acclaim for its dance and fine arts programs. "The strongest single program we have is in the fine arts. And we rank about number three in the country in our dance pro-

gram," explains Bannister, touting the top-notch performance facilities at the university's Clowes Memorial Hall.

Butler is also internationally acclaimed for its Institute for Study Abroad, established in 1988. Students attend programs in Australia, New Zealand, the United Kingdom, and Ireland. "We offer one of the largest study abroad programs in the country," Bannister says. "We have about 1,500 students drawn from all over the United States, including Harvard, Princeton, and Rice University."

A HISTORY OF PROGRESS

Butler's commitment to improve its programs and facilities has been evident throughout its history. In 1855 the university opened its doors as North Western Christian University at 13th Street and College Avenue. Eighteen years later, the school moved to a 25-acre site in Irvington and changed its name to Butler University, honoring attorney Ovid Butler, who wrote the university's charter. In 1923 the campus settled on a beautiful wooded tract north of Indianapolis along the White River and the Inland Water Canal, and three years later the first classes were held in Arthur Jordan Memorial Hall.

Growth and expansion continues today. In May 1995 Butler unveiled a $50 million master plan that proposes four new buildings. The campus will also change to allow more pedestrian freedom and to restrict vehicle passage. The entire project is slated for completion by 2005.

"Our location in the capital city gives us a very special responsibility," says Bannister. "Our mission is to be the premier independent university for the state of Indiana."

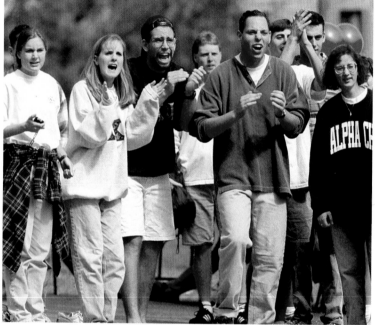

BRENT SMITH

BRENT SMITH

WC RESOURCES CORPORATION HAS A LONG-STANDING partnership with Indianapolis. In recent years, the diversified water utility corporation has expanded service to other communities throughout its own region, nationally, and internationally. ◆ IWC Resources' history dates back to 1871 when its earliest predecessor was incorporated as the Water Works Company. The company operated two wells and used the nine-mile Indiana Central Canal to power its pumps to provide water service to citizens of Indianapolis. However, when financial difficulties forced the company into bankruptcy in 1881, a group of businessmen purchased the failed enterprise and created the Indianapolis Water Company.

Today Indianapolis Water Company is one of IWC Resources' principal subsidiaries, providing quality water service to approximately 235,000 residential, commercial, and industrial customers throughout metropolitan Indianapolis and surrounding areas. IWC Resources' other water utility— Harbour Water Corporation— serves customers north of Indianapolis.

Although providing quality water remains a primary service of the corporation, IWC Resources was formed in 1986 as a holding company to serve other interests, both in the regulated and non-regulated business. In August 1995 IWC Resources reorganized into two divisions—IWC Utilities and IWC Industries.

In addition to Indianapolis Water Company and Harbour Water Corporation, IWC Utilities includes Utility Data Corporation (UDC); Waterway Holdings, Inc.; and IWC Services, Inc. UDC provides data processing and billing services for Indianapolis Water Company and Harbour Water Corporation. UDC also provides sewer billing services for the city of Indianapolis, as well as data processing and billing services for other cities and utilities in Indiana. Waterway Holdings, Inc. holds, leases, develops, and sells real estate for IWC Resources. IWC Services, Inc. is the majority partner of the White River Environmental Partnership, which manages and operates the wastewater treatment facilities for the city of Indianapolis.

IWC Industries includes SM&P Utility Resources, Inc. (SM&P) and Miller Pipeline Corporation (MPC). SM&P was acquired by IWC Resources in June 1993. The company provides underground locating and marking facilities, and preventive maintenance services for utilities in Indiana and several other states.

MPC, which merged with IWC Resources in August 1995, installs natural gas lines and other underground facilities for utilities throughout the United States, as well as international projects through its Construction Division. MPC's Products and Services Division performs technical repair and installation services, and sells sealing products for the natural gas, water, and sewer industries.

IWC Resources has always shown great concern for Indianapolis and the other communities it serves by supporting a myriad of endeavors. The corporation's 2,200 employees are encouraged to become involved and to serve a variety of community activities.

A commitment to quality, fair pricing, public health and safety, community support, shareholder value, and anticipation of future needs of those the corporation serves are the hallmarks of IWC Resources Corporation, its subsidiaries, and its employees.

CLOCKWISE FROM BELOW LEFT: IWC RESOURCES HAS A LONG-STANDING PARTNERSHIP WITH INDIANAPOLIS THAT DATES BACK TO 1871.

A PART OF IWC INDUSTRIES, SM&P UTILITY RESOURCES PROVIDES UNDERGROUND LOCATING AND MARKING FACILITIES, AND PREVENTIVE MAINTENANCE SERVICES FOR UTILITIES IN INDIANA AND SEVERAL OTHER STATES.

MILLER PIPELINE CORPORATION INSTALLS NATURAL GAS LINES AND OTHER UNDERGROUND FACILITIES FOR UTILITIES THROUGHOUT THE UNITED STATES, AS WELL AS INTERNATIONAL PROJECTS THROUGH ITS CONSTRUCTION DIVISION.

▲ MCGUIRE PHOTOGRAPHY, INC.

UST AFTER THE CIVIL WAR ENDED IN 1865, THE LILLY VARNISH Company was founded in Indianapolis by J.O.D. Lilly and his partner, Henry B. Mears. The company's specialty product was a varnish for carriages, with a production capacity of 10,000 gallons per year. ◆ Today Lilly Industries, Inc. is one of the 10 largest North American manufacturers of industrial coatings and

specialty chemicals, supplying customers worldwide from plants in the United States, Canada, Taiwan, Malaysia, Germany, and China.

BUILT ON A SOLID FOUNDATION

In 1872, after purchasing Mears' interest in the company, Lilly brought his sons, Charles and John M. Lilly, into the business. In response to growing demand for the company's coatings, the plant was moved from its original location at the corner of Georgia and Kentucky avenues to South California Street, where the Indianapolis plant is still located today. In 1888 the growing enterprise was officially incorporated as The Lilly Varnish Company.

By 1916 the plant's annual capacity was 2 million gallons, with a storage capacity of 250,000 gallons. The company expanded its market share by supplying varnish to the emerging auto industry, as well as the railway and furniture industries. Lilly's products also included floor varnishes, japans, crystal varnishes, and some shelf goods.

In 1921 Lilly was purchased by a group of men experienced in the manufacture of industrial paint and varnish products. The new

management targeted the industrial coatings market and began the production of customized coatings for a variety of customers who made and painted products such as ladies' hairpins, china pottery, steel oil drums, and locomotives.

GROWTH AND EXPANSION IN THE INDUSTRY

In 1935 a second Lilly plant was built in High Point, North Carolina, to serve the growing furniture industry in that area. By 1938 the company's sales had reached $3 million, and a third plant was built in Gardner, Massachusetts, in 1940. Although the North Carolina plant was destroyed by fire in 1943, it was replaced immediately with a state-of-the-art facility.

In 1944 the company began

to focus on production efficiency and satisfying customer requirements, realizing it was essential for the entire organization to become involved in customer service. Through these efforts, Lilly was able to take a hard look at quality long before quality systems became an industry standard.

MOVING IN NEW DIRECTIONS

In 1963 Lilly purchased C.E. Krieger Company in California to serve a large metal decorating customer on the West Coast. Although this unit's sales and profits grew significantly in the 1970s, the company's primary growth during this time came from supplying the wood furniture business. In 1967 a new satellite facility was built in

In 1990 DOUGLAS W. HUEMME (RIGHT) JOINED LILLY AS PRESIDENT AND CHIEF OPERATING OFFICER OF THE COMPANY AND WAS NAMED CHIEF EXECUTIVE OFFICER A YEAR LATER.

HEADQUARTERED IN INDIANAPOLIS (BELOW), THE COMPANY'S FIVE BUSINESS UNITS INCLUDE WOOD, COIL, POWDER, GLASS, AND SPECIALTY COATINGS.

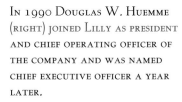

Memphis, Tennessee, but the plant soon was made an independent unit to serve Lilly's strong customer base in Tennessee, Arkansas, Mississippi, and Missouri.

In 1973 a new plant was built in Paulsboro, New Jersey, and soon became one of the most efficient units in the company. As its business grew, the New Jersey plant's major market became coil coating rather than metal decorating.

A small corporate research and development laboratory was established in 1975 in Indianapolis to develop coatings designed to meet new Environmental Protection Agency air pollution regulations. Research and development also targeted new technologies such as high solids, radiation curing, and waterborne coatings.

SIGNIFICANT MILESTONES

In 1989 Lilly's sales exceeded $200 million for the first time in its history. That same year, Lilly set another record by acquiring five new companies. In 1990 Douglas W. Huemme joined Lilly as president and chief operating officer of the company and was named chief executive officer a year later.

Under Huemme's leadership, the 1990s ushered in more prog-

ress. The company's name was changed to Lilly Industries, Inc. in December 1991, reflecting the organization's growing diversity. Lilly has streamlined its operations, established a global presence, and intensified efforts to develop and supply environmentally friendly coatings.

Today the company's five business units include wood, coil, powder, glass, and specialty coatings. Powder coatings have become Lilly's fastest-growing business unit, thanks in part to its environmentally friendly technology. Each business unit has a technical Center of Excellence, with long-term research needs supported by the Corporate Technology Center in Indianapolis.

New markets and new products are continually being evaluated. "Our objective is to focus on programmed innovation," maintains William C. Dorris, vice president of corporate development. "What that means is understanding the markets, their directions, and the forces shaping them, and then using that information to drive technology."

In 1994 Lilly Industries enjoyed record sales exceeding $331 million. Its strong financial performance supports the company's 1994 annual report slogan,

"Building on a Solid Foundation."

"Lilly is proud of its Indianapolis heritage. We have been a part of this growing city for 130 years and have benefited from a variety of city programs," says Huemme. "Supporting Indianapolis is, and will continue to be, a way of life at our company."

A VARIETY OF FAMILIAR PRODUCTS ARE FINISHED WITH LILLY COATINGS.

THE LONG-TERM RESEARCH NEEDS OF LILLY'S BUSINESS UNITS ARE SUPPORTED BY THE CORPORATE TECHNOLOGY CENTER IN INDIANAPOLIS.

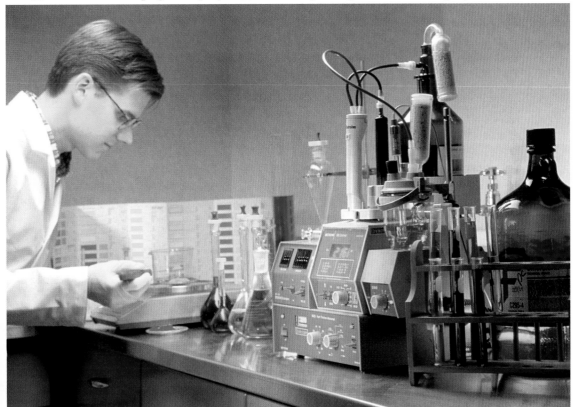

HEN A BANK FOUNDED IN THE CLOSING DAYS OF THE CIVIL WAR merges with one even 20 years older, it conjures up an image of stability and experience—institutions strong enough to survive two world wars, three smaller conflicts, the Great Depression, and at least two major financial panics. ◆ Such was the result in 1992 when Merchants National Bank of Indianapolis—the "baby" of the partners—joined forces with National City Corporation of Cleveland, Ohio, to form National City Bank, Indiana.

Today the Hoosier company—headquartered in the shadow of the State Capitol—includes more than 130 banking centers in 52 cities spanning the length of the state, from East Chicago along Lake Michigan to Madison on the Ohio River.

National City, Indiana draws great strength from its Ohio parent, a $35 billion bank holding company whose principal banks are located in Cleveland, Columbus, Akron, and Toledo in the Buckeye state; in Louisville, Kentucky; and in Indianapolis and surrounds.

The Indiana banking partner offers the full range of banking, financial, and trust services. In addition, through the parent corporation, Indiana businesses can avail themselves of credit cards, retail payment and airline ticket processing, brokerage services, leasing, merchant and mortgage banking, public finance, venture capital, small business and community investment, mutual funds, and credit life insurance.

Coming off 1994's record year in earnings, National City Bank, Indiana continues to pursue constant internal improvement, including the standardization and consolidation of back-office operations, cost containment, and assimilation of acquisitions. It also seeks to build on its traditional banking franchise with innovative products and targeted business initiatives for its corporate banking, trust, and retail banking divisions.

A FULL LINE OF SERVICES

National City's corporate banking division emphasizes lending to small and middle-market businesses. The bank holds a leading market share in this specialty throughout Indiana. National City consistently ranks at or near the top among Hoosier banks in the quality of its cash management services.

Recently National City reorganized its trust division to offer renewed focus on sales, marketing, and improved customer service. Diversified product offerings continue to be developed. A competitive 401(k) employee benefit product for corporate customers was implemented in 1994.

Customer needs in National City's retail banking division have been met through new alternative delivery systems at bank branches already known for quality and efficiency. For example, the organization is investing significantly to enhance telephone banking, supermarket branches, and a wide range of advanced technology.

A LEADER IN COMMUNITY INVOLVEMENT

National City has a statewide reputation for active community involvement—not only in its generous financial contributions but also in the thousands of public service hours given by employees.

"Why do we make this effort? Why do we give both time and money? Simply because National City sees itself as a public trust, dependent on citizen approval for our success in the marketplace," says Vincent A. DiGirolamo, president and CEO. "Giving something back is our way of repaying the people of the state of Indiana for the confidence they continue to show in us."

During 1994 National City's contributions to worthy causes totaled nearly $1.2 million, while approximately 63,000 volunteer hours were given by employees. Civic and community activities comprise the largest block of contributions. Other areas of support include economic development, education, the arts, health and human services, and sports and fitness.

Headquartered in National City Center, just steps away from Circle Centre Mall, National City Bank stands literally at the crossroads of America. But its influence fans out across the Hoosier state, into every nook and cranny of the Indiana heartland.

NATIONAL CITY BANK, INDIANA— HEADQUARTERED IN THE SHADOW OF THE STATE CAPITOL IN NATIONAL CITY CENTER—INCLUDES MORE THAN 130 BANKING CENTERS IN 52 CITIES SPANNING THE LENGTH OF THE STATE.

atCity Investments, Inc. is a full-service regional investment banking and brokerage firm founded in Indiana. The firm, a subsidiary of National City Corporation, has offices throughout Indiana, Ohio, Kentucky, and western Pennsylvania. It is known for its personalized approach with clients when advising them on investment opportunities and financial solutions to their concerns.

In July 1995 National City acquired the business assets of Raffensperger, Hughes & Co., a firm founded in 1937 and regarded as a predominant player in the investment arena. Today NatCity Investments combines independent thinking and institutional strength, making it one of the Midwest's leading investment houses. Its long history of excellence in the municipal and corporate markets, coupled with its extensive knowledge of both local and publicly owned companies, has made NatCity's commitment to personalized client services unsurpassed.

REGIONAL FOCUS

The "small company" approach to service, combined with "big company" performance, is truly the best of both worlds for NatCity's clients. "We have the same capabilities as Wall Street, but we provide these services at the regional level," says Chairman and CEO Herbert R. Martens Jr.

NatCity Investments is noted for having an independent regional focus with a midwestern philosophy. The firm has the region's only comprehensive research that specifically targets companies based in Indiana and other midwestern states. It is among the largest independent market makers of equity securities in the region. Specializing in more than 60 stocks, the firm has managed or comanaged major syndication and marketing efforts for many midwestern companies. The firm is a major underwriter of municipal bonds, ranking among the top managers in the country for bank-qualified issues.

NatCity Investments is prominent in the business community, providing capital to municipalities, school districts, and cities for roads and other infrastructure projects. Its performance in the areas of public and corporate finance is competitive with investment firms throughout the nation. NatCity is a growing organization and, with that growth, expects to see an increase in the services it provides to its clients.

PERSONALIZED SERVICE AND ACCESSIBILITY

In addition to its commitment to regional markets, the company focuses on building long-term relationships with clients and places the utmost importance on maintaining integrity in all its business dealings. Martens says

HERB MARTENS (LEFT), CHAIRMAN AND CEO OF NatCity INVESTMENTS, INC., AND DAVE DABERKO, CHAIRMAN AND CEO OF NATIONAL CITY CORPORATION, NATCITY'S PARENT COMPANY

that emphasis on highly personalized services, including client access to senior executives, is a key reason the firm maintains its position in the marketplace. Clients as well as employees know that if there is ever a need to speak with any member of the senior staff, accessibility is the policy.

Providing insight and guidance unavailable elsewhere, NatCity's exclusive research on local and regional companies is simply unmatched. "Serving our clients with the highest degree of professionalism and utmost respect is the standard within our firm," says Senior Vice President and Retail Managing Director David W. Dunning.

NatCity Investments employs exceptionally experienced, highly disciplined professionals who are supported by state-of-the-art automated systems and technologies. The firm's commitment to maintaining the highest degree of integrity and investing in long-term client relationships places it among the premier investment firms to service the investment needs of the Midwest.

NATIONAL SALES MANAGER DAVE DUNNING (SEATED, FAR LEFT) AND VICE CHAIRMAN GENE TANNER (STANDING) OFFER FINANCIAL ADVICE TO CLIENTS.

LI LILLY AND COMPANY, A RESEARCH-BASED, CUSTOMER-ORIENTED corporation, is a world leader in the pharmaceutical industry. With headquarters in Indianapolis and approximately 26,000 employees worldwide, the company's mission is to create and deliver superior health care solutions—by combining pharmaceutical innovation, existing pharmaceutical technology, disease prevention and management, and information technologies—in order to provide customers worldwide with optimal clinical and economic outcomes.

EARLY BEGINNINGS

Eli Lilly and Company was founded in Indianapolis in 1876 by Colonel Eli Lilly, a pharmaceutical chemist and veteran of the Civil War. Seeking to improve methods of product quality evaluation, Colonel Lilly hired the company's first full-time scientist in 1886, laying the foundation for the firm's ongoing commitment to scientific innovation.

Eventually, Colonel Lilly's son, Josiah K. Lilly Sr., and two of his grandsons, Eli Lilly and Josiah K. Lilly Jr., each served as president of the company. During their tenures, each contributed a unique approach to management, establishing a corporate culture centered on the belief that employees are the company's most valuable asset. This belief still provides the foundation for the organization's corporate philosophy.

PIONEERING SCIENTIFIC INNOVATION

For more than a century, scientific innovation has been paramount to the company's mission. In the early 1920s Lilly scientists worked with researchers Frederick Banting and Charles Best at the University of Toronto to introduce the first insulin product, which revolutionized the treatment of patients with diabetes.

During the 1950s the company developed long-acting, orally administered penicillin products and discovered erythromycin, the first compound in a major class of antibiotics called macrolides. A Lilly research team expanded on discoveries by European scientists in the early 1960s to develop the first agents in another major class of antibiotics, the cephalosporins, which today includes one of the world's most widely used antibacterial products.

In the early 1980s the company introduced human insulin, the world's first human health care product created using genetic engineering technology. In the late 1980s Lilly launched the first product in a major new class of antidepressants.

Over the years, Lilly has evolved from a regional business into an international organization with operations throughout the world. The company entered most Latin American nations during the 1950s and most major European countries during the following decade. In the 1980s Lilly strengthened its presence in Asia, particularly in Korea and Japan.

TURNING TODAY'S STRATEGY INTO ACTION

As customers around the world continue to revolutionize the health care market, Eli Lilly and Company anticipates and responds to these changing needs. Current trends emphasize quality and cost as major issues for health care providers and payers. Concurrently, the costs of bringing new drugs to market continue to rise.

In response to this challenging environment, Lilly charted a new

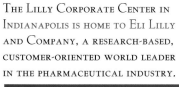

THE LILLY CORPORATE CENTER IN INDIANAPOLIS IS HOME TO ELI LILLY AND COMPANY, A RESEARCH-BASED, CUSTOMER-ORIENTED WORLD LEADER IN THE PHARMACEUTICAL INDUSTRY.

course in 1993 with the strong guidance of its visionary chairman of the board and chief executive officer, Randall L. Tobias. His strategy for the company focuses on five targeted disease categories, on an increased global presence, and on Lilly's own critical capabilities.

"We're not only reinventing our business, but we're reinvigorating our culture, our attitudes, and our thinking. I really believe that the best days at Lilly are not behind us—they are still to come," says Tobias.

The company is currently accelerating the expansion of its global presence. Today, Lilly products are available in more than 150 countries and are manufactured at sites worldwide. Research facilities are located in Belgium, Canada, England, Germany, Japan, and the United States.

"We're looking beyond our traditional strengths and geographic markets to aggressively pursue new global opportunities," says Tobias. "We've picked up the pace of our globalization efforts. In Europe, Latin America, and the Pacific Rim, we've made significant progress in advancing our market position."

In 1994 Lilly established joint ventures in a number of countries, including Greece and Hungary. Products were sold more aggressively in countries of the former Soviet Bloc, and Lilly became the number one pharmaceutical company in Poland. Lilly's presence was reestablished in Argentina and Chile, a new affiliate was opened in Morocco, and operations were extended into the Middle East and Africa.

The company also entered into a global alliance with India's Ranbaxy Laboratories. In addition, business in Indonesia was expanded, and an office in Vietnam was opened. Lilly's position remains strong in Japan, the world's second-largest pharmaceutical market, while operations that started in late 1993 in China and India continue to grow.

TARGETED DISEASE CATEGORIES

Lilly is leveraging current research and development and related resources by focusing them more sharply. Within five broad categories—central nervous system diseases, endocrine diseases, infectious diseases, cancer, and cardiovascular diseases—the company has targeted its discovery research by matching its strengths with the world's most critical health needs. Diabetes, within the endocrine category, is a good example of this focus. As one of the world's major suppliers of insulin, Lilly has long been a global leader in the treatment of diabetes. Unfortunately, the disease continues to cause long-term complications that affect 100 million people worldwide.

Continuing its 70-year history of insulin product development, Lilly is investigating its new insulin

analog, which has undergone clinical trials in 31 countries. The evidence from those trials indicates that this insulin analog may help patients with diabetes achieve better blood-glucose control and more convenience in their daily lives, and may reduce the incidence of complications associated with the disease.

Beyond insulin innovation and leadership, Lilly is also searching for better ways to become a world leader in the management of the entire diabetes disease process. For example, delivery devices are being developed to provide patients with convenient use and more accu-

CLOCKWISE FROM ABOVE: "WE'RE LOOKING BEYOND OUR TRADITIONAL STRENGTHS AND GEOGRAPHIC MARKETS TO AGGRESSIVELY PURSUE NEW GLOBAL OPPORTUNITIES," SAYS RANDALL L. TOBIAS, LILLY'S CHAIRMAN AND CHIEF EXECUTIVE OFFICER. "IN EUROPE, LATIN AMERICA, AND THE PACIFIC RIM, WE'VE MADE SIGNIFICANT PROGRESS IN ADVANCING OUR MARKET POSITION."

THE COMPANY WAS FOUNDED IN INDIANAPOLIS IN 1876 BY COLONEL ELI LILLY, A PHARMACEUTICAL CHEMIST AND VETERAN OF THE CIVIL WAR.

MORE THAN A CENTURY AGO, LILLY LAID THE FOUNDATION FOR ITS ONGOING COMMITMENT TO SCIENTIFIC INNOVATION. PICTURED IS J.K. LILLY SR., SON OF THE FOUNDER.

THE DISCOVERY AND DEVELOPMENT OF INNOVATIVE MEDICINES CONTINUES TO BE CENTRAL TO THE COMPANY'S GROWTH.

rate drug dosage. An agreement with Indianapolis-based Boehringer Mannheim Corporation, the world's leading provider of blood-glucose monitors, will allow Lilly to offer customers more comprehensive and convenient diabetes care.

Lilly is also among the world's largest and most experienced bio-technology companies, with proven abilities to discover, develop, and manufacture small organic molecules and large natural molecules. One exciting new biotech compound, ReoPro™, is a result of the company's collaboration with Centocor, Inc. Cleared for use in the United States, Sweden, and the Netherlands, ReoPro is combined with angioplasty to prevent certain costly, acute complications like heart attacks or repeat angioplasty. This biotech compound, manufactured by Centocor and distributed by Lilly, was launched in the United States in February 1994.

CRITICAL SKILLS AND CAPABILITIES

Foremost among the capabilities Lilly focuses on is innovation in all parts of the business. The discovery and development of innovative medicines continues to be central to the company's growth. For this reason, Lilly acquired Sphinx Pharmaceuticals Corporation in 1994. With that acquisition came a proprietary technology that enables Lilly scientists to generate and screen thousands of diverse compounds more efficiently.

Disease prevention and management is an integral part of corporate strategy and drove a number of strategic actions in 1994, including the purchase of PCS Health Systems, Inc., the largest and fastest-growing managed-pharmaceutical-care company in the United States. Its extensive databases contain comprehensive information on the prescription transactions of more than 55 million members. Today, PCS databases link nearly all the pharmacies in the United States. This technology is also being used increasingly to deliver valuable information to physicians' offices across the country.

Lilly believes that linking its own knowledge of diseases and drugs with PCS information is one critical step in creating total quality health care. To provide the best health care for the least cost, the company believes that the health care system must be equipped to manage the entire course of a disease. Through disease-management programs, payers and providers can better measure and manage the entire health care process. These programs encompass pharmaceuticals as well as a range of other therapeutic and educational interventions.

For example, a disease-management program might help a health maintenance organization

recognize whether its primary care physicians are missing early diagnosis of depression, which results in costly repeated visits to the physician as well as prolonged suffering for the patient. The program would provide improved tools to assist physicians and patients in diagnosing the problem early. Early diagnosis leads to healthier patients, a more efficient system, and lower costs.

Another important capability is cost competitiveness. Countries worldwide are concerned about rising health care expenses. Lilly has responded by controlling company costs and by using its own resources more efficiently.

Yet another vital ingredient in Lilly's success is preeminent organizational effectiveness. Under its current structure, the global capabilities of this large, multinational company will be combined with local expertise to meet specific and diverse customer needs throughout the world.

As part of Lilly's corporate strategy, pharmaceutical global business units were added in 1994, joining the existing animal health global business unit. These units complement geographic and functional organizations by translating strategy into action.

QUEST FOR LEADERSHIP: A VIEW TO THE FUTURE

Looking to the future, Lilly has one of the most exciting new-product pipelines in the industry. The potential exists for breakthroughs in each of the company's targeted disease categories. The company is currently investigating or seeking regulatory approval of new compounds that target, for example, cancer, which causes one of every five deaths in the United States; Alzheimer's disease, a debilitating illness that affects more than 15 million people around the world; schizophrenia, a disease that affects 1 percent of the world's population, or 50 million people; and osteoporosis, a disease that affects 60 percent of all Caucasian and Asian women over age 50.

In the spirit of total commitment to saving lives and satisfying customers, Lilly looks to the future with confidence and enthusiasm. "Together, we've created a vision of global leadership. We have people with talent, energy, and commitment to bring it all to life," says Tobias.

"We will expect to be valued for all that we have achieved in the past, but measured by and rewarded for what we are contributing currently," he adds. "It is, after all, our behavior and not our words that truly reveal what we stand for as individuals and as a company."

WITHIN FIVE BROAD CATEGORIES— CENTRAL NERVOUS SYSTEM DISEASES, ENDOCRINE DISEASES, INFECTIOUS DISEASES, CANCER, AND CARDIOVASCULAR DISEASES—LILLY HAS TARGETED ITS DISCOVERY RESEARCH BY MATCHING ITS STRENGTHS WITH THE WORLD'S MOST CRITICAL HEALTH NEEDS.

THE 1994 ACQUISITION OF SPHINX PHARMACEUTICALS CORPORATION BROUGHT A PROPRIETARY TECHNOLOGY THAT ENABLES LILLY SCIENTISTS TO GENERATE AND SCREEN THOUSANDS OF DIVERSE COMPOUNDS MORE EFFICIENTLY.

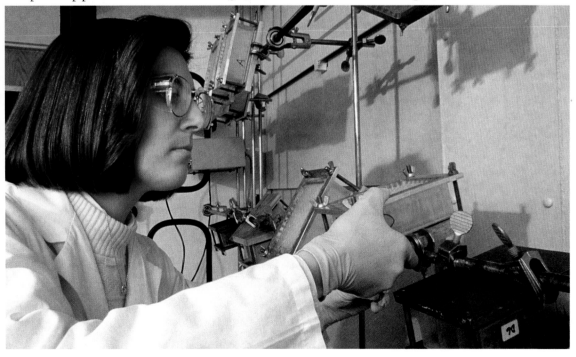

MERICAN UNITED LIFE INSURANCE COMPANY® HAS BECOME known as the "Company with the Partnership Philosophy." This phrase characterizes the organization's relationship not only with its policyholders and clients, but also with its dedicated field sales force and with the city of Indianapolis. ◆ American United Life (AUL)—a mutual company headquartered in the landmark AUL Tower in downtown Indianapolis—is currently licensed to sell its products and services in 46 states and the District of Columbia. This diversified organization has approximately $6.5 billion in assets and provides individual life insurance and annuities, group life and disability insurance, pension products, and reinsurance services. American United Life is one of the country's leading providers of tax-deferred group annuities and pensions, boasting more than $4 billion in managed assets.

THE FOUNDING AND THE DAYS OF KNIGHTS

In the post-Civil War depression era, distrust of corporations and insurance firms was prevalent. Family men turned to fraternal organizations, where low-cost mutual insurance plans offered an incentive to join.

During a convention of the Supreme Lodge of the Knights of Pythias of the World in Cleveland, Ohio, in 1877, Chancellor Stillman S. Davis proposed the Pythian Endowment Rank to create an insurance plan for its members. In November of 1877, the rank—which would later become American United Life Insurance Company—was established.

INNOVATION IN PRODUCTS AND SERVICES

Today AUL offers products and services through four major divisions: pension, individual, group, and reinsurance. Pensions comprise the company's largest product line. Pension assets under management account for more than half the company's assets. With the graying of America and baby boomer concerns over financial security, group and individual products like 401(k) plans and group annuities continue to enjoy explosive growth.

AUL's individual division operates with a career agency system for product distribution. This highly trained, dedicated field force sells AUL products exclusively throughout the country, with emphasis on Indiana and the Midwest.

The group division focuses on the worksite marketing of group products such as group life insurance, group annuities, and group disability. As small and midsize customers continue to grow, AUL increasingly acts as a support consultant, educating employers and employees about available products. Excellent service is a strong focus in all AUL customer relations.

The reinsurance division has been operating for more than 90 years, which makes AUL the oldest life reinsurer in the United States. This division is, in effect, an insurance company for other insurance companies, accepting portions of the risk on policies sold by other reputable companies.

All four divisions benefit from AUL's commitment to state-of-the-art technology. "Companywide, our emphasis on new technology is putting AUL on the information

KNOWN AS THE "COMPANY WITH THE PARTNERSHIP PHILOSOPHY," AUL STRIVES TO CONSISTENTLY EXCEED CUSTOMER EXPECTATIONS (RIGHT).

WORK PROCESSES ARE CONTINUALLY EVALUATED TO ENSURE HIGH LEVELS OF SERVICE AT AMERICAN UNITED LIFE (BELOW).

superhighway, which we believe will be the national road of the future," explains Chairman, President, and CEO Jerry D. Semler. "During the next few years, we plan to invest more than $17 million in new technology with the specific intent of increasing our capacity for service and efficiency."

A STEPPING-STONE FOR DOWNTOWN REVITALIZATION

In the late 1970s, with the approval of the Indiana General Assembly, Indiana Vocational Technical College purchased the location AUL had occupied since 1931. The insurance company then built the AUL Tower and moved to its current location: a downtown site bordered by New York Street, Ohio Street, Illinois Street, and Capitol Avenue. This move relocated AUL in the center of the city's area of highest unemployment and demonstrated the company's strong interest in downtown revitalization. In 1979 Mayor William Hudnut singled out the move as one of the first important steps in the city's long-range plans to revitalize the central business district.

AUL's commitment to the city continues today through its foundation and the company's support of hundreds of organizations and projects involved in health and welfare, education, and urban affairs, as well as local arts and culture. The company's strong partnership with the city of Indianapolis is an integral part of its daily business. "There is a real value system in the Midwest and among the people at AUL," says James W. Freeman, vice president, corporate communications. "We are concerned about our neighbors, whether we have a close personal relationship or not."

PATRIOTISM AND CREATIVITY

AUL's crowning glory, a 20- by 38-foot American flag, flies proudly above its headquarters building—honoring the spirit of patriotism that runs strong in Indianapolis. In good weather, the flag is on display 24 hours a day, waving from its 80-foot aluminum pole. American Legion guidelines for the

removal and care of the flag are strictly observed, and a typical flag lasts about 90 days atop the AUL building.

On a lighter note, the AUL signboard features humorous sayings from a wide spectrum of contributors, helping rush-hour drivers maintain their perspective on the world with a smile. This goodwill effort began with simple messages, such as "Safe Motoring" and "Happy Thanksgiving." Since

1957 these quips have entertained the city, evolving with a sense of creative ingenuity. Many motorists have observed the wit and wisdom of phrases such as "The stork is the bird with the biggest bill," "As a gardener, the only thing I grow is tired," and "People who snore always fall asleep first."

The people at AUL make all this happen. More than 100 years in the insurance industry must be a good sign.

AUL'S CROWNING GLORY, A 20- BY 38-FOOT AMERICAN FLAG, FLIES PROUDLY ABOVE ITS HEADQUARTERS BUILDING—HONORING THE SPIRIT OF PATRIOTISM THAT RUNS STRONG IN INDIANAPOLIS.

MERITECH IS ONE OF THE WORLD'S LARGEST COMMUNICATIONS companies, helping more than 13 million customers keep in touch. The company provides an array of telephone, data, and video services to more than 500,000 customers in the Indianapolis area. Ameritech is creating dozens of new information, entertainment, and interactive services for homes, businesses, and government.

SERVING INDIANA SINCE 1883

Since 1883 Ameritech has provided communications services to home and business customers in Indiana. Originally known as Central Union Telephone Company, and later as Indiana Bell, Ameritech Indiana now employs approximately 5,700 people, including 1,200 who work in Indianapolis. These employees are responsible for keeping Ameritech on the cutting edge of technology, which allows customers to take advantage of many new services, including wireless communications.

With more than 95,000 miles of fiber-optic cable in place in Indiana and with Ameritech's digital call-handling systems, the company can process more than 3 billion calls annually in the state.

Ameritech's Opportunity Indiana plan calls for the investment of millions of dollars in infrastructure to extend advanced communications links to interested schools, hospitals, and major government centers in its Indiana service territory by the year 2000. The company is contributing another $30 million for equipment, software, and training to allow

schools to take advantage of the advanced system.

By January 1996 more than 200 Indiana schools were using Ameritech's two-way, interactive-video technology to expand learning beyond the walls of the classroom. Often referred to as "distance learning," this technology allows schools to conduct joint classes and to take students on "electronic field trips." Teachers are also using the videoconferencing systems to complete continuing education classes on-site rather than traveling to a university.

A TEAM PLAYER AT HOME

Throughout its long history of service in Indiana, Ameritech has been an active corporate citizen. Through its contributions program, Ameritech annually invests about $2 million in Indiana organizations. Major sponsorships have included the Ameritech Hoosier Academic Super Bowl, a statewide academic competition for high school students; Ameritech's Yuletide Celebration, a holiday tradition in conjunction with the Indianapolis Symphony Orchestra; and

Ameritech's Animals and All That Jazz, a series of summer jazz concerts at the Indianapolis Zoo.

"We've been here a long time, and throughout that history we've had a very proud heritage of partnering with the communities we serve, like Indianapolis," says Kent Lebherz, president of Ameritech Indiana. "And for that reason we have been actively involved in both the public and private sectors in helping to contribute to the development of Indianapolis. It's a good place to live and work."

FOR MORE THAN A CENTURY, THE INDIANAPOLIS MUSEUM OF Art (IMA) has contributed to the exceptional quality of life in its hometown and the state of Indiana. Since its founding as the Art Association of Indianapolis in 1883, the IMA has built one of the finest collections of art in the country and has become a showcase for national and international exhibitions.

MASTERPIECES FROM AROUND THE WORLD

Among the IMA's priceless individual collections are the Eli Lilly Collection of Chinese art, the Clowes Fund Collection of old masters, the Kurt F. Pantzer Sr. Collection (one of the largest collections of works by J.M.W. Turner outside Great Britain), the W.J. Holliday Collection of neo-impressionist paintings, the Eiteljorg Collection of African and South Pacific art, and the Joseph Cantor Collection of contemporary European art. Works from these collections are sought by museums around the world for special exhibitions. In addition, the IMA has mounted many exhibitions of its own that have included prized works lent by other institutions and major collectors.

The IMA's magnificent setting, unique for an art museum, consists of 152 acres including the historic grounds of Oldfields, a rare representative of an important period of landscape design. In addition to Oldfields, the Eli Lilly Gardens include the grounds surrounding the museum; the Garden for Everyone, which is accessible to all visitors; and the Richard D. Wood Formal Garden.

CULTURAL LEADER

The IMA is a community leader in cultural programming and a center of learning for both children and adults. Classes related to the permanent collections and special exhibitions, as well as art survey classes, are offered in the spring and the fall. Lectures and seminars are presented throughout the year by distinguished guest speakers on diverse topics such as postmodern culture, art glass, horticulture, and the art of Zen.

The education division of the IMA offers programs, workshops, and tours for children, and resource kits about the collections help those who teach art. The more than 32,000 reference books, periodicals, films, and videos housed in the Stout Reference Library and the 157,000 slides in the IMA's slide collection are valuable resources for scholars and others.

Special events such as AfricaFest, Artventures in Victorian England, and Artventures in Japan have provided insight into other cultures, while concerts of classical and contemporary music feature local, regional, and international performers.

Admission and parking are free; however, there is an admission

◀ WILBUR MONTGOMERY

charge for selected exhibitions, except on Thursdays. The museum is open daily from 10 a.m. to 5 p.m., on Thursdays from 10 a.m. to 8:30 p.m., and on Sundays from noon to 5 p.m. The IMA is closed on Mondays and on major holidays. The Alliance Museum Shop, the Rental Gallery and Better Than New Shop, and the Madeline F. Elder Greenhouse offer interesting shopping experiences. Dining is available at the Garden on the Green restaurant, while snacks, sandwiches, and a variety of beverages are offered at Caffe Pietro.

The IMA is committed to enriching the lives of the more than 400,000 visitors who come to the museum yearly to participate in its programs and activities. Indeed, the Indianapolis Museum of Art makes it possible for people to explore the world of art around them and to enjoy a special aspect of the cultural life in Indianapolis.

CLOCKWISE FROM TOP:
THE IMA IS RECOGNIZED AS THE SEVENTH-LARGEST GENERAL ART MUSEUM IN THE UNITED STATES.

ITS MAGNIFICENT SETTING, UNIQUE FOR AN ART MUSEUM, CONSISTS OF 152 ACRES INCLUDING THE RICHARD D. WOOD FORMAL GARDEN.

AMONG THE IMA'S PRICELESS INDIVIDUAL COLLECTIONS IS THE ELI LILLY COLLECTION OF CHINESE ART.

ITIZENS GAS & COKE UTILITY IS THE ONLY U.S. UTILITY THAT operates as a public charitable trust. This not-for-profit organization fulfills its trust responsibilities by providing Marion County citizens with prompt and safe service, adequate natural gas supplies, and some of the lowest natural gas rates in the country. Having experienced many transitions throughout its

history, the Indianapolis-based utility has consistently maintained its status as a public trust and consequently has passed on many advantages to the community it serves.

HISTORY OF A PUBLIC TRUST

More than a century ago, Indianapolis was a leading center for manufacturing. A group of prominent citizens formed a trust to provide low-cost natural gas for residents of Marion County, hoping to avoid a utility monopoly.

A quarter century before the formation of this trust, on February 12, 1851, the Indianapolis Gas, Light and Coke Company was incorporated and was granted permission by the state legislature to "supply the city of Indianapolis and its inhabitants with artificial

gas for lighting purposes for the term of 20 years." A parcel of land on Pennsylvania Street was obtained, and a retort house and gas holder were built for $27,000. On January 10, 1852, the first artifical gas for public use was provided by the utility. By 1853, 115 residences were lighted by artifical gas, and by May 1860, 8.5 miles of city streets were illuminated by 265 street lamps. Natural gas was finally discovered in Indiana during the mid-1880s, and was first used in Indianapolis in December 1887.

That same year, citizens of Marion County responded to rising gas rates by holding a public meeting to discuss the possible formation of a new gas system that would be operated for the benefit of the consumer. The resulting proposal led to the establishment of Consumers Gas Trust Company, which was

formed as a nonprofit corporation and public trust. The utility was then franchised by the city of Indianapolis, and distribution of natural gas to customers began in May 1888. But by 1904 the company's natural gas supplies had been exhausted, wasted by inefficient street torches and consumption without the benefit of meters. Customers often regulated their heating by raising and closing windows while the gas heat remained on.

In 1905 the city of Indianapolis exercised a provision from its 1887 franchise agreement allowing it to purchase Consumers Gas Trust Company outright, and in 1906 the operation was renamed Citizens Gas Company. That same year, the company preserved its original goal when the Chicago Federal Court of Appeals deemed the utility to

CITIZENS GAS & COKE UTILITY'S GENERAL OFFICE AND CUSTOMER SERVICE CENTER ARE LOCATED ON NORTH MERIDIAN STREET IN INDIANAPOLIS.

be a public charitable trust. This arrangement freed the utility from political control and put its assets in trust for Marion County residents. Formed in the public interest, the trust cannot be broken and will continue to exist as long as it serves a viable purpose.

In 1929 the Indiana General Assembly granted exclusive management, regulation, and control of the trust assets to Citizens Gas Company. Even if the utility's authority could be changed by the General Assembly, the natural gas plant and property would remain subject to the trust terms. In 1935 ownership of Citizens Gas Company was conveyed entirely to the city of Indianapolis, and the name was changed to Citizens Gas & Coke Utility.

Today Citizens Gas & Coke is governed by a five-member board of trustees and a board of directors. Each trustee is nominated by the prior board and appointed by the mayor. Trustees serve four-year terms, and seven members of the board of directors—who are elected by the board of trustees—are given general supervision and control of the utility.

Citizens Gas & Coke pays local property taxes and several million dollars annually in Indiana gross receipts taxes. However, as a public charitable trust, income from the utility's services is not subject to federal tax. This exemption allows the utility financial flexibility. For example, Citizens Gas & Coke enjoys lower borrowing costs and uses tax-free bonds to purchase equipment. Operating as a public charitable trust sets the tone for everything done at the utility. Its history still has meaning today.

CONTINUOUS SERVICE TO CUSTOMERS

Customers today enjoy many benefits provided by Citizens Gas & Coke. In January 1994, amid the coldest winter on record in Indianapolis, the utility supplied adequate service to all its customers, including industrial customers. Local businesses and residents were delighted with this kind of reliable service. In fact, in a recent survey, 87 percent of the 250,000 Marion County residents served by the utility favored leaving the trust intact.

Citizens Gas & Coke customers also benefit from the reliable supplies of natural gas that remain available through the utility. Two interstate pipelines, Panhandle Eastern and Texas Gas, currently supply the utility. Additionally, Citizens Gas & Coke maintains underground storage for natural gas in Greene County and two liquefied natural gas facilities in Marion County.

The utility is the only natural gas distribution company in the United States to operate a coke manufacturing plant. Net income from the plant, located at 2950 Prospect Street, is added to revenues to keep gas costs to customers as low as possible. Revenues at the coke plant are supplemented by the sale of by-products recovered in the coke manufacturing process. These include coke oven gas, which is mixed with natural gas and supplied to the utility's customers.

As Citizens Gas & Coke continues to grow, its vision extends beyond paradigms about the natural gas industry. "These are exciting and challenging times, and Citizens Gas & Coke Utility is determined to stay competitive to ensure future growth," says President and Chief Executive Officer Don Lindemann. "We intend to reinforce our commitment to total customer satisfaction."

COMMITTED TO MAINTAINING RELIABLE SUPPLIES OF NATURAL GAS FOR CUSTOMERS, THE COMPANY OPERATES THIS COKE MANUFACTURING PLANT AND GAS MIXING STATION ON PROSPECT STREET.

NION FEDERAL SAVINGS BANK—WITH ASSETS EXCEEDING $2 billion—has been providing financial services in Indianapolis since 1887. As a result of an aggressive expansion program, Union Federal now operates more than 40 full-service offices in central Indiana, including Lafayette and Anderson. ♦ "Union Federal is proud of our 108-year heritage of serving the financial needs of the people of Indiana, and we remain committed to meeting those needs in the future," says President Jerry Von Deylen. "Our goal is to maintain a clear focus on expanding our operation throughout the entire state and to become an even stronger financial partner for the people of Indiana."

PROUD HERITAGE

Founded in 1887 as the Indianola Building and Loan Association (with an office on West Washington Street), Union Federal is one of the few remaining Indiana-owned and -operated banks in Indianapolis. In 1937 the institution was converted to a federal savings and loan association and moved to East Market Street. Rapid growth led the bank to another East Market Street location in 1941. In 1948 Union Federal opened the city's first savings and loan branch on East Maple Road.

Assets of the company increased by more than $11 million in 1959 when Union Federal merged with Colonial Savings and Loan Association. In 1962 Union Federal announced plans to construct a new building on the corner of Pennsylvania and Market streets. The facility, completed in 1964, still houses the bank's main branch and much of its management operations.

In September 1984, when Union Federal was acquired by the principals of Waterfield Mortgage Company, mortgage banking operations expanded significantly, making the bank a leader in home financing. The downtown Union Federal building underwent extensive renovation in 1985, including a new reflective glass exterior, a remodeled lobby, and new modular workstations.

UNION FEDERAL'S "NEW" MAIN OFFICE AS IT APPEARED SHORTLY AFTER ITS COMPLETION IN 1964 (BELOW)

THE REMODELED HEADQUARTERS AS IT APPEARS TODAY (RIGHT)

In January 1986 the organization was granted permission from the Federal Home Loan Bank Board to change its name to Union Federal Savings Bank. As a savings institution, Union Federal expanded the range of its banking services and became the largest federal savings bank in Indiana with the 1987 acquisition of Community Federal Savings and Loan Association of Ohio. Branch offices increased to include 33 locations in Indiana and Ohio.

Union Holding, the parent company of Union Federal Savings Bank, grew in 1988 with the acquisition of Arsenal Savings Association, F.A., Indianapolis, and Frankton Federal Savings and Loan Association. Union Federal remains the state's largest federal savings bank, achieving total assets of more than $2 billion in fiscal 1995.

PEOPLE-ORIENTED SERVICE

Union Federal offers a full range of financial products and services designed to meet the needs of personal and business customers, including checking and savings products, consumer and commercial lending, residential mortgage lending and construction loans, charge cards,

ATMs, alternative investment opportunities, and trust and private banking. "We continue to seek new opportunities to increase the scope and depth of our branch operations. This includes not only expansion within our existing markets, but also the development of new markets within Indiana," says Senior Vice President Lonnie Frauhiger.

Union Federal prides itself on being a friendly, customer-driven organization. Employees are dedicated to making the bank's slogan, "All your bank should be," a reality. It is not uncommon for Union Federal tellers to recognize customers and call them by name. Building trust and providing excellent, personalized service are longtime goals that have remained unchanged.

Reflecting increased efforts to provide convenience for its customers, Union Federal opened its first Marsh Supermarket branch in 1981 at 62nd Street and Allisonville Road. Today, the bank operates a total of 22 Marsh Supermarket branches. Union Federal also offers extended lobby hours—10 a.m. to 7 p.m. Monday through Friday, and 10 a.m. to 5 p.m. on Saturday. Additionally, the bank operates an extensive network of 24-hour ATMs, as well as the InTouch 24 telephone account information service.

To help customers better understand and select appropriate bank services and products, Union

Federal has compiled a catalog-style handbook that gives information on checking and savings accounts, credit cards, loans, mortgages, insurance, investments, personal trust services, private banking, and business services.

COMMUNITY BANK

A great bank is a great community neighbor. Union Federal makes community involvement a priority, offering support to more than 200 projects through personal involvement and corporate donations.

For example, Union Federal was the proud sponsor of WTTV's "Do the Right Thing"—a multilevel educational campaign designed to help children avoid the perils of drugs, abduction, and other crimes that affect children. Other community projects include sponsoring a Multiple Sclerosis Society benefit, a room at the Children's Museum Haunted House, and the SuperCities Walk. In addition, Union Federal brings the Dolce Trio to downtown Indianapolis annually for the holiday season. The bank has also been strongly involved in support of the Day Center, an organization dedicated to assisting the homeless through the holidays.

Union Federal's commitment to its customers and the city has created tremendous loyalty in the community. It is the kind of bank that is destined to prosper because of its great heritage, its people-oriented philosophy, and its generous contributions to Indianapolis.

CUSTOMERS ENJOY THE CONVENIENCE OF FULL-SERVICE BANKING AT ONE OF UNION FEDERAL'S MARSH SUPERMARKET LOCATIONS (ABOVE).

THE BANK'S BROAD RIPPLE OFFICE IS A WELL-RECOGNIZED LANDMARK IN THE COMMUNITY (BELOW LEFT).

OR MORE THAN A CENTURY, THE INDIANAPOLIS CHAMBER of Commerce has articulately voiced the needs and concerns of the local business community, creating a dynamic environment for thriving businesses within central Indiana. The efforts of this distinguished organization have elevated Indianapolis to a place of national prominence, positioning

the growing city as an attractive and vibrant place to establish and conduct business.

In its early days, the Chamber targeted campaigns to improve the city's infrastructure and to protect business interests. Today the organization remains an essential partner to more than 3,300 businesses and corporations in central Indiana.

TRADITION AND SERVICE

The Indianapolis Chamber of Commerce has led numerous successful programs throughout its 106-year history. Originally founded by 27 business leaders as the Commercial Club of Indianapolis on February 6, 1890, the group's initial mission was "to promote prosperity and work for the general welfare of Indianapolis." The organization's charter was signed two days later, and Colonel Eli Lilly was elected as its president.

In its first week of operation, the Commercial Club sponsored the Street Exposition of Indianapolis, resulting in the paving of the major streets in the downtown area. Other early accomplishments include creating a city park system, supporting the first city hospital, facilitating a

major cleanup of downtown property, securing a location for the airport, and revising the city charter to establish the mayor/city council system. Renamed the Indianapolis Chamber of Commerce in December 1912, the organization also responded to the needs of businesses, protecting manufacturing interests during the war years and assisting veterans with job placements in the 1950s and 1960s.

In the 1970s the Stanley K. Lacy Executive Leadership Series was developed, offering training to the city's promising young business leaders. During the 1980s the Chamber focused on the environ-

ment, introducing a program to increase awareness of air quality problems and to promote voluntary vehicle emission inspections. In addition, the Chamber launched a campaign urging parents to become more involved in their children's education. The Chamber also actively lobbied the Indiana General Assembly for legislation that led to the construction of the RCA Dome.

THE 1990s—
SUCCESSFUL SOLUTIONS

Indianapolis has always been blessed with business leaders and companies who see the big picture, who have a vision of

CLOCKWISE FROM TOP LEFT: JOSEPH D. BARNETTE JR. IS THE CHAMBER'S 1995-96 CHAIRMAN OF THE BOARD.

JOHN S. MYRLAND SERVES AS THE CHAMBER'S PRESIDENT.

FROM ITS EARLIEST DAYS, THE CHAMBER HAS BEEN INVOLVED WITH INDIANAPOLIS' AIRPORT.

FOUNDED IN 1890, THE CHAMBER HAS LONG BEEN A PART OF THE CITY'S GROWTH AND PROSPERITY.

where the community ought to be headed, and who are willing to support efforts to fulfill that vision," says John S. Myrland, Chamber president.

Throughout its history, the Indianapolis Chamber of Commerce has encountered internal and external challenges while successfully moving the local business community toward a promising and progressive future. Today's growing membership enjoys a full range of targeted products and services, including an annual Chamber directory, access to the city's largest electronic database of local market information, hundreds of workshops, and more than 35 different networking opportunities each year.

Members also have access to the Internet through IndyLink, the Chamber's on-line information server. Through IndyLink, each member's company profile is available to international and domestic businesses, serving as a resource for locating products and services and enhancing business. IndyLink users can communicate via private electronic mail and can post public messages to a forum.

Individuals and companies interested in relocation information and employment opportunities in the Indianapolis area can log onto IndyLink to obtain details on businesses, demographics, and the region's quality of life. In addition, a library of multimedia information—including images, motion graphics, and videos of the area—is easily accessible on IndyLink for downloading by remote users.

The Chamber has positioned its membership on the cutting edge of technological, marketing, and business promotion with its homepage on the World Wide Web. This resource includes a database of all members, a calendar of Chamber events, on-line membership applications, an index of other U.S. chambers of commerce, and business advertising opportunities.

The Chamber also offers a research library. Books, maps, newspaper clippings, subject files, brochures, research reports, magazines, and local and national newspapers covering various aspects of Indianapolis and the business community are available for review to any

EACH MAY THE CITY PLAYS HOST TO THE WORLD-RENOWNED INDIANAPOLIS 500 (ABOVE).

THE CHAMBER ACTIVELY LOBBIED THE INDIANA GENERAL ASSEMBLY FOR LEGISLATION THAT LED TO THE CONSTRUCTION OF THE RCA DOME (LEFT).

Chamber member. The collection also includes subject and title access to materials ranging from foreign trade directories, telephone books, and government documents to company annual reports, business periodicals, and directories.

Additional membership benefits include representation in local and state government, and opportunities to meet local elected officials.

THE CHAMBER'S MAGIC

The Indianapolis Chamber of Commerce coordinates the Metropolitan Association of Greater Indianapolis Communities (MAGIC), a group of more than 300 representatives from area chambers, local economic development organizations, and regional employers established to collec-

tively address problems that limit the region's ability to foster business growth and expansion.

"One of the more exciting activities for the years ahead is the further development of MAGIC," says Joseph D. Barnette Jr., the Chamber's 1995-96 chairman of the board. "Success will require awareness and collaboration by community and township governments to create a high quality of life for all of our citizens. In the future, the new base of support will come from the growing groups of small, medium, and large businesses throughout central Indiana that share the vision. Business leaders will step up to the plate and provide what is needed. And the Indianapolis Chamber of Commerce will continue to support those efforts."

TATE LIFE'S SUCCESS OVER THE PAST CENTURY CAN BE DIRECTLY attributed to its people. The company's reputation in large part is defined by combining the reputations of the men and women involved with the organization—both in the home office and in the field. Especially important have been the thousands of agents who have sold billions of dollars' worth of insurance to

State Life policyholders. The company continues to depend on these individuals for its success in the 1990s.

Currently, State Life sells life insurance and annuities through a Personal Producing General Agent (PPGA) network of independent contractors. The company is licensed in 44 states and the District of Columbia. Additionally, State Life has a wholesale brokerage marketing agreement for impaired risk insurance with State Systems, Inc., a Texas-based marketing organization.

STATE LIFE IN INDIANAPOLIS

In 1894 eight prominent citizens founded State Life in Indianapolis and served as its first agents. Among the founders were an Indianapolis mayor, an Indiana Supreme Court judge, and a dean of the DePauw University Law School. The business grew and flourished during its early years in the firmly established American insurance industry. But the company's leaders were forced to conduct business in a challenging environment because the state of Indiana had few laws regulating insurance companies.

State Life earned the distinction of becoming Indiana's first "legal reserve" life insurance company early in its history. Company leaders voluntarily deposited monetary sums equal to the cash value of the company's insurance in force with the State Insurance Commissioner in order to honor obligations to policyholders.

This focus on integrity and an unblemished reputation has served the company well. State Life has grown from a start-up firm with no premiums and an operations budget of $500 to a thriving company with approximately $300 million in assets and $2.4 billion worth of insurance in force. State Life's

ARTHUR L. BRYANT, FSA, A VETERAN OF STATE LIFE FOR MORE THAN 30 YEARS, HAS SERVED AS PRESIDENT SINCE 1983 (RIGHT).

SINCE ITS FOUNDING, THE COMPANY'S EFFORTS HAVE BEEN DIRECTED BY PROMINENT INDIANAPOLIS BUSINESS AND CIVIC LEADERS. PICTURED BELOW ARE EARLY BOARD OF DIRECTORS MEMBERS.

financial strength is further represented by the superior quality of its investment portfolio.

Still headquartered in Indianapolis, the company has occupied five different downtown offices since its inception. The first one-room office was in the Journal Building at 8 East Market Street. After several other short-term locations, the company moved to 15 East Washington Street in 1904. In 1969, during its 75th anniversary year, the company settled into its current headquarters at 141 East Washington Street.

In 1982 State Life purchased a former downtown branch of Merchants National Bank at 117 East Washington Street, including its parking lot. Now the company owns approximately 95 percent of a triangular city block. State Life has directly contributed to the growth and development of the

city by maintaining its headquarters in downtown Indianapolis for more than 100 years.

AGENT RELATIONSHIPS: A PRIMARY COMPANY GOAL

State Life's main emphasis has always been building quality, long-term relationships with its agents. With that goal in mind, the company offers certain benefits to its agents that other companies do not. For example, State Life is small enough to encourage feedback from agents, and can incorporate this valuable information in its planning. This personal approach has been a company trademark and has contributed to State Life's success through an underlying philosophy of making it as easy as possible for agents to conduct the company's business. "People, not places, have made State Life a dynamic and stable company for the last 100 years," says President Arthur L. Bryant.

STRATEGIC ALLIANCE

In 1994 State Life entered into a strategic alliance with Indianapolis-based American United Life Insurance Company® (AUL) to meet the challenges of a changing marketplace. AUL is a mutual company with $6.5 billion in assets. The alliance is a permanent relationship between State Life and AUL in which both companies remain separate but share administrative resources and staff.

Bryant notes that the purpose of the alliance is to position State Life to deal effectively with the challenges and competitiveness of the market today and into the future. Benefits of the alliance include lower unit costs; increased ratings from A.M. Best (A+), Standard & Poor's (AA-), and Duff & Phelps, Inc. (AA+); and improved new agent recruitment. In addition, policyholders benefit from competitive dividends due to greater savings in operations costs.

Bryant further explains the intent of the alliance as "having the best of both worlds—the economies of scale that a merger brings and the focus, flexibility, and synergy available through separate companies."

State Life has demonstrated its ability to change with the times as evidenced by its recent alliance with AUL. However, the one thing that will not change is the company's firm belief that its most important responsibility is servicing customers. State Life continues to find ways to exceed expectations. Bryant is optimistic about the future of the company and the insurance industry. "State Life's success in meeting challenges is directly attributable to its commitment to quality service and to the value it places on relationships with both policyholders and agents."

STATE LIFE HAS BEEN HEADQUARTERED IN DOWNTOWN INDIANAPOLIS SINCE ITS FOUNDING IN 1894. THE CURRENT HOME OFFICE BUILDING, AT THE CORNER OF WASHINGTON AND DELAWARE STREETS, WAS COMPLETED IN 1969.

EXECUTIVE VICE PRESIDENT LARRY R. ROBINSON, FSA, HAS BEEN WITH STATE LIFE SINCE GRADUATING FROM COLLEGE.

LEXANDER & ALEXANDER OF INDIANA INC. (A&A) HAS A Hoosier heritage. In 1896 Edward E. Barton opened an insurance agency in Indianapolis. Barton later joined with Marvin E. Curle and Edward E. McLaren to form Barton, Curle & McLaren. In the 1920s Ben O. Aspy opened an agency and later joined Alex Sommerville, forming the Aspy-Sommerville agency.

The combined agencies became part of Alexander & Alexander in 1974. The Herman C. Wolff Company was acquired in 1975, completing the successful acquisition of major community leaders in the insurance business.

A&A's Indianapolis office handles retail commercial insurance brokering and consulting, with specialization in risk management services for industrial, construction, and Japanese businesses. The Alexander Consulting Group specializes in human resource management consulting, group benefit brokerage and consulting, special risk coverage, and executive compensation. The Alexander Howden Group is A&A's London-based specialty and reinsurance operation.

A&A-Indianapolis looks at problems through the eyes of its clients and offers solutions specifically tailored to their needs, rather than offering services and products "off the shelf."

Over the years, this approach has earned A&A the trust of its clients. The firm has continually done business with one municipality since 1954, a utility since the 1930s, and a steel fabricator since 1924.

In a nutshell, A&A does business better, faster, and smarter by putting the client first.

CULTIVATING A CULTURE OF INTEGRITY

Among A&A's performance goals, uncompromising integrity is number one. In the service arena, the firm understands that a company's image and long-term success ultimately rest on the integrity and professionalism of its employees.

A&A believes that industry leadership and superior results will be impossible to sustain without a corporate culture committed to uncompromising ethical behavior. A&A employees worldwide work within established integrity and professional practice guidelines in their dealings with clients, colleagues, and suppliers. The firm's financial performance will always be measured against how those results were achieved.

SPECIAL SERVICES FOR DISTINCTIVE NEEDS

Regardless of size or location, growth companies, midsize firms, and global conglomerates all have access to the full range of international consulting and technical resources of A&A.

At A&A, every risk management, benefits, and consulting assignment is supported by a broad spectrum of dedicated resources concentrated in key industry groups, risk management disciplines, and global insurance markets.

Industry segments have been the cornerstone of A&A's service strategy. Through the decades, the firm has organized its expertise into distinctive groups such as aviation, transportation, construction, energy, financial services, forestry and other natural resources, health care, and utilities.

Two of A&A's newer specialties reflect a determination to keep pace with—or move ahead of—important public policy and economic trends. A&A's global Privatization Consulting Group is helping clients capitalize on the deregulation/privatization movement, particularly in Latin America and Central Europe. AlexEnvironmental was formed in recognition of growing environmental liability concerns worldwide.

For many clients, captive insurance companies are a viable alternative to the traditional insurance market. Alexander Insurance Managers is one of the largest captive management networks in the world. A new option for captive owners is Alternative Reinsurance for Captives (ARC), offered exclusively by the Alexander Howden Group.

In the increasingly strategic human resources arena, The Alexander Consulting Group (ACG) continues to expand capabilities that complement its traditional benefits-related brokerage and actuarial services. ACG specialists in health care management, retirement planning, information technologies, compensation, communications, and organizational effectiveness are helping clients address both immediate and long-range business needs related to workforce management.

Doing Business Faster, Better, Smarter

The new A&A is reconfiguring itself to establish new standards of speed, quality, and innovative service.

Commercial insurance brokering—like many other service industries—is showing all the signs of revolutionary change. An onslaught of new technology, a relentless drive for value on the part of A&A clients, and their increasing reliance on self-insurance and other less traditional alternatives are driving a fundamental redefinition of the risk management industry.

A&A is emerging as the acknowledged industry leader—in service, in results, and in profession-

alism. One of the firm's most ambitious internal initiatives is The A&A Way. The A&A Way involves rethinking and redesigning the firm's service delivery process for maximum efficiency and quality.

About Alexander & Alexander

Alexander & Alexander Services Inc. provides professional risk management consulting, insurance brokerage, and human resource management consulting services from offices in 80 countries.

Risk Management Consulting and Insurance Services

Alexander & Alexander designs and implements integrated insurance and risk management programs globally. The firm has the expertise to help businesses of all sizes, as well as associations and governmental agencies, address their risk assessment, risk control, and risk financing requirements.

Specialist and Reinsurance Brokering

The Alexander Howden Group places large and complex risks that require access to wholesale and specialist insurance markets worldwide. This division also provides a range of brokering and associated services to insurance and reinsurance companies as well as Lloyd's syndicates.

Human Resource Management Consulting

The Alexander Consulting Group provides integrated advisory and support services in human resource management, including retirement strategies, health care and total remuneration, Human Resource information technologies, organizational effectiveness, compensation, and communications.

ACG also offers brokerage services for group health and welfare, special risk, and executive planning insurance coverages.

t. Elmo Steak House has a long-standing history not many in the business can boast. Nautically inclined Joe Stahr opened the doors in October 1902, naming the establishment after the patron saint of sailors. The restaurant has remained one of the most popular eateries in downtown Indianapolis for more than 90 years. ◆ Famous for its steaks, fine wine, and shrimp cocktail, St. Elmo draws nationwide attention. Just mention your destination is Indianapolis, and someone within earshot will point you to 127 South Illinois Street. The restaurant has won the praise of the *New York Times*, *Car and Driver* magazine, and *Indianapolis Monthly*, which has frequently named it the "Best Downtown Restaurant."

The St. Elmo Steak House (right) has remained one of the most popular eateries in downtown Indianapolis for more than 90 years.

Over the years, St. Elmo's dining area has been expanded and now seats up to 250 people, with both public and private dining rooms (below).

Expanding with Indianapolis

Over the years, St. Elmo's dining area has been expanded and now seats up to 250 people, with both public and private dining rooms. The entryway has been refurbished so that the circa 1872 building blends well with the historical facades of the new Circle Centre Mall development. The dark green exterior and the oak-wainscoted interior of the entryway open the door to the turn-of-the-century atmosphere inside. The massive, 30-foot tiger oak bar recalls a time when groups of men gathered at the bar, eating sandwiches and drinking nickel beers. Through the dimly lit atmosphere, beige tin ceilings give way to dark-paneled walls that feature hun-

dreds of celebrity snapshots, historical photographs, and other artwork.

The restaurant has long been a mainstay in the community—from the days of the bustling wholesale district, through the times when buildings were torn down and only holes surrounded the restaurant. "And now the Circle Centre Mall," says co-owner Jeff Dunaway. "Hopefully, if we do our part, St. Elmo will live on." He and partner Stephen M. Huse purchased the restaurant in 1986 from Harry Roth and Isadore Rosen, who had owned the establishment for more than 40 years.

Where the Rich and Famous Go

A perennial favorite among Indianapolis residents and visitors, the restaurant has been a hot spot for sports celebrities as well, including heavyweight boxing champion Joe Lewis and such present-day stars as Indianapolis Motor Speedway regulars Paul Newman and Roger Penske. Musicians and actors also frequent the establishment, including Bon Jovi, Billy Joel, Elton John, Hank Williams Jr., and Bette Midler, among many others. Rock group Van Halen has even ordered take-out shrimp cocktail when they've performed in Fort Wayne, Indiana, or Dayton, Ohio.

And while the shrimp cocktail is well worth mentioning (and ordering), the steaks are what draw in the crowds. Wet aging—performed in-house by the staff—is the secret behind the mouthwatering, tender cuts. St. Elmo also boasts a wine list with more than 300 fine wines ranging from affordable to very expensive. In fact, *Wine Spectator* has recognized St. Elmo with its second-highest award every year since 1988.

"A good steak and a good bottle of wine complement each other," says Dunaway—much like St. Elmo Steak House and Indianapolis.

ERRILL LYNCH, ONE OF THE WORLD'S LARGEST AND MOST respected financial services organizations, has changed the way it does business. This innovative firm now offers complete planning-based financial services for its clientele. Merrill Lynch—rated the best-managed nonbank retailer by Towers Perrin—is represented in all 50 states. In Indianapolis,

the Merrill Lynch office is the headquarters for the Midwest District, encompassing 40 offices in 10 states.

The Indianapolis Complex, established in 1915, continues the international firm's 109-year-old commitment to excellence. The Complex, which includes the Indianapolis, Carmel, and Lafayette offices, has been named Complex of the Year for two consecutive years. The Midwest District was awarded District of the Year honors for 1994. Several Indianapolis financial consultants have been recognized among the top performers in the entire firm. An active supporter of civic and charitable organizations, Merrill Lynch continues to build trust and respect throughout the community.

The company achieved its second most profitable year in 1994, with net earnings of $1.02 billion. This success differentiates Merrill Lynch in terms of earning power, client service, and global market leadership. The firm's successful marketing strategies continue to enhance lifelong client relationships. These strategies include focusing on core business, achieving a broad revenue base, expanding the firm's global presence, and strengthening its capital base and liquidity positions.

COMMITMENT TO CLIENTS

To ensure strong client relationships, Merrill Lynch published its Client Commitment in 1994, underscoring the firm's resolve to become the world's premier planning-based financial management company. The Client Commitment comprises six pledges: client dedication, personal service, a financial plan, suitable recommendations, full disclosure, and the integrity of Merrill Lynch.

To fulfill this commitment, Merrill Lynch created business units to work closely with its financial consultants. The goal of these units is to serve the needs of clients throughout the changing financial cycles of their lives. Merrill Lynch addresses the needs of younger investors through the Next Generation Group, which provides solutions that help them build assets and manage credit in order to meet lifetime financial goals. The Priority Client Group concentrates on the needs of established investors, from building and managing wealth to retirement planning. The Private Advisory Group serves clients with substantial investment portfolios who require specialized financial and estate planning. This division provides sophisticated assets and liability management, including financing, discretionary investment, advisory, and philanthropic services.

A commitment to this level of personal service begins with highly trained Merrill Lynch financial consultants. Additionally, clients have access to specialists in areas such as mortgages, personal credit, insur-ance, estate planning, trusts, and small-business and employee benefit services.

HELPING BUSINESSES OF ALL SIZES

Small and midsize businesses enjoy a variety of new product lines that have been designed with Merrill Lynch expertise. In 1994 the Business Financial Planner service was introduced, along with a computer-based account reporting and electronic funds transfer system. The Middle Markets Group was created in 52 offices nationwide to deliver these services to midsize financial institutions and corporations.

Whether assisting with mergers and acquisitions for large corporations or consulting with a young couple just beginning a financial portfolio, Merrill Lynch leads the way in providing trusted advice based on financial expertise, global perspective, and a long-term view. The principles embodied in the Client Commitment are effectively guiding the firm towards a successful future.

THE INDIANAPOLIS COMPLEX, ESTABLISHED IN 1915, CONTINUES MERRILL LYNCH'S 109-YEAR-OLD COMMITMENT TO EXCELLENCE. THE INDIANAPOLIS TEAM OF SPECIALISTS SUPPORT MORE THAN 60 FINANCIAL CONSULTANTS WITH MORTGAGE, TRUST, CREDIT, INSURANCE, AND BUSINESS FINANCIAL SERVICES.

ITHIN THE CONGENIAL ATMOSPHERE THAT PERMEATES THE 60-acre campus of the University of Indianapolis, it is apparent that people are valued. The rush seems to slow down a bit, and there is time to explore, to be encouraged, to change, to grow, and to reach goals. ◆ Situated in a neighborhood five miles south of downtown Indianapolis, the campus is home to a compre-

hensive academic institution of moderate size with offerings that range from associate to doctoral degrees. Class sizes that average between 20 and 30 students illustrate the university's focus on the individual student. Qualified faculty members offer personal attention to the changing needs of their students. Professors instruct without the help of teaching assistants and often give students their office and home telephone numbers for further assistance.

"We are a people-oriented institution," says Dr. G. Benjamin Lantz Jr., president of the university. "People are the most important thing we deal with. There is a real sense of family here." No one demonstrates the people-oriented philosophy more than Lantz himself. This university president encourages an open-door policy and is readily available both to students and to visitors.

About the University

The University of Indianapolis is a private, residential institution affiliated with the United Methodist Church. There are more than 65 major fields of study in the College of Arts and

Sciences and the schools of business, nursing, and education. The university offers 12 graduate programs, including the first Executive MBA program in Indiana and doctoral studies in clinical psychology. The Krannert School of Physical Therapy ranks as one of the best in the nation.

The University of Indianapolis also maintains strong international ties, offering associate, bachelor's, and master's degrees in the arts and sciences and in business at its overseas branch campuses in Cyprus

and Greece. Faculty and student exchange is encouraged and facilitated between campuses. There are also collaborative relations with Taiwan-Tunghai University through the Regional Development Institute, as well as sister relationships in mainland China.

The diverse student population at the university includes individuals from 42 countries. "We embrace all religions, acknowledging their dignity and worth," explains Lantz. "John Wesley said, 'If your heart is as my heart, give me your hand.'

CLOCKWISE FROM TOP RIGHT: STUDENTS CELEBRATE GRADUATION AT THE UNIVERSITY OF INDIANAPOLIS.

BONES AND SKULLS ARE EXAMINED IN THE UNIVERSITY'S ARCHAEOLOGY AND FORENSIC LABORATORY.

THE TRADITIONAL TUG-OF-WAR BETWEEN STUDENTS AND FACULTY TAKES PLACE ON BROWN COUNTY DAY, AN ANNUAL AUTUMN EVENT WHEN THE UNIVERSITY CLOSES FOR A DAY OF FELLOWSHIP IN A NEARBY STATE PARK.

This affirms the religious experiences of all humankind."

LOOKING BACK

The University of Indianapolis was founded as Indiana Central University in 1902 by the St. Joseph and the White River conferences of the Church of the United Brethren of Christ and the Evangelical Church. The university has always been church-affiliated, and since 1968—when the Evangelical United Brethren and Methodist churches merged—it has been affiliated with the United Methodist Church.

Although incorporated in 1902, academic instruction began September 26, 1905, after the first building—now Good Hall—was completed. In those days, the university had three divisions, including the academy, the normal school, and the liberal arts college. The last academy class graduated in 1926, and the normal school was discontinued in 1938. The liberal arts college was restructured in 1983 to include the undergraduate College of Arts and Sciences; the undergraduate schools of business, education, and nursing; and the Graduate School.

In 1986 the institution became known as University of Indianapolis. "The name is reflective of what we are," says Lantz. "We have the same entrepreneurial spirit as the city of Indianapolis. We are responsible to the city, an asset to the city, and a part of the city."

A HOLISTIC APPROACH TO STUDENT LIFE

All facets of student life at the university are equally important for each student's personal growth and sense of well-being. The university's approach to student life is holistic, since its central mission is to prepare individuals for effective, responsible, and articulate membership in a complex society, as well as in their chosen professions or occupations.

Having a strong 30-year history, the university's Center for Continuing and Management Development makes programs available to more than 5,000 professionals and community residents each year. Noncredit educational programs include areas such as the Women Aware Series, Law Enforcement, and Fire and Safety.

The university provides many classes on an as-needed basis. For example, through a joint effort with Eli Lilly and Company, the University of Indianapolis developed a program and trained laboratory technicians for the company. This proactive, responsive approach is typical of the university. "Our goal is to maintain the strengths of our traditions and to exhibit them in a creative and dynamic way, so we can respond to and contribute to change all around us," says Lantz.

CHRISTEL DEHAAN FINE ARTS CENTER

In early April 1994 the Christel DeHaan Fine Arts Center opened at the University of Indianapolis. Located at the main campus entrance, this $10.2 million educational and arts facility includes a two-tiered, Viennese-style performance hall. With this 59,000-square-foot facility, the university and the city of Indianapolis gained another venue for fine arts events. The center also houses the prestigious Faculty Artist Series, featuring artists from the music faculty and guests from the Indianapolis Symphony Orchestra.

The University of Indianapolis has experienced a renaissance in its growth and philosophy. Both the city and the university have awakened to the exciting possibilities that lie ahead. Maintaining his focus on the needs of the community and the day-to-day business of the university and its students, Lantz adds, "We can anticipate and help to make the future. However, a lot of the future is what we make of the present."

OPENED IN APRIL 1994, THE $10.2 MILLION, 59,000-SQUARE-FOOT CHRISTEL DEHAAN FINE ARTS CENTER INCLUDES A TWO-TIERED, VIENNESE-STYLE PERFORMANCE HALL.

THE FIRST HEART TRANSPLANT IN INDIANA . . . THE NATION'S first kidney stone crusher . . . the state's first baby conceived through micro sperm injection . . . the hospital of choice for Indy race car drivers. ◆ Methodist Hospital has been a leader in delivering technologically superb and compassionate health care in Indiana for nearly a century. It's a role the organization con-

tinues to take seriously today. As managed care brings new emphasis on preventing illness and managing disease, Methodist is developing new ways to deliver care.

After 86 years as Methodist Hospital, the health care organization changed its name and organizational structure to the Methodist Health Group in 1994. Banding together with physicians and home health and occupational health services, Methodist is working to establish a single system offering the full spectrum of health services.

Part of that system is a network of outpatient centers Methodist has built since 1992 near the Indianapolis suburbs of Carmel and Greenwood and in the Eagle Highlands area. Plans call for another outpatient center on the east side of Indianapolis. Methodist also has established medical plazas with physician offices, and lab and radiology services in Brownsburg,

METHODIST IS THE FIFTH-LARGEST NOT-FOR-PROFIT HOSPITAL IN THE NATION (RIGHT).

A RADIOLOGIST EXAMINES MAMMOGRAPHY FILM (BELOW).

the Glendale area, Zionsville, and Mooresville. Another medical plaza is planned for the Geist area.

The goal: To provide 90 percent of health care services within 15 minutes of where people live and work. The outpatient centers and medical plazas allow Methodist

to continue to provide excellent patient care in a lower-cost environment that is convenient for patients. Many surgeries—such as gallbladder and cataract operations—now can be done on an outpatient basis and are routinely performed at the Methodist outpatient centers.

At the same time the health group has expanded throughout the suburban area, it has focused on reducing hospital costs. Methodist is now one of the lowest-cost health care systems in the area. For example, in 1993, 1994, and 1995, hospital price increases averaged less than 2 percent a year compared with as much as four times that percentage for other large local health systems.

UNITED METHODIST HERITAGE LIVES ON TODAY

Methodist began its mission "to treat the sick, wounded, and injured and dispense charity for the poor" in 1899 when the Methodist Episcopal Church donated $4,750 to build the hospital.

The link with the United Methodist Church has endured, with the board of directors ap-

pointed by a committee that includes the bishop and other United Methodist leaders. The original mission remains intact today and has expanded to include a dedication to preventing injuries, and studying and improving the health of the communities served by Methodist.

Each year, Methodist spends about $70 million on programs that directly benefit the Indianapolis community and surrounding area. Some of these programs help school-age children understand the importance of wearing a helmet while riding a bicycle, and show high school and college students the dangers of drinking and driving. Other areas of emphasis include educating people with chronic diseases how to manage their illnesses; providing primary health care services to low-income residents near downtown Indianapolis through five HealthNet Community Health Centers; offering prenatal care and parenting classes to needy women; and making affordable housing available in the neighborhoods surrounding the hospital.

These programs, and many like them, help the health group accomplish part of its mission to reduce the human and financial cost of illness and injury.

Expertise Unmatched in Indiana

While Methodist dedicates itself to serving the people in its surrounding area, many patients travel from other parts of the state and nation to take advantage of the top-notch care the nation's fifth-largest not-for-profit hospital provides.

With more than 20 clinical programs, Methodist has more than 300 physicians specializing in such areas as heart and lung, orthopedics, diabetes, cancer, neurology, and mental health. The hospital handles more than 45,000 inpatients each year.

Methodist is one of two hospitals in the state that has been verified as a Level I trauma center. The emergency department sees more than 80,000 patients a year, 25,000 of them trauma cases. Some 100 times a month, Life Line helicopters transport the critically ill and injured to Methodist. Since 1979 the airborne emergency medical service has made approximately 15,000 flights.

Methodist delivers more than 3,500 babies each year. In 1970 Methodist was the first hospital in Indiana to begin a comprehensive neonatal program to care for premature infants and newborns with serious illnesses, and continues to have one of the largest neonatal intensive care units in the state.

For children, Methodist houses the state's only in-house pediatric rehabilitation facility. Methodist also operates the Indiana Poison Center, which fields some 80,000 calls a year—60 percent concerning childhood poisonings.

Working toward a Statewide Health Care System

Methodist is leading a charge throughout Indiana to develop a statewide system of health care providers. In this system, hospitals and other organizations would join together to offer a coordinated system of care.

This system would allow patients to move freely and easily among institutions because the participating organizations would share common information systems and diagnostic and care guidelines. In some cases, hospital services might be streamlined to reduce costs.

Physicians and other practitioners would be able to share expertise. This statewide system could help participants respond to the economic pressures facing health care organizations today and could provide the best opportunity to keep Indiana health care providers based in the state.

Just as it has for nearly a century, Methodist continues to lead the way by responding to challenges in health care delivery in innovative ways.

Since 1979 Life Line helicopters have been transporting the critically ill or injured to Methodist for treatment (below left).

Each year, Methodist Hospital caregivers treat more than 45,000 inpatients (below right).

N 1910 WALTER G. JUSTUS BUILT HIS FIRST BRICK AND STONE homes in Indianapolis using teams of horse plows to dig basement foundations. With these efforts, he founded Justus Contracting Company, which grew to become The Justus Companies. Today this fourth-generation, family-owned organization touts an 85-year track record for producing successful residential and commer-

cial developments, including construction, development, management, and marketing.

The Indianapolis-based firm has planned, constructed, and developed single-family home subdivisions; apartment and condominium villages; business offices and shopping centers; industrial parks; nursing homes and retirement care communities; and hotel/resort developments throughout Indiana, Michigan, Ohio, Tennessee, Florida, and California.

"Our company is firmly rooted in the belief that successful results are achieved through boundless perseverance, sound financial management, and an unyielding commitment to quality performance," says Chairman of the Board Walter G. Justus. "My grandfather established those company precepts when he founded Justus Contracting Company. They formed the basis for his success as a home builder known for quality craftsmanship. My father, Walter E. Justus, refined and honed those principles to an even greater degree during his more than 40-year leadership of The Justus Companies. Today those policies are being carried on by my son, Walter E. Justus Jr., as an integral part of our reputation as a financially successful, results-oriented firm."

THIS FOURTH-GENERATION, FAMILY-OWNED ORGANIZATION, ESTABLISHED IN 1910 BY WALTER G. JUSTUS (RIGHT), TOUTS AN 85-YEAR TRACK RECORD FOR PRODUCING SUCCESSFUL RESIDENTIAL AND COMMERCIAL DEVELOPMENTS, INCLUDING CONSTRUCTION, DEVELOPMENT, MANAGEMENT, AND MARKETING.

JUSTUS HOSPITALITY PROPERTIES, INC., A HOTEL/RESORT DEVELOPMENT FIRM ESTABLISHED IN 1980, BUILT THE 250-ROOM MARRIOTT INN OF INDIANAPOLIS (BELOW).

STRENGTH THROUGH DIVERSIFIED SERVICES

The company is comprised of a family of interrelated enterprises that work together to provide a complete spectrum of real estate services. Each of the corporate divisions addresses a different specialty within the firm. One of these divisions, Justus Construction Company, has built a reputation of integrity and service in handling all aspects of construction, from engineering design and planning to developing innovative construction concepts and effective project management. Initially known for quality craftsmanship in its single-family residences, Justus Construction expanded its expertise to the development of

commercial facilities and planned residential communities. Because most of these development ventures are managed and owned by Justus, the company is consistently successful in maintaining cost controls and timely project completions.

Justus Rental Property Management, Inc. was a major force behind the multifamily industry in Indianapolis when it was founded 28 years ago. Now it is the third-largest property management group in Indiana and the 18th-largest in the United States. This division manages 4,300 residential units and diverse commercial/retail properties throughout seven states. Another division, Justus Company Realtors, Inc., is one of the oldest real estate service companies in Indianapolis, specializing in the sale of new and existing residential and commercial real estate.

Justus Construction Company/ Justus Homes, Inc. was established as a single division in order to meet the market demands of the shelter industry in each of the regions it serves. Within this division, Justus Home Builders of Indiana and Justus Homes, Inc. of Florida were established to respond to market demand throughout Indiana, Florida, Michigan, Tennessee, and Ohio. More than 20,000 residential units have been planned, developed, and constructed throughout the Midwest and Southeast. In addition, this division has built numerous commercial office buildings, shopping centers, restaurants, hotel/ resorts, and automotive retail centers.

The Commercial/Retail Division handles marketing, leasing, development, and sales of properties ranging from shopping centers to office buildings. This division provides a complete package of services for prospective tenants to ensure that transactions match client needs.

In 1980 Walter G. Justus founded Justus Hospitality Properties, Inc., a hotel/resort development firm. The company built the 250-room Marriott Inn of Indianapolis, which has consistently won the AAA Four Diamond Award. In Florida, the company developed the $30 million Galt Ocean Club of Fort Lauderdale and has developed the $30 million Radisson Inn/ Justus Aquatic Center in Orlando.

SPECIALISTS IN SENIOR HOUSING

For the past 30 years, Justus has been redefining its shelter and nursing care programs for senior citizens. Ranked among the top 20 national senior housing providers, Justus has designed, constructed, and managed adult retirement communities and health care/nursing facilities with services for nearly 3,500 elderly residents. More than 50,000 Indianapolis seniors have been served by these communities since 1962.

Retirement communities developed by Justus in Indiana, Tennessee, and Florida are focused on three specific types of housing: active adult communities, compre-

hensive senior citizens villages, and nursing/convalescent facilities. With four Indianapolis locations, Crestwood Village provides an excellent example of one of the company's highly successful active adult communities. Some of its special amenities include nondenominational worship services, libraries, landscaped courtyards, a visiting lounge/television media room, a personal care beauty/barber salon, free transportation, housekeeping services, and home-delivery cafeteria meals.

Justus has also provided more than 4,500 government-sponsored housing units. These communities were planned, developed, and constructed by Justus throughout Indiana, Michigan, Florida, and Tennessee.

"Our primary business is the sheltering of people—be it single-family homes and condominium complexes, nursing homes and life care retirement communities, or luxury hotel/resorts. We plan to become even more deeply involved in the development of elderly life care and active retirement communities," says Walter G. Justus. "Most of all, we intend to maintain our enviable profile as a solid growth company that is a recognized leader known for its proud past, proven track record, and dynamic future."

CLOCKWISE FROM TOP: JUSTUS HAS PLANNED, CONSTRUCTED, AND DEVELOPED SINGLE-FAMILY-HOME SUBDIVISIONS, SUCH AS MAPLE CREEK IN INDIANAPOLIS.

THE JUSTUS CORPORATE SHEILD, A RECOGNIZED SYMBOL OF QUALITY, HAS STOOD THE TEST OF TIME SINCE 1910.

CRESTWOOD VILLAGE IN INDIANAPOLIS PROVIDES AN EXCELLENT EXAMPLE OF ONE OF THE COMPANY'S HIGHLY SUCCESSFUL ACTIVE ADULT COMMUNITIES.

T TAKES VISION AND COURAGE—LOTS OF BOTH—TO SELL A PROFIT- able company your family had built up over more than 70 years in order to embark on a wholly new direction. But that is what the Lacy family did, with remarkably successful results. Clearly, the Lacys are an extraordinary family. And their company, Lacy Diversified Industries (LDI, Ltd.), is an exceptional organization.

The dramatic shift in direction came in the early 1980s. Andre B. Lacy, whose grandfather had founded U.S. Corrugated Fibre Box Company in 1912, with $343, was elected president in 1978 (he is now chairman and chief executive officer). Over the previous few years he had pushed through a restructuring that got rid of unprofitable facilities and focused on healthy operations. The result: The company had grown into the second-largest independent box manufacturer in the United States. "But it was part of an industry that had a lower appetite for making money than I did," Lacy says.

He saw greater opportunities elsewhere; specifically, in the distri- bution industry. "Distribution was a new industry," says Lacy. "Most distribution businesses were started after World War II, and a lot are owned as family businesses. Now, as they've grown older, they've

CLOCKWISE FROM RIGHT: ANDRE B. LACY TODAY SERVES AS LDI'S CHAIRMAN AND CHIEF EXECUTIVE OFFICER.

IN 1912 HOWARD J. LACY SR. FOUNDED U.S. CORRUGATED FIBRE BOX COMPANY, THE PREDECESSOR TO TODAY'S LACY DIVERSIFIED INDUSTRIES.

RETAILERS CAN ORDER BY PHONE OR COMPUTER, OR COME INTO MVC'S WAREHOUSE TO PURCHASE VIDEO- CASSETTES FOR THEIR STORES.

slowed down their investments. So there was a great potential there."

LDI had already begun to diversify; in 1972 it acquired the Jessup Door Company, one of the nation's largest producers of wooden door products for the home build- ing and remodeling industries.

The company stepped up diver- sification efforts, beginning in 1987

with the purchase of Major Video Concepts (MVC), a wholesale dis- tributor of prerecorded videocas- settes. Over the next few years LDI acquired four other distributors and merged them into MVC. Now MVC is one of the nation's largest companies in this field, and the chances are good that the movie you watched on your VCR last night was purchased by the video store from MVC.

Today LDI, a closely held investment management firm, encompasses not only Jessup Door and MVC, but two other wholly owned operating companies: Tucker-Rocky Distributing, the world's largest wholesale distributor of aftermarket parts, apparel, and accessories for motorcycle, water- craft, and snowmobile enthusiasts, and Answer Products, a manufac- turer of Manitou bicycle frames and suspension forks, as well as a manufacturer and/or distributor for a wide range of apparel and parts for those who love off-road motorbikes and bicycles.

LDI also manages its own in- vestment portfolio of stocks, bonds, and other securities valued at more than $125 million. LDI generates annual sales of more than $560 million through its diversified hold- ings. Headquartered in Indianapolis,

KEVIN ATHERTON COMPLETED A PICTURE-PERFECT RACE ON AUGUST 19, 1995, AT THE INDIANAPOLIS STATE FAIRGROUNDS TO WIN THE INDIANAPOLIS MILE. AMONG HIS RACING SPONSORS ARE TUCKER-ROCKEY, NEMPCO, MSR, AND SILLCOLENE (LEFT).

it employs 1,400 people spread among 36 facilities, which sell in all 50 states and Canada.

What's the most striking measure of the wisdom of LDI's corporate strategy? A share of LDI stock that was worth $2.27 in 1983 is now worth more than $48. The company has a compounded growth rate of more than 18 percent.

"Our vision for LDI," says Lacy, "is to identify and satisfy customer needs profitably and better than any competitor. This is our commitment to excellence and to the continuous improvement of everything we do."

That can't be—and isn't—just lip service, for the company's customers are primarily retailers who are dependent on shipments that are on time and accurate. Many of LDI's market niches are in product/service areas that are often avoided by its competitors.

Another element in the company's success is Andre Lacy's strong adherence to the principle of participative management. There are only 17 people at the Indianapolis headquarters, which inevitably results in a high degree of autonomy among the subsidiaries. Lacy believes in a work environment in

which people feel free to disagree, to propose ideas that may not mesh with ideas of others, and to be as creative as possible.

"I try to listen as much as I can," Lacy says. "I try to let people operate their businesses. I give people authority and responsibility, and I ask for profit and accountability. I don't get into looking at how they do everything."

That's a far cry from how his grandfather, Howard Lacy Sr., ran the original company. "He was rough-hewn," Andre Lacy says, "a risk taker. An entrepreneur." Andre Lacy, too, is entrepreneurial and a risk taker, but certainly not rough-hewn. He tends to take after his father, Howard Lacy II, who had a more contemporary and collegial style. But his father died in 1959 after only seven years of running the company. At that point, everyone assumed the widow of Howard II, Edna Balz Lacy, would sell the company. Instead, she decided to run it with the help of her son.

"We ended up building the company leadership together," Andre Lacy recalls.

Edna Lacy was not only a phenomenally successful businesswoman, but she was also widely

honored as a leader in civic, cultural, and political activities. For example, she was the first woman elected to the board of directors of the Indianapolis Chamber of Commerce. But the heritage of Edna Lacy, her husband, and his father, the founder, lives on in the corporate culture of LDI.

"The founder's word and a handshake were an iron-bound contract," Andre Lacy says. "That same sense of honor and integrity is a part of our business style today."

ANSWER MANITOU BICYCLES AND SUSPENSIONS CONTINUE TO SET THE STANDARD FOR THE OFF-ROAD CYCLING COMMUNITY (ABOVE LEFT).

JESSOP DOOR PRODUCTS MAINTAIN THEIR TOP-OF-THE-LINE POSITION BECAUSE OF LDI'S INVESTMENT IN SOPHISTICATED TECHNOLOGY (ABOVE RIGHT).

N ITS HEYDAY THE HOTEL SEVERIN, A 13-STORY DOWNTOWN "skyscraper," offered telephone-equipped barber chairs, panic-proof bedroom doors, one of the most beautiful and modern cigar stands in the country, and silver newspaper racks at breakfast so that guests did not have to interrupt their reading while dining. From its beginnings in 1913 to the late 1930s,

the Severin, located across the street from Union Station, throve on business brought to Indianapolis by the 300 passenger trains that arrived daily.

Today the renovated and expanded hotel stands as a historic landmark in the Indianapolis Union Station Wholesale District and is listed on the National Register of Historic Places. Walking from the original portion of the hotel to the newly constructed areas is like taking a brief trip through time. The interior styling of the contemporary lobby facing Union Station is classic in its design. The eclectic approach blends a European influence with its clean, modern look.

New Owners Bring About Renovation

Ownership of the Severin has changed hands several times over the years. In 1966 the property was purchased by Warren M. Atkinson, underwent a $2.5 million renovation, and was renamed the Atkinson Hotel. The urban blight of the 1970s left the hotel struggling, and by the 1980s new construction throughout Indianapolis made the old property seem outdated by comparison.

With plans to develop the newest—and oldest—hotel in downtown Indianapolis, Mansur Development Corporation bought the Atkinson Hotel in July 1988. The subsequent $40 million restoration and expansion of the city's only remaining "grand hotel" created a beautiful, historic landmark in harmony with the downtown renaissance. Renovation of its distinctive architectural features was carefully and conveniently executed. The old part of the hotel boasts the original chandelier and was painted in keeping with its historic period.

Known today as the Omni Severin Hotel, the property has 423 spacious guest rooms, 38 suites (including bilevel penthouse suites), and plaza suites that feature walk-out balconies. The restored classical Severin ballroom is booked throughout the year, with wedding

receptions and holiday parties reserved well in advance.

Restaurants include the upbeat 40 West Coffee Cafe, where drop-in customers and hotel guests alike enjoy the varied and unusual gourmet menu at this popular carryout restaurant. A few tables and a long countertop at the window offer seating. Fresh and tasty ingredients abound. Sandwiches, salads, soups, desserts, and distinctive beverages tempt diners with quick and delicious fare.

The newest dining spot at the Omni Severin is Hot Tuna—seafood with a sizzle. The restaurant offers the diner in the downtown area the freshest seafood available. The award-winning chef has created a menu that is unparalleled in the Indianapolis area.

The Omni Severin's modern, newly designed fitness room is equipped with exercise and aerobic equipment—from treadmills to Life Cycles to weight machines. This contemporary room is designed with a panoramic window overlooking the hotel's indoor swimming pool.

Other amenities offered at the Omni Severin include business-class rooms equipped with fax ma-

THE OMNI SEVERIN'S MODERN FITNESS ROOM IS EQUIPPED WITH EXERCISE AND AEROBIC EQUIPMENT—FROM TREADMILLS TO LIFE CYCLES TO WEIGHT MACHINES (RIGHT).

THE GRAND STAIRCASE LEADS TO THE MEZZANINE LEVEL, WHERE THE HOTEL IS NOW CONNECTED VIA SKYWALK TO THE CIRCLE CENTRE MALL DEVELOPMENT (BELOW).

chines, modem jacks for laptop computers, and extra-large desks. Nonsmoking floors are available throughout the hotel. All 423 guest rooms have irons and ironing boards, coffeemakers, hair dryers, and makeup mirrors. To accommodate an increasing corporate clientele, the hotel offers 16,000 square feet of meeting space, as well as the Business Center located off the lobby.

"Our mission is to be the hospitality hotel most preferred by discerning customers, dedicated employees, and investing partners who share our vision," says Stephen A. Rosenstock, the hotel's general manager.

Ensuring Satisfaction— across the Board

The dedicated associates of the Omni Severin make it a point to remember returning guests and their personal requests by maintaining a computerized customer database. The "What's Important to You" cards filled out by guests are taken seriously; the philosophy of the hotel and its staff is to provide the best in personalized service. "Our strength," maintains Rosenstock, "is attention to personalized service and meeting our customers' individual needs."

Associate satisfaction is another strong emphasis at the Omni Severin. The hotel has a "Power of One" program allowing staff members to make a decision to benefit a guest without obtaining supervisory approval. Another practice that is well received among hotel associates is the monthly ambassador meeting. An associate representing each hotel department has the opportunity to meet with the general manager to discuss on-the-job concerns or to contribute new ideas. Programs like these at the hotel have made a difference. According to staff surveys from the 45 Omni properties in the country, the Indianapolis hotel ranks number one in associate satisfaction.

Positioning itself as the premier business travel hotel in Indianapolis, the Omni Severin serves as an anchor hotel for Circle Centre Mall and is connected to the new development via a skywalk. Steeped in more than eight decades of history, this elegant downtown hotel offers guests the perfect blend of fine cuisine, gracious surroundings, and meticulous service.

CLOCKWISE FROM TOP LEFT:
THE OMNI SEVERIN'S 423 SPACIOUS GUEST ROOMS INCLUDE A COMFORTABLE SITTING AREA.

THE HOTEL'S LOBBY BRINGS THE OPULENCE OF THE PAST TO THE PRESENT.

THE RESTORED CLASSICAL SEVERIN BALLROOM IS BOOKED THROUGHOUT THE YEAR, WITH WEDDING RECEPTIONS AND HOLIDAY PARTIES RESERVED WELL IN ADVANCE.

ONSISTENTLY RANKED AMONG THE NATION'S TOP HOSPITALS BY *U.S. News & World Report* and many other guides to health care, Indiana University (IU) Medical Center is widely recognized for its clinical excellence in cancer, medical and molecular genetics, cardiology, and pediatrics. With a tradition for providing quality health care since 1914, IU Medical

ROBERT W. HOLDEN, M.D. (ABOVE), DEAN OF IU SCHOOL OF MEDICINE AND DIRECTOR OF IU MEDICAL CENTER

LOCATED DOWNTOWN ON THE CAMPUS OF INDIANA UNIVERSITY-PURDUE UNIVERSITY INDIANAPOLIS, IU MEDICAL CENTER INCLUDES UNIVERSITY HOSPITAL & OUTPATIENT CENTER, A HIGHLY SPECIALIZED ADULT HOSPITAL (BELOW).

Center is made up of Indiana's only comprehensive pediatric hospital, Riley Hospital for Children; the nation's second-largest and the state's only medical school, IU School of Medicine; and a highly specialized adult hospital, University Hospital & Outpatient Center. The medical center is conveniently located downtown on the campus of Indiana University-Purdue University Indianapolis.

Relationships with dozens of managed care organizations, such as HMOs, help IU Medical Center provide the highest-quality care efficiently and cost-effectively—important features in today's health care market. David J. Handel, director of hospitals, says, "Our network of physicians, hospitals, managed care organizations, and businesses enables us to provide the most comprehensive services available. Patients receive individualized care for a wide range of health problems all in one convenient setting."

Continuously enhancing the quality of patient care is a system-wide priority at IU Medical Center and has resulted in high patient satisfaction and significant cost reductions. Riley Hospital for Children and University Hospital & Outpatient Center receive no state funds for patient care services.

As a major referral center, the medical center makes consultations easily attainable for physicians and patients via specially dedicated telephone lines. With a single call to IMACS, physicians have toll-free, 24-hour direct access to more than 600 faculty members, the Ruth Lilly Medical Library, the Continuing Medical Education office, and other resources.

IU On-Call assists members of the general public in scheduling appointments with the medical center's primary care physicians or specialists. Based on their specific need for medical services, individuals can receive information about programs and physicians. Resource

Coordinators offer callers the names of doctors who match the callers' preferences and who can best provide the care needed, as well as background information on each physician.

Established in 1903, the IU School of Medicine serves as the nucleus of a medical education network that extends to regional centers in South Bend, Gary, Fort Wayne, Muncie, West Lafayette, Terre Haute, Bloomington, and Evansville. Approximately two-thirds of Indiana's physicians received all or part of their education from the IU School of Medicine.

Riley Hospital for Children, a Level I trauma center, is Indiana's only comprehensive pediatric hospital. Riley operates one of the largest pediatric intensive care units in the country, and has the only pediatric burn unit in Indiana. Riley is also the only hospital in the state that provides pediatric renal dialysis and an advanced technique called extracorporeal membrane oxygenation. The latter is a support system for children with serious lung disorders that allows their lungs to heal by "breathing" for them.

A pediatric bone marrow transplant unit with 10 dedicated beds was recently constructed at Riley to better accommodate the number and variety of pediatric cancer patients. Riley is a national model for parental participation and education. In addition, the Ronald McDonald House provides a place to stay for families of pediatric patients.

The IU Cancer Center is home to some of the nation's leading cancer clinicians. Today more than 90 percent of testis cancer patients are cured because of an innovative platinum-based drug therapy developed by IU Medical Center oncologist Lawrence H. Einhorn, M.D. Advances against this complicated

disease require collaboration among physicians and researchers from a wide variety of health care disciplines.

IU Cancer Center embodies the interdisciplinary approach to patient care for adults and children with cancer of the lung, skin, central nervous system, breast, head, and neck. Other comprehensive programs address gynecologic, gastrointestinal, prostate, and urologic cancers as well as blood and bone disorders.

University Hospital & Outpatient Center houses a high-technology imaging center, the only facility in Indiana that offers all the

high-tech modalities—such as positron-emission tomography (PET) and magnetic resonance imaging (MRI)—in one location. Transplant teams perform more transplants than any other Indiana hospital, and offer seven transplantation programs for adults and six for children. To care for bone marrow transplant patients, University Hospital & Outpatient Center has a dedicated 14-bed adult bone marrow transplantation unit.

A comprehensive adult kidney program treats all forms of congenital and acquired renal disease. The Indiana Diabetes Center is the only comprehensive care center in Indi-

ana that offers education, research, exercise, obstetric, and treatment programs for diabetes patients of all ages.

The IU Breast Care and Research Center—designed to help detect breast cancer, conduct research, and encourage collaboration among all breast care specialists—offers a multidisciplinary approach to diagnosis and treatment.

IU Health Care is a primary care group practice that provides pediatric, family practice, obstetric, gynecological, and internal medicine services. Locations in Indianapolis—in addition to IU Medical Center—include the Broad Ripple Center, Avon Internal Medicine, Eagle Highlands Center, Banta Road Center, and Post Road Center. In central Indiana, IU has facilities in Frankfort and Anderson.

Prevention of illness and injury is also an integral part of IU Medical Center's approach to health care. Programs such as that at the Bowen Research Center not only examine lifestyle choices that lead to disease and death, but investigate methods of behavior modification as well, contributing to generations of better health for the citizens of Indiana and for people around the nation and the world.

CLOCKWISE FROM TOP LEFT: MARILYN BULL, M.D., DIRECTOR OF THE IU MEDICAL CENTER DIVISION OF DEVELOPMENTAL PEDIATRICS, IS NATIONALLY RECOGNIZED FOR HER EXPERTISE IN EVALUATING AND MANAGING INFANTS WITH HANDICAPPING CONDITIONS.

HUGGING HER SON JONATHAN, WENDY W. WEIDBERG, BREAST CANCER SURVIVOR, TELLS HER DOCTOR, GEORGE W. SLEDGE JR., M.D., IU MEDICAL CENTER PROFESSOR OF MEDICINE AND PATHOLOGY, "I WOULD NOT BE HERE WITHOUT YOU, IN A VERY REAL SENSE. I NOW HAVE A SECOND CHANCE AT LIFE."

STEPHEN WILLIAMS, M.D., DIRECTOR OF IU CANCER CENTER, TEACHES MEDICAL STUDENTS AT IU SCHOOL OF MEDICINE, THE SECOND-LARGEST MEDICAL SCHOOL IN THE UNITED STATES.

AVING FOR THE FUTURE AND OWNING A HOME HAVE BEEN PART OF the American Dream for generations of Indianapolis families. First Indiana Bank, along with its holding company First Indiana Corporation, has made that dream a reality for more than 80 years. ◆ From its roots as a neighborhood building and loan association, First Indiana has grown into the largest

publicly owned bank based in Indianapolis, with a presence in the state's major markets and throughout the country. At the same time, the bank's local ownership has created a unique opportunity to advance home financing and community reinvestment.

In 1915 a group of Indianapolis businessmen invested $100,000 to form Ashland Savings Association, making home financing available to residents on the city's near east side. In 1934 E. Kirk McKinney Sr., whose family still holds controlling interest in the bank, reorganized Ashland as First Federal Savings and Loan Association of Indianapolis under New Deal laws that established federal deposit insurance and a ready source of funds for home lending.

The business of lending money for home financing was simple and straightforward for the next five

decades. First Federal grew slowly, holding fast to key values about the importance of thrift and housing. Federal laws restricted savings accounts, interest rates, and even advertising copy. The formula was simple: pay a fixed rate on deposits, lend money to home buyers at a fixed rate, and repeat the cycle when the loan is repaid. Following this basic framework, First Federal's assets rose to more than $400 million by 1980.

Deregulation in the late 1970s and early 1980s, along with record high interest rates, forced banks and savings institutions to rethink their strategies. Competition intensified among banks, money market funds, and other providers of financial services. For the first time, savings institutions could offer the same products as their bank competitors. Other banking laws authorized interstate bank mergers, setting the stage for a wave of consolidations nationwide.

At the center of these major changes was First Indiana's chairman, Robert H. McKinney, who served as chairman of the Federal Home Loan Bank Board during President Carter's administration. As the nation's top thrift regulator,

McKinney helped position the industry for competitive changes.

After returning to Indianapolis and First Federal in 1980, McKinney led the bank through several major changes that helped it withstand the recession of the early 1980s. First, the bank reorganized as a shareholder-owned (rather than depositor-owned) company in 1983. Second, the bank adopted a new name, First Indiana Bank, to reflect the modern age of financial services. Third, the bank expanded into new markets, including Evansville, Indiana; Charlotte and Raleigh, North Carolina; and Tampa and Orlando, Florida.

By the early 1990s, the banking horizon in Indianapolis had changed dramatically. The community's three largest banks had been acquired by holding companies from other states. Although First Indiana had grown to more than $1 billion in assets, its size was eclipsed by eight superregional banks vying for customers and market share. Recognizing that First Indiana could compete more effectively by offering something different, the bank's management closely examined ways to set the

RIGHT: FIRST INDIANA'S MANAGEMENT TEAM INCLUDES (FROM LEFT) ROBERT H. MCKINNEY, CHAIRMAN AND CHIEF EXECUTIVE OFFICER; OWEN B. MELTON JR., PRESIDENT AND CHIEF OPERATING OFFICER; AND MARNI MCKINNEY, VICE CHAIRMAN.

IN ADDITION TO SERVING METROPOLITAN INDIANAPOLIS AND EVANSVILLE, FIRST INDIANA BANK HAS A PRESENCE IN MANY SMALL TOWNS THROUGHOUT THE STATE, INCLUDING THIS BANKING CENTER IN FRANKLIN (BELOW).

organization apart. After extensive analysis of customer needs and trends, First Indiana chose to tie its fortunes to its heritage as a real estate lender.

By centering its strategy on real estate finance, First Indiana is in a unique position to build on its longtime expertise, with new angles designed for today's markets. The bank now has a large share of the custom construction market in Indianapolis and other cities. Home equity lending occupies center stage in the bank's retail banking, with enhanced technologies that ensure quick action on loan applications. Commercial real estate lending, business loans to selected niches, and traditional housing finance round out First Indiana's emphasis on real estate finance as its core strategy.

This commitment appears most dramatically in First Indiana's market position. The bank is central Indiana's largest mortgage lender, despite competition from national mortgage banking companies and huge regional banks. First Indiana's community lending team works side by side with grassroots organizations to make housing finance available to home buyers who fall outside the traditional loan systems. Innovative financing packages, including lease/purchase programs, special savings accounts, and low-down-payment loans, have made the American Dream of home

ownership a reality for thousands of families. The bank also offers special checking accounts for home owners, with reduced fees and other convenient services. These accounts reinforce the bank's image as a real estate specialist and help build profitable long-term banking relationships.

Although many believe that bigger is better, First Indiana maintains that smaller can be better, too. Toward that end, the bank has invested heavily in systems for improving efficiency and designing the most cost-effective processes for delivering products to the customer. Every employee

is involved in process improvement, and jobs are routinely redesigned to yield maximum efficiency. Process improvement will bring the same benefits to First Indiana that economies of scale bring to the bank's mass-market competitors.

In today's changing world, successful banks must set themselves apart from the competition. First Indiana plans to stay out in front by capitalizing on local ownership, real estate expertise, and market focus. These strategies will help keep the American Dream within reach for generations to come.

FIRST INDIANA PLAZA IS THE HEADQUARTERS OF FIRST INDIANA CORPORATION, THE HOLDING COMPANY FOR THE LARGEST PUBLICLY OWNED BANK BASED IN INDIANAPOLIS.

CHRISTMAS CLUB ACCOUNTS WERE A FIXTURE OF FIRST INDIANA FOR SEVERAL DECADES. IN THIS PHOTO FROM THE EARLY 1960S, CHAIRMAN ROBERT H. MCKINNEY MAKES A DEPOSIT. CONSUMER PREFERENCES HAVE SHIFTED OVER THE YEARS, AND FIRST INDIANA HAS EXPANDED ITS PRODUCT OFFERINGS TO REFLECT CHANGING TASTES.

HE APPEARANCE OF TODAY'S WORKPLACE IS EVER-CHANGING. As companies grow, downsize, rightsize, and flatten, the layout of the contemporary office is hardly recognizable from even a few years ago. Changes in fabrics, colors, and finishes as well are the result of the industry's response to the style preferences of end users. At the same time, sales trends often follow fluctu-

ations in the economy, and value drives most purchases in the 1990s.

Business Furniture Corporation—the largest and oldest office furniture dealership in Indiana—boasts a distinguished, 74-year history of providing both productive work environments and superior value. The company's focus continues to be on customer satisfaction, just as it was during the 1920s.

A LONG AND PROUD HISTORY

In 1922 C.S. Ober founded the company, opening the doors for business at 42 South Pennsylvania Street. In 1924 Business Furniture Corporation moved to 112 East Maryland Street, where it operated for 32 years. Rapid growth resulted in the addition of more sophisticated office, warehousing, installation, and project management facilities.

Over the years, C.S. Ober's son, John, assumed the role of president and chief executive officer, and the Obers moved their entire operation to 101 South Pennsylvania Street. This unique downtown

building has been placed on the National Register of Historic Places. The company's distribution center, centrally located at 1300 North Meridian, provides easy access to customers throughout the Indianapolis area.

NEW OWNERS ENSURE A BRIGHT FUTURE

When Dick and Deb Oakes bought the company in 1987, they recognized its growth potential for the future. Both Dick and Deb came from Steelcase Inc., the industry's manufacturing leader in office furniture, where they held management positions. They found the Indianapolis business climate to be positive, cooperative, and long-term in its thinking, an ideal foundation for success.

The owners set an example for excellent customer service by personally calling on many of their customers. During each visit, they got to know their customers and asked for feedback on how to achieve their goal of total customer satisfaction. They put into place a management group consisting of diverse, aggressive individuals who shared their business philosophy of a customer- and employee-driven company in a team-based environment. "Our reason for being here is to make a difference to our customers," says Richard Oakes. "It really doesn't matter what I think; it's what the customer thinks."

Business Furniture also put its customer-driven philosophy into action by forming the Customer Advisory Council, where members strive to incorporate customer focus

RIGHT: THE COMPANY'S LEADERSHIP TEAM INCLUDES (SEATED, FROM LEFT) MARY BETH SCHNECK, VICE PRESIDENT MARKETING AND COMMUNICATION; KENDRA BENNETT, CHIEF FINANCIAL OFFICER; (STANDING, FROM LEFT) RANDY HARLAN, VICE PRESIDENT OPERATIONS; BRET WATTS, VICE PRESIDENT MARKET DEVELOPMENT; MICHELLE HOPPES, SENIOR VICE PRESIDENT CORPORATE SERVICES; RICHARD OAKES, PRESIDENT/CEO; AND BOB KOEHNE, VICE PRESIDENT SALES AND GENERAL SALES MANAGER.

THE COMPANY'S 25,000-SQUARE-FOOT WORKING SHOWROOM DISPLAYS THE MOST RECENT TRENDS IN SYSTEMS FURNITURE, ALONG WITH A VARIETY OF CASEGOODS AND SEATING OPTIONS (BELOW).

into the company's business plans. With corporate clients representing 50 percent of the client base and smaller entrepreneurial businesses comprising the remaining 50 percent, Business Furniture Corporation realizes the importance of thoroughly understanding customer profiles to determine their strategic business goals.

In July of 1993 Business Furniture purchased the office furniture division of IOS Office Furniture at 2330 North Meridian, diversifying the company's range of products and services even more. The new showroom boasts 20,000 square feet of space for Business Furniture to display a wide variety of products for the walk-in customer to browse.

PRODUCTS AND SERVICES

To meet the needs of its diversified clientele, the company offers furnishings from a variety of top-of-the-line manufacturers, including Steelcase Inc., Brayton, Vecta, and Metro, in addition to Indiana manufacturers such as OFS and National. With a growing trend for home-based businesses, Turnstone, a line of office furniture especially for the home, is also available at Business Furniture.

Since 40 percent of businesses in America either move to a new space or renovate their existing space, the need for furniture services has never been greater. Renting furniture is ideal for businesses experiencing growth while planning for future expansion. Business Furniture rents brand-name furniture at competitive prices, with quick delivery. Furniture refurbishing, inventory, and storage alternatives are also available for customers looking for cost-effective solutions for enhancing their office environments.

THE OFFICES OF THE FUTURE

The company views selling office furniture as the beginning of a long-term, successful customer relationship. To meet future customer needs, Business Furniture stays ahead of the times by searching out innovative and value-driven solutions. The company is active in the community through employee involvement in volunteer programs and events.

Relationships with such prestigious companies as Eli Lilly, Thomson Consumer Electronics, Boehringer Mannheim, PSI Energy, National City Bank, and MacMillan Publishing have not happened overnight. Years of dedicated service have gone into building the city's oldest and most respected office furniture dealership. As the company approaches its 75th anniversary, its reason for being in business is as simple as it was in 1922—quality and customer service.

BUSINESS FURNITURE CORPORATION OFFERS A VARIETY OF SOLUTIONS TO REFLECT CONSTANTLY CHANGING ENVIRONMENTS IN THE WORKPLACE.

BUSINESS FURNITURE CORPORATION'S DELIVERY TRUCKS ARE LOCALLY RECOGNIZED FOR THEIR INNOVATIVE GRAPHICS.

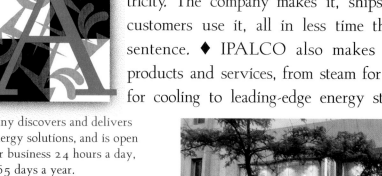

A IPALCO Enterprises, Inc. the principal product is electricity. The company makes it, ships it, and sells it, and its customers use it, all in less time than it takes to read this sentence. ◆ IPALCO also makes and sells other energy products and services, from steam for heating and chilled water for cooling to leading-edge energy storage devices. The com-

pany discovers and delivers energy solutions, and is open for business 24 hours a day, 365 days a year.

IPALCO and its subsidiaries operate with a business philosophy rooted in getting the basics right. The company has a sustained and significant involvement in the communities where it does business. IPALCO cares about the environment. It creates value for its customers and shareholders, and strives to act in the public interest.

Company officials say they feel fortunate to provide energy solutions to a vibrant city where their priorities—jobs, economic prosperity, good schools, and a better life for residents—are shared by the business community and the city administration.

Electric service began in Indianapolis in the 1880s, pioneered and developed by the predecessors of Indianapolis Power & Light Company (IPL), IPALCO's regulated subsidiary. These were practical businessmen, not dreamers. At first they thought of themselves as operating only a lighting business.

IPALCO's CORPORATE HEADQUARTERS IS LOCATED IN THE HEART OF DOWNTOWN INDIANAPOLIS ON MONUMENT CIRCLE (TOP RIGHT).

MARK DAVIS, A SUPERVISOR IN TRANSMISSION AND DISTRIBUTION SUPPORT, IS ONE OF THE THOUSANDS OF EMPLOYEES WHO HELP KEEP IPL'S ELECTRIC SERVICE AMONG THE LOWEST-COST AND MOST RELIABLE IN THE COUNTRY (BELOW).

Their primary goal was to provide the public with better light at lower cost. While that basic idea has motivated the entire development of electric service in Indianapolis, IPALCO has grown to become more than just "the light company."

Incorporated in October 1926, IPL provides retail electric service to more than 400,000 residential, commercial, and industrial customers in Indianapolis, as well as portions of other central Indiana

communities surrounding Marion County. IPL also generates and sells steam to 275 customers in downtown Indianapolis. IPL's steam operations are more than a century old.

During its long history, IPL has supplied its customers with some of the lowest-cost, most reliable power in the country. IPL also provides critical economic and energy-related information and services to businesses looking to expand or relocate into the Indianapolis area. And IPL works with customers to help them use electricity more efficiently, save energy costs, and improve productivity.

In addition, the company has a long history of concern for the environment. In the 1970s IPL drew up an environmental charter and pledged to "adapt existing and proposed facilities to meet the vital requirements of a clean environment." The company continues to keep that promise.

In 1977 IPL was one of the first utilities in the Midwest to install sulfur dioxide control devices—called scrubbers—at its Petersburg power plant. Two more scrubbers were added in 1996 to comply with new environmental laws

◄ RON HOSKINS

▲▼ MICHAEL VAUGHN

and provide cleaner air for Indiana. IPL was also instrumental in the formation of the Indianapolis Air Pollution Control Board and in 1988 received the Clean Air Award from the Indianapolis Clean Air Committee.

Mid-America Capital Resources, Inc., the holding company for IPALCO's unregulated subsidiaries, was created in April 1984. After a successful, two-year venture in cable television, Mid-America expanded into district cooling systems, which provide chilled water for air-conditioning services in downtown Indianapolis and Cleveland. Mid-America's Indianapolis district cooling system is one of the largest in the country. Its customers include the Circle Centre Mall, Indiana Convention Center and RCA Dome, and Indiana University-Purdue University Indianapolis.

Mid-America's subsidiary SHAPE Energy Resources is involved in the development of cutting-edge energy storage applications. SHAPE technology is able to capture and store waste energy from many different sources and then reuse it to heat or cool.

Another Mid-America subsidiary, Indianapolis Campus Energy, Inc. provides cooling to Eli Lilly and Company's Indianapolis technology center. The cooling center allows Eli Lilly to focus capital and resources on its core business of pharmaceutical research and produc-

tion, while IPALCO manages and assumes responsibility for a vital portion of Eli Lilly's growing energy needs.

In all, IPALCO has more than 2,400 employees, making it one of the larger employers in Marion County. These dedicated, hard-working individuals contribute thousands of hours each year to various organizations and charities. Their efforts are aligned with those of IPALCO, which has long served the community through programs that focus on education, the environment, health and welfare, and the arts.

The Golden Apple program recognizes outstanding teachers who are able to integrate math, science,

▲ MICHAEL VAUGHN

and technology into classroom subjects and create excitement among their students in the process. Each year, 25 of the best and most able of these teachers are recognized in an awards ceremony attended by community and corporate leaders, parents, and the families of the winning teachers.

The Golden Eagle Grants program, instituted in 1994, is designed to help fund worthwhile projects aimed at resource conservation and environmental awareness. The IPALCO grants have gone to groups and communities all around the state. The company designed this program to make a growing and positive contribution to a better, richer life for all citizens of Indiana.

CLOCKWISE FROM TOP LEFT: JESS BILLINGS (LEFT), IPALCO'S AMBASSADOR TO PIKE COUNTY, AND IPL EMPLOYEE CARLA LEVY TALK TO PETERSBURG MAYOR RANDY HARRIS. THE AMBASSADOR PROGRAM PARTNERS IPALCO EMPLOYEES WITH COMMUNITIES THROUGHOUT INDIANA.

IPL USES THE SERVICE OF JENNIFER JOHNSON (RIGHT) TO TRANSCRIBE UTILITY BILLS INTO BRAILLE TO HELP BLIND CUSTOMERS BECOME MORE INDEPENDENT. ALSO PICTURED IS YVONNE RONEY, AN IPL CUSTOMER SERVICE REPRESENTATIVE.

KEVIN GREISL (LEFT), MID-AMERICA'S VICE PRESIDENT OF SALES, TALKS WITH CUSTOMER BARNEY LEVENGOOD, EXECUTIVE DIRECTOR OF THE INDIANA CONVENTION CENTER AND RCA DOME. THE CONVENTION COMPLEX RECEIVES ENVIRONMENTALLY FRIENDLY DISTRICT AIR-CONDITIONING SERVICE FROM MID-AMERICA.

ROM THE TIME THE PILGRIMS FIRST CAME TO AMERICA, THE
name Mayflower has been synonymous with moving. Over
the centuries, people have picked up their possessions and
carried them any way they could in search of better lives in new
lands. With the arrival of the motorized vehicle in the early
years of the 20th century and the development of paved roads,

the modern moving business began to evolve. As part of that evolution, Mayflower Transit was founded by Indiana grocer Conrad M. Gentry and his friend Donald Kenworthy in 1927.

A HISTORY OF INNOVATION

Immediately establishing a reputation for innovation, Gentry and Kenworthy sold their first trucks to contract drivers with the promise of helping them obtain moving orders. In the process, they created a service supply method that is still used today. Promoting their service as an alternative to the railway system, they quickly attracted customers who were interested in moving their belongings across the country on the newly paved roads. Providing safe door-to-door pickup and delivery, the enterprise became a success.

It was soon apparent that additional capitalization was necessary to take advantage of the growing market. Gentry sought the help of Indianapolis businessman Burnside Smith, who contributed capital and management expertise. In 1928 Smith reincorporated the business as Aero Mayflower Transit Company, and he became the firm's president one year later.

By the company's 10th anniversary, annual revenues approached

the $2 million mark. In 1940 Mayflower received the nation's first 48-state operating authority from the Interstate Commerce Commission. Mayflower continued its push for progressiveness by developing corrugated wrapping (instead of using messy shredded paper) in the 1950s. In the '60s Mayflower became the first company to equip its vans with "air ride" suspension systems—now an industry standard.

With business continuing to expand, Mayflower moved from its downtown Indianapolis location to its current 200-acre headquarters campus in Carmel, Indiana, in 1974.

THE NUMBER ONE NAME IN MOVING

Today the Mayflower family has more than 750 worldwide agents and 1,400 employees and is the most recognized name

in moving, according to a 1995 national survey. To achieve and maintain that status, the company has positioned itself as a well-rounded transportation service provider, with household relocations still the heart of Mayflower's service offerings. Performing more than 80,000 interstate household relocations a year, Mayflower serves three primary markets: national accounts, including major corporations that are relocating employees; customers who are paying for the move themselves; and the U.S. military, Mayflower's largest single customer.

MOVING MORE THAN HOUSEHOLD GOODS

To meet the increasingly diverse needs of its customers, Mayflower provides services not often expected of a typical

TODAY THE MAYFLOWER FAMILY
HAS MORE THAN 750 WORLDWIDE
AGENTS AND 1,400 EMPLOYEES, AND
IS THE MOST RECOGNIZED NAME IN
MOVING, ACCORDING TO A 1995
NATIONAL SURVEY.

"mover." For example, the company recently delivered more than 170 truckloads of exhibits to COMDEX, the world's largest trade show attended by more than 225,000 computer industry professionals. Mayflower also moved the space equipment for the Russian cosmonauts when they joined forces with NASA in the space shuttle program. The company has even moved a professional football team.

To service shipments other than household goods, Mayflower created a separate division called Special Transportation Systems (STS). Delivering more than 75,000 shipments each year, STS handles product distribution and trade show exhibit transportation.

Mayflower is also on the leading edge of transportation with its specialized logistics services. Backed by a network of agent support, Mayflower Logistics, Inc., a subsidiary of Mayflower Transit, provides comprehensive warehouse and transportation capabilities for corporate accounts, including individual product service to full-service supply chain management.

SMOOTH SAILING TOWARD THE NEXT CENTURY

In early 1995 Mayflower underwent an ownership change when it was purchased by St.

Louis-based UniGroup, Inc., the parent company of United Van Lines and other transportation-related subsidiaries. Considered an industry first, the transaction formed the nation's largest household goods moving organization. Although they remain business rivals in the marketplace, both van lines are benefiting from the new relationship by forging a shared foundation of standardized business practices and common internal support services. The partnership is helping Mayflower to realize enhanced financial strength and to focus on the goals of increased business, utilization of emerging technologies, and growth into new market segments.

GIVING BACK TO THE COMMUNITY

A proud member of the Indianapolis corporate community, Mayflower is active in many charitable causes, including the United Way, Easter Seals, and United Christmas Service. Mayflower employees also give back to the community by serving as Junior Achievement representatives. Through Junior Achievement, the company adopts local schools, and its employees instruct classes on business practices, as well as

business operations and career opportunities available to students when they complete their education.

With a history rich in innovation, growth, and quality service, Mayflower continues to move ahead as a leader in the transportation industry. Even though the Pilgrims' original mode of transportation in 1620 did not include 18-wheelers, it did represent a safe, reliable way to transport their possessions to their new homes. It is this similar dedication to quality service that makes the Mayflower of today the number one name in moving. With a philosophy of exceeding customer expectations with quality, professional service, Mayflower is positioned to lead the way along the world's highways into the 21st century.

CLOCKWISE FROM TOP LEFT: THERE ARE NO LIMITS TO MAYFLOWER'S PRODUCT DISTRIBUTION COVERAGE.

MOVING MORE THAN HOUSEHOLD GOODS, MAYFLOWER IS A LEADER IN THE TRADE SHOW TRANSPORTATION INDUSTRY.

AN ACTIVE CORPORATE MEMBER IN THE INDIANAPOLIS COMMUNITY, MAYFLOWER ADOPTS LOCAL SCHOOLS THROUGH ITS INVOLVEMENT WITH JUNIOR ACHIEVEMENT.

HE CANTERBURY HOTEL—REFLECTING OLD-WORLD EUROPEAN traditions and the charm of Canterbury, England—has received the AAA Four Diamond Award each year since 1986. Listed on the National Register of Historic Places, the Canterbury astonishes travelers with its attention to detail and highly personalized service. It is estimated that of more than 3,000 resorts and hotels worldwide, only 104—among them the Canterbury—can claim Preferred Hotels membership. Preferred is an independent member organization that sets and maintains the highest quality standards for fine resorts and hotels around the world. The Canterbury's impeccable service and its outstanding credentials earned it Preferred Hotels membership in 1986 and continue to bring it distinguished travelers.

RICH IN HISTORY

The Canterbury Hotel celebrates a long and noteworthy history. In 1858 prominent Indiana architect Frances Costigan designed, built, and operated the Oriental Hotel on the corner of Illinois and Chesapeake streets, the site of today's Canterbury Hotel. Its name was later changed to the Mason House and then to the Oxford Hotel. In 1928 Costigan's hotel was razed to make room for the Lockerbie, a 12-story, 200-room hotel. Eight years later, hotelier Glenn F. Warren changed the name of the property to the Warren Hotel, operating the facility until 1973.

The Warren Hotel was purchased in 1983 by Indianapolis Realtor Fred C. Tucker Jr. and Donald L. Fortunato of Chicago. The new owners envisioned transforming the historic property into an intimate luxury hotel with European ambience. Project architects Browning, Day, Millins, Dierdorf, Inc. created 25 spacious guest suites and 74 guest rooms, while meticulously preserving the hotel's original 12-story red brick exterior and elegant two-story atrium.

A HOME AWAY FROM HOME

Today, the Canterbury Hotel seems more home than hotel. Rather than the traditional lobby, guests can gather in intimate rooms, inviting and comfortably furnished. The parlor, much like a comfortable English sitting room, features a carved wooden fireplace. This unique space lends itself to reading and quiet conversation.

Guest rooms are furnished with elegant Chippendale four-poster beds, marble vanities, and gold-plated fixtures. Luxurious private suites and duplex penthouses include modern whirlpool baths, wet bars, and elegant adjoining sitting rooms.

Special amenities abound: valet parking, complimentary overnight shoeshine, 24-hour room service, full concierge service, twice-a-day housekeeping service, nonsmoking rooms, barrier-free rooms, private mini bar, hair dryers in each room, complimentary Continental breakfast, telephone and television in each bathroom, fine hand-milled soaps, complimentary morning newspaper, and plush terry cloth robes.

For the business traveler, a variety of office equipment is readily available. Complete audiovisual services and equipment, telex and secretarial services, interpreters, and fax machines are provided by the hotel. Limousine, butler, babysitting, and dry cleaning services, as well as sight-seeing/shopping tours, can be arranged by request.

THE CANTERBURY'S 1980S RENOVATION METICULOUSLY PRESERVED THE HOTEL'S ORIGINAL 12-STORY RED BRICK EXTERIOR AND ELEGANT TWO-STORY ATRIUM (BELOW LEFT).

OLD-WORLD EUROPEAN TRADITIONS AND CHARM ARE EVIDENT IN THE HOTEL'S BAR (BELOW RIGHT).

BANAYOTE PHOTO

The Canterbury Hotel was designed with comfort and elegance in mind. Attention to detail is unsurpassed, from intimate gatherings to groups of up to 120 people.

Outstanding reviews of the Canterbury's delicious American and Continental cuisine prepared by award-winning chef Volker Rudolph lure discriminating diners from around the state. The Restaurant—the hotel's quiet, wood-paneled dining room with soft rose upholstered chairs and banquettes—offers a peaceful haven for enjoying expertly prepared meals. Reservations are required for afternoon tea at the Canterbury, a favorite among locals, particularly during holiday seasons.

Directly adjoining the magnificent Circle Centre Mall and located within blocks of Union Station, the Indiana Convention Center and RCA Dome, Market Square Arena, Monument Circle, and the Indianapolis Repertory Theatre, the Canterbury Hotel is ideally situated in the heart of Indianapolis.

"The Canterbury Hotel enjoys a reputation for being 'the hotel of choice' for Hollywood stars, dignitaries, and government VIPs," says Letitia Moscrip, general manager.

"Our hotel staff is trained to assist our guests during their stay with us. We cater to their individual needs and make sure every detail is well organized. When Robert Goulet and his wife requested a coffeepot and a microwave oven for their room, we went out and got them. Those items have now become permanent fixtures."

The Canterbury staff have also become security experts, and on more than one occasion have discreetly whisked a star out of the hotel's back entrance to a waiting limousine. The hotel's VIP list is an impressive read, including Paula Abdul, Cher, Bob Dylan, Elton John, David and Julie Nixon Eisenhower, Whoopi Goldberg— and the list goes on.

The Canterbury, steeped in old-world tradition and charm, welcomes visitors to Indianapolis in style. Mark Twain once commented, "All saints can do miracles, but few of them can keep a hotel." Considered a wonderful home away from home by more than one of its guests, the Canterbury Hotel takes pride in making miracles happen every day.

THE CANTERBURY OFFERS A NUMBER OF MEETING ACCOMMODATIONS FOR GROUPS OF VARIOUS SIZES (ABOVE).

GUEST ROOMS (LEFT) ARE FURNISHED WITH HIGHLY POLISHED CHIPPENDALE FOUR-POSTER BEDS, CRISP IRISH LINEN, MARBLE VANITIES, AND GOLD-PLATED FIXTURES.

ETROIT-BASED GENERAL MOTORS (GM), FOUNDED IN 1908, IS best known as the world's largest full-line vehicle manufacturer. The company makes and sells cars, trucks, automotive systems, and locomotives worldwide. GM's other substantial business interests include Electronic Data Systems Corporation (EDS), GM Hughes Electronics Corporation, and General Motors Acceptance

Corporation and its subsidiaries. The Allison Transmission and Metal Fabricating divisions have represented GM's presence in Indianapolis for more than 66 years.

ALLISON TRANSMISSION DIVISION

The Allison Transmission Division of General Motors is the world's leading designer, producer, and assembler of medium- and heavy-duty automatic transmissions for trucks, buses, off-road vehicles, and military equipment. Applications of Allison Automatics include school buses; city and transit coaches; pickup and delivery vehicles; beverage trucks; refuse haulers; dump trucks; fire and rescue vehicles; recreational vehicles; oil field, mining, and

logging equipment; military recovery vehicles; medium- and heavy-tactical trucks; and the M1A1 Abrams tank.

Allison Transmission has a significant customer base of original equipment manufacturers (OEMs) and end users, such as Ford Heavy Truck, Navistar, Freightliner, and GMC. A myriad of municipalities and transit companies throughout North America and Mexico look to Allison Automatics to equip their vehicles.

In 1915 James Ashbury Allison—who was dedicated to quality and known for risk taking—established the Indianapolis Speedway Team Company to redesign and rebuild race cars. This small shop in Speedway grew to become a multimillion-dollar company known as Allison Transmission. General Motors purchased the

company on April 1, 1929, in order to closely evaluate the development of the aircraft industry. Allison, along with three others, was also a founder of the Indianapolis Motor Speedway in 1909.

During World War I, Allison offered the technical expertise of his company to do for the wartime effort whatever projects others could not or would not undertake. By the end of World War II, more than 70,000 Liberty engines had been produced by Allison Engine Company, thrusting the company into becoming the predominant power of the U.S. military fighter force.

By 1946 the Allison division had designed and produced its first heavy-duty torque converter/planetary gear transmission for military and commercial applications. By the mid-1950s Allison had pro-

ALLISON AUTOMATICS, THE BEST TRANSMISSIONS IN THE WORLD, ARE MADE IN INDIANAPOLIS.

duced more than 30,000 transmissions for the military and 100,000 commercial units. Today the company has produced considerably more than 2 million units worldwide.

In 1973 General Motors merged the Allison division with Detroit Diesel, naming the unit Detroit Diesel Allison. In 1983 GM separated the gas turbine portion of the business and established it as Allison Gas Turbine Division. December 1987 brought yet another change as GM established the transmission business as a stand-alone division, naming it Allison Transmission. Roger Penske purchased the Detroit Diesel portion.

Changes within General Motors brought about a possible monumental impact when it put the Allison Transmission Division up for sale in 1992. The U.S. Justice Department ultimately blocked the sale to Zahnrudfabrik Friedrichshuten (ZF), and the company continues to thrive as an important division within GM.

More than 4,000 employees

within six plants covering 3.75 million square feet comprise Allison Transmission's Indianapolis facility, which occupies 225 acres of land. Allison Transmission has more than 1,600 distributors and dealers worldwide; three international business segments in Europe, Latin America, and the Asia/Pacific region; operations in 81 countries; and seven established licensees in China, Spain, Italy, England, Turkey, India, and South Korea. Its factory warehouses are located in Indianapolis, Brazil, Singapore, and Belgium. The company expects to increase international sales substantially in the near future.

Allison Transmission's research and development effort is supported by approximately 150,000 square feet of R&D space and includes component, subassembly, transmission, and vehicle level testing. Engineering evaluation and durability testing are performed in the engineering test facilities, which are separate from the production test facilities. Allison Transmission has developed and implemented a methodology to remain the world

leader and to improve transmission technology rather than respond only to product problems. This allows the company to pursue new technologies, such as electric drive systems, and to investigate innovative peripherals, such as electromechanical starting devices.

Allison Transmission, along with the GM Metal Fabricating Division, supports its local and statewide community through the United Way, Junior Achievement, Children's Museum, Minorities in Engineering, Boy Scouts of America, and many other educational, artistic, health and human services, and community-oriented organizations.

METAL FABRICATING DIVISION

The current Indianapolis Metal Center on White River Parkway first established its local presence in 1930 when Chevrolet Motor Division purchased a factory from Martin Perry Carriage Works. Since that time, the Indianapolis plant—which produces sheet metal stampings

and metal assemblies for General
Motors' truck products—has mod-
ernized equipment and expanded
facilities, growing to its current
2.1 million-square-foot size.

For the first 52 years, the
facility was part of the Chevrolet
Motor Division of General Motors.
In 1982 it became part of the
Truck and Bus Group. In 1994,
after a brief association with the
Cadillac Luxury Car Division, the
Indianapolis facility finally settled
in as part of the recently formed
General Motors Metal Fabricating
Division, which now includes 13
stamping and metal-assembly opera-
tions throughout the United States
and Canada.

The Indianapolis plant, with
a workforce approaching 3,000
employees, is one of the largest-
volume metal stamping facilities in
the United States. Approximately
2,000 tons of steel per day are
consumed for production of parts,
which are shipped in more than
60 rail cars to 10 assembly plant
customers in the United States,
Canada, and Mexico. These parts
include major sheet metal panels
and assemblies, such as doors, roofs,
dash panels, and most pickup box

metal for GM's popular line of
pickup trucks and utility vehicles.
A variety of truck products present
today on the streets of Indianapolis
bearing nameplates such as Blazer,
Jimmy, S-10, Sonoma, Suburban,
Tahoe, and Yukon all wear sheet
metal proudly produced by the
men and women of the Indianapolis
plant.

Today the plant is a strong
contributor to the economic health
of the city of Indianapolis and surrounding communities. An annual

payroll of approximately $180
million, combined with annual
purchases from local area suppliers
of $60 million, illustrates the impor-
tant but sometimes invisible role of
the Indianapolis facility. Additionally, the plant helps support local
government budgets to the tune of
$5.5 million through payments of
annual property taxes. Many charitable and civic organizations and
programs also receive support
annually through the plant's
involvement in the GM India-

napolis Community Relations Committee.

Over the years, the plant has matured along with the industry, adding modern technology as it has become available in order to stay at the forefront of the stamping business. The Indianapolis plant led the industry in the 1980s as it invested millions of dollars in transfer press technology. The transfer presses, weighing hundreds of tons each, were purchased in Germany and Brazil, shipped across the ocean, transported by barge on the Ohio River, and then loaded onto 96-wheel trailers for the last leg of the journey to Indianapolis. A philosophy of investing in new technology such as transfer presses and automation has contributed to making the Indianapolis plant a premier General Motors press metal center. It is also one of the world's largest. Ongoing improvements in equipment systems and in synchronous manufacturing processes, coupled with a dedicated Hoosier workforce, have helped it sustain a leadership role in the industry.

"Technology is important, but dedicated employees are essential," explains Plant Manager Hank

ALLISON TRANSMISSION IS THE LEADING PRODUCER OF AUTOMATIC TRANSMISSIONS FOR MEDIUM- AND HEAVY-DUTY TRUCKS, BUSES, AND MILITARY EQUIPMENT (LEFT).

Hale. "We owe our current success to our people. Their involvement and participation in process improvements on the manufacturing floor have helped form us into the company we are today and will determine the course of our future." Thus, in conjunction with its UAW Local #23 partners, the General Motors Metal Fabricating Division intends to continue building quality parts for quality GM vehicles for years to come.

1930-1969

1930	The Heritage Group
1930	Indianapolis Symphony Orchestra
1930	Zimmer Paper Products Incorporated
1935	Farm Bureau Insurance
1935	National Wine & Spirits Corporation
1937	NatCity Investments, Inc.
1938	Best Lock Corporation
1944	Inland Mortgage Corporation
1946	Chrysler Corporation Indianapolis Foundry
1947	Hamilton Displays, Inc.
1950	Carrier Corporation
1953	DowElanco and DowBrands
1956	Community Hospitals Indianapolis
1957	Marsh Supermarkets, Inc.
1957	WTHR, Channel 13
1960	MSE Corporation
1961	R.W. Armstrong Associates
1961	CSO Architects Engineers & Interiors
1963	Ivy Tech State College, Central Indiana Region
1964	Boehringer Mannheim Corporation
1967	Service Graphics Inc.
1968	ITT Educational Services, Inc.
1969	Hoosier Orthopaedics and Sports Medicine, P.C.
1969	Indiana University-Purdue University Indianapolis

OR MORE THAN 60 YEARS, THE HERITAGE GROUP HAS BEEN A family-owned organization, managing a comprehensive list of prominent companies from its home base in Indianapolis. Today, it is best known for its involvement in environmental services, oil refining and marketing, asphalt refining, aggregate production, and construction. ◆ In 1930 John Fehsenfeld Sr. founded

Crystal Flash Petroleum Corporation in Indianapolis and began selling kerosene and axle grease. Crystal Flash expanded into the retail and commercial marketing of fuels and lubricants. Around 1960 Fehsenfeld and his sons acquired an asphalt refinery and several stone quarries, one of which was performing environmental reclamation work long before it became fashionable. This laid the foundation for The Heritage Group, which today consists of more than 20 companies with operations throughout the country. The group's Indianapolis research and development offices are housed in the Heritage Environmental Plaza on West Morris Street, while Crystal Flash and Asphalt Materials have their operations on the northwest side of the city.

"Over time, we've just expanded into various types of businesses," says Mac Fehsenfeld, president of Crystal Flash, one of Indiana's largest independent suppliers of petroleum products. Mac and his older brothers, Fred and Frank (now retired), were the original trust-

ees of Heritage. Fred previously led the environmental division, and Frank headed the Crystal Flash division in Michigan. They both remain active as consultants to Heritage.

STRENGTH THROUGH SYNERGY

The strength of The Heritage Group is in the synergy created when its affiliated companies join forces. Together they hold one vision—to build long-term relationships with customers based on trust and confidence. This synergy also allows Heritage to be flexible, anticipate change, and proactively respond to customer needs. By pooling resources and technology, the companies are able to take an idea, explore its possibilities, and make it work for the customer.

The Heritage Group's team approach to management allows it to provide creative, effective solutions that benefit not only customers, but the community as well. For example, Heritage Environmental Services, Inc. hosts Tox-Away Days in Indianapolis. This program allows residents to dispose of hazardous materials—such as paints and

other household supplies—in an environmentally responsible manner, free of charge.

NATIONAL PRESENCE, LOCAL ROOTS

While Heritage was founded in Indiana, its presence is felt nationally in a variety of industries and globally in the oil marketing arena. Although growth and expansion have made it an industry leader, Heritage never forgets its roots.

In addition to bringing many needed services and products to Indianapolis, The Heritage Group's Education Foundation produces an environmental science curriculum, Partners with the Earth, that is taught in many local schools. Also, Crystal Flash sponsors an annual golf tournament to benefit the Muscular Dystrophy Association of Indiana.

As it has for more than six decades, Heritage will continue to thrive on the synergy that has brought it success. In each of the industries in which its companies operate, The Heritage Group will lead the way with environmental stewardship and product innovation.

FIRST IMPRESSIONS ARE IMPORTANT, AND HAMILTON DISPLAYS has carved a niche in the trade show exhibit industry by helping its clients make the best possible first impression. ♦ Large and small businesses in various fields—such as health care and pharmaceuticals, automotive, and home building—rely on Hamilton to design, produce, market, and service their exhibits. Customers

include Allison Transmission, Cummins Engine Company, Eli Lilly and Company, Boehringer Mannheim, and Cook, Inc. Hamilton has also designed retail and museum installations for the Indiana Pacers Store and the Indianapolis Museum of Art, among others.

LOCAL BEGINNINGS

The company was started in Indianapolis in 1947 by Renzie Hamilton, who originally focused on the construction of trade show exhibits. In the 1990s the business has expanded to encompass trade show marketing, program management, and a variety of services.

"We are one of the few nationally recognized exhibit and display companies that focuses on trade show marketing," says James Obermeyer, director of sales and marketing. "We work with our clients to determine their trade show marketing plan. We still design and build displays just like everybody else. But when we present a solution to a prospect, we present not just the design, but also how they're going to use it—the preshow, at-show, and postshow activity that

will achieve objectives and justify the investment."

Hamilton Displays is currently owned by Daniel Cantor, who purchased the company with partner Joel Coleman in January 1990. Hamilton acquired one of its largest competitors, Dimensional Designs, in January 1991. This transaction prompted a move in December of that year to the new, 195,000-square-foot headquarters at 9150 East 33rd Street. In addition, Hamilton operates sales offices in St. Louis and Louisville. Cantor became sole owner in December 1993.

AN INDIANA LEADER

Building on nearly five decades of success, the $10 million company has a strong foothold in the community. In addition to its original corporate clients like Citizens Gas and Indiana Bell, Hamilton once produced about 70 percent of the Indianapolis 500 Festival Parade floats.

Today Hamilton is Indiana's largest custom trade show exhibit company and employs approximately 110 people. Although 80 percent of its business is generated in central Indiana, technological

advances have made geography less of an issue, allowing Hamilton to gain an edge in the national and global trade show marketplace.

An awareness of the global market and design trends enhances the services Hamilton offers its clients who attend shows overseas. Obermeyer explains that European designs favor paneled "systems," which can be configured according to individual needs. The company is a distributor of the German-manufactured OCTANORM systems, as well as several other portable and modular display units. Hamilton recently made its first overseas appearance at EuroShop '96, International Trade Fair & Congress for Storefitting, Display, and Merchandising in Düsseldorf.

The company has designed numerous award-winning exhibits for its clients, and in 1994 and 1995 received two "Best of Show" awards from the Exhibitor Show for its own exhibit. Many of Hamilton's designers have architectural and industrial design backgrounds, which lend a special quality to their eye-catching designs.

While moving into the global market is one of the company's primary goals, it will not occur at the expense of local clients. "We still want to be number one in Indiana," maintains Obermeyer. "We do not want to give that position up."

FROM ITS 195,000-SQUARE-FOOT INDIANAPOLIS HEADQUARTERS (TOP), HAMILTON DESIGNS, PRODUCES, MARKETS, AND SERVICES EXHIBITS FOR LARGE AND SMALL BUSINESSES IN VARIOUS FIELDS.

W HEN THE INDIANAPOLIS SYMPHONY ORCHESTRA (ISO) HOLDS AN audition to fill the position of a principal chair, it can expect to receive applications from up to 250 musicians from all over the United States, and even from other countries. Of those applicants, close to 90 musicians typically are invited to Indianapolis to audition. Many of the musicians have been playing for

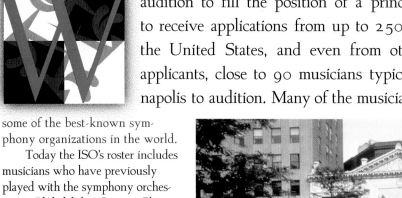

some of the best-known symphony organizations in the world.

Today the ISO's roster includes musicians who have previously played with the symphony orchestras in Philadelphia, Boston, Chicago, Moscow, Tel Aviv, and 13 other major cities, as well as the Metropolitan Opera Orchestra, the Bolshoi Theatre Orchestra, the Rome Opera Orchestra, and other highly respected opera or chamber orchestras.

That so many fine artists want to be part of the Indianapolis Symphony Orchestra is an indication of its quality. It is not surprising, then, that the orchestra is so popular. So many people attend ISO concerts (annual attendance exceeds half a million) that the orchestra could fill the RCA Dome eight times every year.

The impact of the orchestra is also felt outside Indiana through its tours of Europe and other regions of the United States; its recordings (eight compact discs are currently

available); and *Indianapolis-on-the-Air*, a 13-week, syndicated radio program that is heard over 200 stations in 41 states and Puerto Rico, including the 10 largest markets. The total population of the markets reached by *Indianapolis-on-the-Air* exceeds 92 million.

Founded in 1930, the Indianapolis Symphony Orchestra is a

full-time, 52-week orchestra. With 87 full-time musicians, it performs some 200 concerts annually. Its budget of more than $14 million makes it the 17th-largest among America's professional symphony orchestras.

The ISO's music director is Maestro Raymond Leppard, guest conductor of many of the world's most famous orchestras, composer of film scores, Cambridge don, music scholar, and conductor on more than 150 recordings including winners of Grammys and other awards. Leppard clearly enjoys conducting the orchestra, and his commentaries, witty and informed, add spice and fun to concertgoing.

Music critics give every evidence of enjoying the orchestra's performances as much as regular concertgoers. During an ISO concert tour of Europe, the *Daily Telegraph* of London said, "The Indianapolis Symphony Orchestra is remarkably polished, athletic, and precise in its articulation but with a burnished tone which is more resonant of a European than an American sound." *La Suisse* of Geneva said, "Because of the individual quality of its musicians and the supple perfection of the ensemble, the Indianapolis Sym-

THE ISO CONDUCTS 25 DIFFERENT EDUCATION AND OUTREACH PROGRAMS. THESE ARE SOME OF THE 25,000 SCHOOLCHILDREN, FROM AS FAR AWAY AS LAKE MICHIGAN AND THE OHIO RIVER, WHO ATTEND THE YOUNG PEOPLE'S DISCOVERY CONCERTS IN THE CIRCLE THEATRE.

phony Orchestra joined today the level of the orchestras of Chicago or Boston." The *Times* of London said, "Much fun was had by all. Leppard has honed his orchestra's strings to a warm, willing transparency, ready for the cultivated phrasing and buoyant rhythms which are so much his own conducting hallmark. The band, in turn, responds to him with ebullience and sometimes bravado."

Of the ISO's recordings, Byron Belt, music critic of the Newhouse chain of newspapers, said, "Major league." Mortimer H. Frank, commenting favorably in *Fanfare* on the orchestra's recording of Schubert's Symphony No. 3 in C, praised the "stylish conducting," and the *Stevenson Classical Music Compact Disc Guide* called the same recording "a winning release." The *American Record Guide* agreed, saying of the ISO's musicians, "They. . . sound like a first-class ensemble."

The home of the ISO is the Circle Theatre on Monument Circle in the heart of downtown Indianapolis, one block away from the Circle Centre Mall. Constructed in 1916—in the heyday of the great movie palaces—the Circle Theatre was one of the first buildings west of New York erected specifically for the purpose of showing feature-length films. From 1916 to 1981 it presented live stage shows and classical concerts, in addition to motion pictures. Among the many celebrities who performed there were Frank Sinatra, Tommy Dorsey, Glenn Miller, Dizzy Gillespie, Stan Getz, Fred Waring, and Beverly Sills. In 1961 Jack Benny played his violin with the ISO at a benefit concert in the theater.

In 1981 the movie palace, then run down, closed its doors and seemed headed for demolition. But it was saved by the combined efforts of the Historic Landmarks Foundation of Indianapolis; the Commission for Downtown; and the theater's next-door neighbor, the Indianapolis Power and Light Company, which succeeded in having the building placed on the National Register of Historic Places. Then a $9.2 million adaptive reuse project, in which highly skilled craftsmen from various parts of the country were brought to Indianapolis, restored and preserved the theater's decor, which is in the elegant style developed in the 18th century by British architects James and Robert Adam. In 1984 the Indianapolis Symphony Orchestra opened its season in the newly converted concert hall. In 1990 the theater became the property of the orchestra.

Since 1983 the president and chief administrative officer of the ISO has been Robert C. Jones. In a little more than a decade, attendance has increased nearly 200 percent, Annual Fund contributions have more than doubled, and $42 million has been added to the endowment. With a balanced budget, strong management controls, aesthetic vision, and notable artistic growth, the Indianapolis Symphony Orchestra is a major cultural asset of the state.

FOUNDED IN 1930, THE INDIANAPOLIS SYMPHONY ORCHESTRA HAS 87 FULL-TIME MUSICIANS AND PERFORMS SOME 200 CONCERTS ANNUALLY.

INCE 1930 ZIMMER PAPER PRODUCTS INCORPORATED HAS pioneered the development of new techniques for coating paper and other flexible materials. The success of this third-generation, family-owned business can be attributed to a strong commitment to quality and a strategy of concentrating on market niches that other companies find difficult to serve.

The company's beginnings were bold. When Karl Zimmer Sr. left a secure executive position to start his own waxed paper business during the depression of 1930, old-timers in the industry (while praising his audacity) seriously questioned his timing. Fortunately, the founder's courage and integrity were more than a match for the depressed economy. Within a few short years, Zimmer Paper Products became a leading manufacturer of the colorfully printed waxed bread wrappers used by commercial baker-

ies throughout the Midwest. For almost 40 years, until his death in 1967, Karl Zimmer's dedication to his employees, his customers, the industry, and the community in which he lived was like a strong beacon whose light still guides the company through the difficult course of responsible private enterprise.

From 1965 until 1988, following a successful career as a publishing executive in the United States and Europe, Karl Zimmer Jr. served as company president. The bread

wrappers gave way to a wide variety of more sophisticated products, including specially coated packaging for butter and margarine, tamper-resistant inner seals for instant coffee, and even sticker trading cards for bubble gum and breakfast cereal in-packs. New laboratories for ink and coating development were built, while expanded production facilities were added in Indianapolis and California. Yet Zimmer Paper remained entrepreneurial. In an era during which many of its competitors were absorbed by large firms

THREE GENERATIONS OF LEADERSHIP: CHAIRMAN KARL ZIMMER JR. AND HIS SON, PRESIDENT AND CHIEF EXECUTIVE OFFICER KARL ZIMMER III, ARE SEATED BEFORE A PORTRAIT OF COMPANY FOUNDER KARL ZIMMER SR. (ABOVE).

IN ALL AREAS OF THE COMPANY, ZIMMER EMPLOYEES MAINTAIN A STRONG COMMITMENT TO QUALITY (RIGHT).

ZIMMER'S CONTINUING INVESTMENT IN ADVANCED PRODUCTION EQUIPMENT ASSURES THAT THE COMPANY'S CUSTOMERS GET THE BEST PRODUCTS AVAILABLE (LEFT).

in or out of the industry, Zimmer remained independent, convinced that despite the advantages that might accompany becoming part of a giant corporation, outstanding service and employee dedication do not always survive. As Karl Zimmer Jr. put it at the time, "We believe that our customers deserve the best products we are able to make, service that is second to none, and prices that are advantageous to both buyer and seller."

Karl Zimmer III took over as president in 1988 and has led the company to the forefront of new technologies. Three state-of-the-art hot-melt coater-laminators and high-tech, eight-color flexographic process printing have significantly broadened the product mix. Karl's younger brother, Erik, came on board in 1991 and now heads the company's Special Products ventures. The company enjoys a leading position as a supplier of paper and film wraps for frozen novelties (for example, Drumsticks and "desserts on a stick" like Popsicles and Good Humor bars), which are produced in its Sacramento, California, and its Indianapolis and Plymouth, Indiana, facilities. In addition, Zimmer has developed highly specialized pressure-sensitive

(self-adhesive) laminations that are further transformed by the company's label-converter customers into printed labels affixed to tires, automobile batteries, pharmaceutical bottles, and the myriad products people use every day.

A key role in the firm's progress continues to be performed by Financial Vice President Tom Terry, who joined Zimmer in 1973 after a career in public accounting. He, along with dedicated operations, sales, and customer service specialists, is looked to by a board of distinguished outside directors to continue the successful conduct of the firm.

As a caring corporate citizen, Zimmer supports many not-for-profit civic and cultural organizations. The company, for example, is a corporate sponsor of the Indianapolis Museum of Art, the Indianapolis Symphony Orchestra, and the Indianapolis Opera. Zimmer also serves as a Partner in Education with neighborhood schools, where employees volunteer their time to tutor pupils and help maintain playground equipment that the company has supplied.

"More than 65 years have elapsed since I watched my father supervise the unloading of the

second-hand printing press and waxing machine that formed the productive nucleus of Zimmer Paper Products," says Chairman Karl Zimmer Jr. "I am proud that my two sons continue the legacy of ethical business practices and dedication to our customers that inspired him when he founded our company in 1930."

SINCE 1930 THE COMPANY HAS PIONEERED THE DEVELOPMENT OF NEW TECHNIQUES FOR COATING PAPER AND OTHER FLEXIBLE MATERIALS (ABOVE).

FARM BUREAU INSURANCE

 STABLISHED IN 1935, FARM BUREAU INSURANCE WAS FOUNDED by Indiana Farm Bureau, Inc. to serve its members' insurance needs. Farm Bureau Insurance continues in its tradition as a company dedicated to serving the people of Indiana. Farm Bureau is not only the largest writer of farm insurance in Indiana, but also the state's second-largest insurer of automobiles and

homes. The business continues to evolve, evaluating and developing new products to match the changing needs of its members and policyholders.

Members of the Indiana Farm Bureau family of companies include United Farm Family Life Insurance Company, United Farm Mutual Insurance Company, and UFB Casualty Insurance Company. The Indianapolis headquarters functions as a service site for agency and claims service centers conveniently located throughout the state.

"The strength of the Farm Bureau organization lies in the value and philosophy of its members," says Harry L. Pearson, president. "The purpose of our organization is to serve the needs of our members and clients. The relationship between Indiana Farm Bureau and the Farm Bureau Insurance Companies is a strong one based on this underlying principle."

HOOSIER BEGINNINGS

Initially, Farm Bureau insured only farms throughout the state, but in 1955 the company began to sell insurance to the urban market as well. Business growth was dynamic, and by 1970 the com-

pany's total insurance in force reached $1 billion—a figure that had doubled just seven years later. By 1987 the Farm Bureau organization reported more than $7 billion worth of life insurance in force. At year-end 1995, United Farm Family Life Insurance achieved the goal of $1 billion in assets, an indication of the company's strength and financial performance. The Farm Bureau companies' complete line of insurance products includes life, auto, home, disability, retirement planning, annuities, farm, crop, business, business life, and pensions.

The A.M. Best Company, based on its current opinion of Indiana Farm Bureau's financial status and operating performance, has assigned a rating of A (Excellent) to the United Farm Family Life Insurance Company and A- (Excellent) to the United Farm Mutual Insurance Company and its property/casualty subsidiaries.

A COMMITMENT TO THE CITY

Long a supporter of downtown Indianapolis, Indiana Farm Bureau made a major commitment to the city in 1988 with its

relocation to new offices in the former Indianapolis Rubber Company plant on South East Street. Renovation and new construction began in July 1990 on the headquarters site. Initial work consisted of major demolition and environmental cleanup of 38 structures—in addition to a smokestack occupying 9.5 acres—by F.A. Wilhelm, Inc. Designed by Indianapolis-based Ratio Architects, the new headquarters features a three-story atrium with extensive use of granite, marble, maple, and glass finishes.

Farm Bureau was the first to occupy space in what has since become a 50-acre corporate and science development park. The move was hailed by city officials as a necessary revitalization of a deteriorated neighborhood that would subsequently attract improved housing and further development in the area.

"As our company is domiciled in the state of Indiana, we feel it is important to support the city of Indianapolis, where our home office is located and where a great number of our employees work and live," says Pearson. "As we were looking at possible locations for a new home

INDIANA FARM BUREAU MADE A MAJOR COMMITMENT TO THE CITY IN 1988 WITH ITS RELOCATION TO NEW OFFICES IN THE FORMER INDIANAPOLIS RUBBER COMPANY PLANT ON SOUTH EAST STREET (BELOW LEFT).

THE RENOVATED HEADQUARTERS FEATURES A THREE-STORY ATRIUM WITH EXTENSIVE USE OF GRANITE, MARBLE, MAPLE, AND GLASS FINISHES (BELOW RIGHT).

260

office a few years ago, it was the overwhelming desire of management and staff that we stay in the downtown Indianapolis area because we have a strong commitment to the city."

VISIONS FOR THE FUTURE

Farm Bureau's ongoing, community-oriented commitment manifests itself throughout the organization. The company created the Teenage Driver Safety and Education Program, the only initiative of its kind in the country. Any teen covered by Farm Bureau Insurance can earn a $1,000 savings bond by driving three years with no claims or traf-

fic convictions. "If this program saves just one life, it will be worth it," says CEO Donald E. Henderson. This is just one of the ways this innovative company has demonstrated its commitment to Indiana youth.

The company also sponsors a competition called Project XL, open to all Indiana high school students. Emphasis is on creativity and communicating a positive, motivational message to young people. Judges, under the supervision of Cranfill & Company advertising agency, look for originality, honesty, powerful emotional appeal, factual basis, and creative style. The six contest categories include writing, video art, poster design, original music, fine art, and performance. Farm

Bureau Insurance awards a $1,500 scholarship to the state winner in each category. Second-place winners receive a $1,000 scholarship, and a $500 scholarship is awarded to third-place winners.

The company is also involved in the Southeast Neighborhood Development Corporation and is a Partner in Education with School 78, a public grade school on Indianapolis' east side.

Since 1935 Farm Bureau Insurance has pledged to provide high-quality products and services to its members, while participating as a responsible corporate citizen of Indianapolis. The company continues to support this commitment with its ongoing financial strength and stability.

ATIONAL WINE & SPIRITS CORPORATION ENJOYS ITS REPUTA-
tion as the largest liquor and wine wholesale distributor in Indiana.
"The customer's economic justification for dealing with us really
hinges on products and service," says President James R. Beck.
"Our emphasis has always been on service." ◆ National Liquor
Corporation was incorporated in Indiana on April 9, 1935.

The original shareholders were
Jules Fansler, and George and
Laura Galm. Subsequent owners included the Frank McHale
and Frank McKinney families,
Marven Lasky, Charles Johnson,
and William and R. Cameron
Johnston. The current shareholders are James E. LaCrosse and
Norma M. Johnston. Their ownership was purchased in 1973.

National's success has been the
result of careful strategic planning.
The company has been the only
wine and liquor wholesale distributor in Indiana to expand market by
market throughout the state, purchasing the assets of eight other
wholesalers since 1973 and acquiring their sales organizations. These
organizations provided the company
with an instant presence in their
respective markets as well as a
viable market share of many small
to medium-sized accounts.

As a result of these acquisitions, National's sales increased
dramatically from $14 million to
$185 million between 1973 and
1995, while the company's asset
base increased from $4 million to
$135 million.

NATIONAL IS TODAY LED BY
PRESIDENT JIM BECK (STANDING)
AND CHAIRMAN JIM LACROSSE.

THE COMPANY'S BRAND MANAGERS
AND VICE PRESIDENTS MEET WITH
CO-OWNER AND SECRETARY NORMA
JOHNSTON (SEATED AT CENTER).
ALSO PICTURED ARE (FROM LEFT)
DAVE PETROFF, JON SCHUTZ, JOHN
COREY, BOB WALLACE, PHIL
FRAME, NORM TROUTT, AND
RON BURNS.

◄ JOHN FRAME

EMERGING NEEDS IN THE MARKETPLACE

In 1975 there were 17 liquor
and wine wholesale distributors
operating in Indiana, 14 of which
were out of business by 1988.
These wholesalers had failed to
serve the total market, either by
not expanding statewide or by
not providing adequate focus to
both the large volume chain retailers and the small to medium-sized
accounts. National's statewide
acquisition strategy not only provided the chain operators with
consistent statewide competitive
pricing and service, but also maintained the local sales personnel,
who were critical in servicing the
small to medium-sized accounts.

NEW MARKET RESPONSIBILITIES

In 1982 company management
identified several emerging
industry demands. Distributors

had to be held accountable to
suppliers for all distribution
activities. To assume this type
of responsibility, the distributor
needed exclusive authority from
the suppliers to distribute their
products in each market. Since
state regulations prohibited suppliers from designating exclusive
territories, the concept of multiple individual markets was not
viable. Therefore, the only exclusive market that could be effectively established was statewide.

To this end, National implemented a statewide sales and delivery organization in 1984, which
enabled suppliers to grant the
company exclusive franchises
in Indiana.

Today National occupies a
235,000-square-foot facility on
West Morris Street and employs
500 people. The company was
formerly housed in a 40,000-
square-foot building on East 16th

Street until its move in 1982. National also operates an 80,000-square-foot warehouse in South Bend, Indiana, and has five sales offices throughout the state.

In 1991 the company purchased Chicago-based Union Liquor, which operates a distributorship in Illinois. Revenues for this subsidiary are expected to reach $300 million in fiscal 1997. National will continue its focus on expansion in the Chicago/Illinois market.

National also owns Cameron Springs, a $6 million bottled water company, which began operations on West Morris Street in 1991. Cameron Springs also maintains an office in Evansville. The bulk of the company's business is home and office cooler placements. Cameron

Springs also has a retail bottled water division that provides the official water of the Indianapolis Colts.

COMMUNITY RESPONSIBILITY

As a corporate citizen, National supports numerous charitable and not-for-profit organizations such as the Kidney Foundation, Youth Links, Noble Centers, Meals on Wheels, Indianapolis Symphony, Indianapolis Museum of Art, and Junior Achievement. The company also enthusiastically supports the Indianapolis Pacers and Colts.

National enjoys a significant role in the city's entertainment community by sponsoring sporting events and concerts. National also devotes much effort to promoting responsible drinking practices with

a focus on younger consumers. LaCrosse is active on the board of directors for the Wine & Spirits Wholesalers of America (WSWA), having served as its president in 1993 and chairman in 1994. WSWA helped establish the Century Council in 1992, an association formed among wholesalers and suppliers of liquor in a cooperative effort to address responsible drinking.

"For the past few years, alcohol-related traffic accidents have declined as a result of people becoming aware of the need for the responsible use of alcohol," says Beck. "The key is moderation."

Beck also cites the connections being established between moderate alcohol use and health benefits. "The French have a much lower rate of heart problems than do Americans, despite their rich diet. Red wine consumption is part of the solution. Findings also show that other alcoholic beverages are beneficial," says Beck. "Again, the key is moderation."

Careful strategic planning and execution, in addition to an ongoing campaign to promote responsible drinking practices, have made National Wine & Spirits Corporation a model for others within the industry. Looking to the future, the company plans to maintain its position as the largest liquor and wine distributor in the Great Lakes region, while also sharing its resources with the communities it serves.

CLOCKWISE FROM TOP LEFT: NATIONAL'S WINE STAFF INCLUDES (FROM LEFT) SALESPERSON SUSAN SAGE, VICE PRESIDENT MIKE PYLE, MANAGER TOM DRAKE, AND VICE PRESIDENT ROB HENKE.

MANAGER BOB FREELAND CHECKS ORDERS ON THE CONVEYOR SYSTEM AT NATIONAL'S INDIANAPOLIS WAREHOUSE.

THE COMPANY'S ADMINISTRATIVE STAFF INCLUDES (FROM LEFT) VICE PRESIDENT PAT TREFUN, CREDIT MANAGER CINDY SULLIVAN, AND DATA PROCESSING MANAGER KEVIN COX.

JOHN FRAME

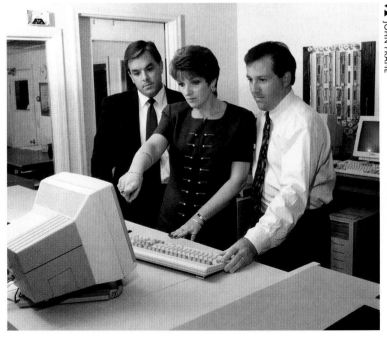

HE SECURITY INDUSTRY CONTINUALLY EVOLVES, SHAPED BY INNOvative technological advancements. Today electronic access, biometric controls, and integrated systems reflect some of these important breakthroughs. ◆ Best Lock Corporation, a world-class security company and a leading manufacturer in its industry, had its early beginnings in Seattle, Washington. In 1918

BASED IN INDIANAPOLIS SINCE 1938, BEST LOCK IS HEADQUARTERED ON EAST 75TH STREET (BELOW).

THE COMPANY OFFERS LOCKS FOR EVERY APPLICATION, INCLUDING ELECTRONIC SYSTEMS, INTERCHANGEABLE CORE ACCESS PRODUCTS, AND AUXILIARY PRODUCTS (BOTTOM).

Frank E. Best, an industrial arts teacher in the Seattle school district, soon tired of carrying a cumbersome key ring, heavily laden with a key for each lock in the school. Frustration inspired ingenuity and the entrepreneurial spirit. In 1925 the successful designer founded the Best Universal Lock Company. In that same year, Best designed and patented the now-famous inter-

changeable core and master-key system. The remarkable invention revolutionized the security industry, providing the foundation for the company's mechanical access control products.

Under the visionary leadership of Frank's son, Walter Best, the Best system was improved and the product line was expanded. To accommodate growing demands for the company's products, Walter implemented a unique distributor network of exclusive Best Locking System representatives. This network soon became the envy of the industry, providing the most comprehensive service in the United States and Canada. In 1994 Walter's son, Russell Best, became CEO, guiding the $100 millionplus company in the traditions of his father and grandfather while exploring new directions for future growth.

The company's solid reputation is based on a long history of commitment to total quality and the customer. This dedication includes

responsiveness to the customer's needs, efficiency and effectiveness in providing high-quality products and services, flexibility in accommodating changes in both the security industry and the industries of customers, and a well-targeted focus on conducting business with integrity.

With its East 75th Street headquarters and manufacturing facility occupying more than 300,000 square feet and with nearly 650 employees locally, this company—based in Indianapolis since 1938—is firmly entrenched. The local and national business climate has been excellent, and international demand for Best products continues to grow each year.

PAVING THE WAY FOR A BRIGHT FUTURE

The Best interchangeable core allows customers to easily change lock combinations at minimal cost. This core can be removed, and a new core can be inserted with a special "control" key. No lock disability is required. New keys can then be issued and records updated. When this system is in place, lock disassembly and expensive service calls are eliminated.

Best's customized master-key plan and key control program, designed to meet the unique requirements of each facility, offers convenience and highly controlled access. With the use of Best special service equipment, key blanks, and cores, customers can conveniently manage distribution of keys and record updates.

The system can be maintained manually or with Best's proprietary G600 Key and Core Control software package. This user-friendly software provides a basic recordkeeping system, a cross-referencing capability, and a historical maintenance feature. Benefits of the

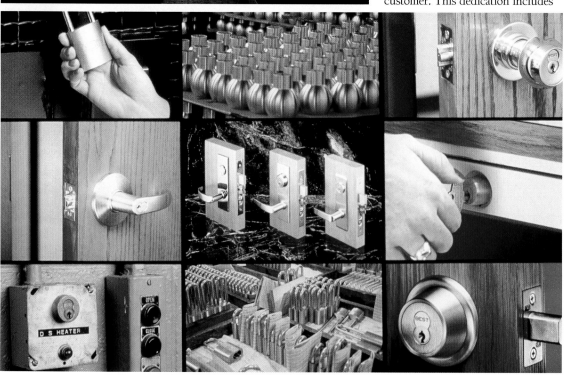

record-keeping system include solutions for many probable circumstances. For example, if a key is lost, the system records can quickly identify which cores need to be changed and what doors and personnel are affected.

Unique Distributorships Provide Quality Service

To further enhance security, Best's interchangeable core and master-key plan are available through authorized Best representatives. Experts in mechanical and electronic access products, these representatives can survey a facility and then design, install, and maintain a customized, flexible security system that not only meets a customer's present needs, but also can be adapted to future needs. The versatility of the Best system allows for expansion within the original system design, and Best representatives remain available to the customer throughout the life of a system.

Best maintains distributorships in more than 30 strategically located offices, with additional satellite offices in the United States and Canada. The company is also represented internationally in England, South America, Australia, the Caribbean, and the Middle East.

Installations and Self-Service Packages Empower Customers

A typical installation includes a control key that inserts or removes any system core, a grand

master key that unlocks any lock in the system, a master key and a submaster key that unlock only specified groups of locks, and an operating key that opens only single locks. Best's self-service package empowers customers by providing the capability to

"combinate" or "recombinate" cores and to cut new keys quickly and cost-effectively without security compromises.

The company offers locks for every application, including electronic systems, interchangeable core access products, and auxiliary products. Best ranks as an industry leader, as evidenced by its distinguished clientele and repeat business. Of the top 100 companies in the Fortune 100 rankings, Best sells security systems products to 96 of them.

Given its long history of innovation and success, it is clear that there is no end in sight for this dynamic company as it forges ahead into an exciting future. As Best Lock continues to invest in research, development, and technology, it will no doubt lead the way in innovation and quality in the security industry. One could easily say the company has a "lock" on its longtime leadership position.

Best Lock markets its products through exclusive factory representatives who also act as security consultants before, during, and after the installation (top left).

The company's manufacturing facility occupies more than 300,000 square feet (below).

A S ONE OF AMERICA'S MAJOR MORTGAGE LEADERS, INLAND Mortgage Corporation has never lost sight of the old-fashioned values that characterize the great state of Indiana. ◆ Inland Mortgage originates and services FHA, VA, and conventional mortgage loans, as well as commercial loans primarily for multifamily properties. The company also offers credit life insurance to its customers, while Inland's Community Lending Department provides mortgages and financial counseling to citizens with low and moderate incomes. Additionally, Inland plans to extend its mortgage lending activities into Mexico in 1996.

The firm, which was established in 1944 as Inland Mortgage Company, originally operated out of a single office in Indianapolis. In 1981 it became a subsidiary of Irwin Financial Corporation, a Columbus, Indiana-based bank holding company. At that time, Inland had annual loan production of $65 million, and its servicing portfolio totaled approximately $140 million.

INLAND MORTGAGE EMPLOYS MORE THAN 400 PEOPLE IN THE INDIANAPOLIS AREA AND HAS ITS CORPORATE HEADQUARTERS ON THE NORTH SIDE OF THE CITY (RIGHT).

"CUSTOMER SERVICE IS THE REASON WE'RE OPEN," SAYS PRESIDENT RICK L. McGUIRE (BELOW). "WE ATTRACT OUR CUSTOMERS BECAUSE OF THE QUALITY OF OUR SERVICE."

ED MOSS

FROM MERCHANT TO MORTGAGE BANKING

Inland's parent company came to life as a result of the tireless efforts of Joseph I. Irwin. In 1850 he opened a mercantile store in downtown Columbus, and residents soon began asking him to keep their money in his store's safe. A short time later, Irwin received a note asking that payment be made from one person to another, and hence, his life as a banker began. A few years later, he established the Irwin Union Bank and Trust Company.

Today the Inland network of mortgage providers spreads across the nation. In fact, Inland Mortgage produces 75 to 80 percent of Irwin Financial Corporation's total revenues, with annual production of more than $3 billion and a servicing portfolio of more than $10 billion.

Favorable market conditions over the past 10 years have allowed Inland to expand into the national market. The corporate expansion strategy included the acquisition of several smaller mortgage companies in various parts of the country. Inland also acquired a medium-sized mortgage bank in California, which added 40 offices to its loan production branch network. For its future expansion, Inland intends to remain on the cutting edge of technological advances. Plans call for the steady and orderly growth of the network by building upon Inland's strength in existing markets, as well as by entering into new markets that possess excellent potential for success.

Currently, Inland maintains 106 offices in 27 states, with more than 1,200 employees throughout the country. In the Indianapolis area, the company employs more than 400 people and has its corporate headquarters on the north side of the city. Because Inland's growth has outpaced its work space, the company plans to relocate to either a north side or downtown location in the near future.

SUCCESS BUILT BY EMPLOYEES

Top company administrators are quick to credit Inland's employees with the phenomenal success of the business. Knowing that satisfied employees make for satisfied customers, Inland provides an excellent benefits package and recognizes outstanding

employees on a regular basis. More than one-fourth of its management team have 10 years of service with the company. Inland also has a policy of retaining the employees of newly acquired branch offices. This approach allows the company to maintain strong ties to all of the communities it serves.

With the goal of improving customer service, Inland has a large training staff that provides high-quality programs to enhance employee performance. "Customer service is the reason we're open," says President Rick L. McGuire. "We attract our customers because of the quality of our service."

But the employees of Inland Mortgage do more than provide the capital for people in search of the American dream. They also work hand in hand with the communities they serve, building homes through their volunteer efforts with Habitat for Humanity. Likewise, the company donates 2 percent of its pretax earnings to local charities and its parent company's foundation, Irwin Financial Foundation. In addition, many employees raise money for other worthy organizations, including the March of Dimes and the Central Indiana Easter Seal Society, among a host of others.

"We are a people-oriented company," says McGuire. "We care about our customers and we care about our employees. We are doing everything we can to be an industry leader so we can keep helping the people of the communities we serve."

HE CHRYSLER CORPORATION INDIANAPOLIS FOUNDRY IS forging ahead in high-volume production, churning out record numbers of engine blocks for its owner, Chrysler Corporation. In an intense effort to meet market demand, the foundry runs two shifts, six days a week. The future continues to look bright. Today the Chrysler Corporation Indianapolis Foundry produces about 90 percent of all Chrysler domestic engine blocks.

The 366,000-square-foot foundry is situated on 32 acres on the west side of Indianapolis. Its 1,140 employees are an integral part of the company's long and proud history. Some are third-generation workers, and the oldest employee is a productive 78 years old.

COMPANY ORIGINS

The foundry began in 1890 as the American Foundry Company. In 1901 it began manufacturing engine blocks for the emerging automobile industry. Through the early 1920s, engine blocks and heads were cast for the Marmon, Chalmers, Maxwell, and Apperson automobiles and for Stutz autos and fire trucks. Blocks were also cast for the Caterpillar tractor.

In 1925 Chrysler Corporation became a very important customer. The foundry's production jumped to producing Chrysler 60 and 70, and Imperial 80 series motor blocks. In 1928 Chrysler began manufac-

turing the Plymouth and DeSoto autos, with the engine blocks being produced at the Indianapolis foundry. A long-term relationship was established.

During the 1930s the foundry also cast engine blocks for International Harvester, as well as large refrigerator compressors for the

Chrysler Airtemp Division. Later, castings were made for the Humber and Austin automobile companies when their own foundries in Coventry, England, were destroyed during World War II.

The American Foundry Company was purchased by Chrysler in 1946. Operating as a wholly

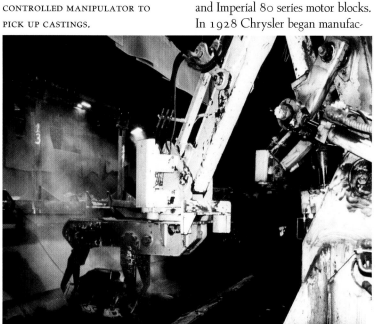

CLOCKWISE FROM RIGHT: CHRYSLER'S 366,000-SQUARE-FOOT INDIANAPOLIS FOUNDRY IS SITUATED ON 32 ACRES ON THE WEST SIDE OF THE CITY.

AFTER SHOT BLASTING, CASTINGS ARE TRANSPORTED TO A CLEANING AND FINISHING ROOM.

THE FOUNDRY USES A HUMAN-CONTROLLED MANIPULATOR TO PICK UP CASTINGS.

owned subsidiary until 1958, the foundry was then designated a Chrysler plant. Major modernization programs were completed in 1964, 1978, and 1988. Today, through planning, commitment, modernization, and investment in employees, the foundry is preparing for the future of the local operation, Chrysler, and the people of Indianapolis.

EXPANSION, PRODUCTION, AND DEDICATION

The number of foundries in the United States today is significantly lower than it was just a few years ago," says Plant Manager Ken Brune. "We are one of the major foundries in the country, and we are continuing to expand. We have maintained a competitive edge by continuously improving quality and productivity. Demand has increased year after year, and we will continue to increase well into the year 2000."

Brune not only speaks proudly of the plant's expansion and productivity levels, but notes with pride the dedication of foundry employees. During peak demand times, the company has experienced the lowest absenteeism rates in recent history. While others are sleeping, these dedicated, hardworking people are pouring castings throughout the night and into the early hours of the morning. Dusk and dawn have little meaning at the foundry.

Inside, the heat of blaring furnaces and the industrial clang of machines overwhelm the senses with the clamor of constructive, focused labor. During the casting process, scrap metal is melted in a coke-fired cupola, and alloys are added to provide the required metallurgical composition. As one of the largest and most effective recyclers in Indiana, the foundry uses scrap metal from shredded automobiles, engine blocks, discarded and dismantled equipment, and other similar sources.

The casting process actually begins with a prototype pattern made of wood, metal, or polyurethane. This pattern duplicates the final casting and is used to form the exterior surface of the finished product in the mold. The mold consists of sand mixed with a binder material. The vast majority of sand is recycled many times.

To assemble the mold, the pattern is placed in a flask. The top of the mold is the cope and the bottom is the drag. The pattern is covered with the sand mixture, which is compacted into the mold. The top and bottom are separated, and when the pattern is withdrawn, a negative cavity remains to form the outside of the block.

In a separate process, sand "cores" are produced, which are placed inside the drag half of the molds. These cores form the internal configuration, including water and oil openings.

Molten metal is then poured into the mold. The metal follows a series of channels, called a gating system, during the pouring. Gases that are produced are burned off, and risers are provided for extra liquid metal to prevent shrinkage. Once the filled mold has solidified and cooled, it is transferred to a shakeout area where the solid metal casting and external disintegrated molding sand are removed. The gating system and risers are also removed, usually by breaking them off and grinding the surface smooth. After the gating system is removed, the surface undergoes a form of shot blasting to remove any attached sand.

Once shot blasted, the casting is transported to a cleaning and finishing room. Here, every casting undergoes a series of quality checks while being processed. After inspection, the casting is ready for painting, machining, and assembly. In 1982 the plant produced 1.5 million castings. In 1995 production rates soared to 2 million.

After five decades under Chrysler operation, the foundry remains ablaze with activity, and production is moving forward in record volume. This momentum continues to challenge the plant and its employees with hard work and little rest, but dedication runs strong and production seems never to stop. The Indianapolis foundry remains a vital entity in the production of Chrysler vehicles, and, insists Brune, with its dedicated workforce, it will remain so for a long time to come.

MOLTEN IRON IS TRANSFERRED FROM A 5-TON LADLE TO A POURING FURNACE (BELOW LEFT).

SAND CORES ARE MOVED TO THE MOLD LINE, WHERE MOLTEN METAL IS POURED INTO THE MOLD TO FORM THE INTERNAL CONFIGURATION OF THE CASTING (BELOW RIGHT).

ITH 30 PERCENT MORE MARKET SHARE THAN ANY OF its nearest U.S. competitors, Carrier Corporation is the world's largest manufacturer of heating and cooling systems. The company's North American Operations Residential Products Group—which maintains administrative offices and manufacturing facilities in Indianapolis as well as a world-class

research and development center—has helped the company maintain its leading edge by investing nearly $500 million over the past five years in the development of core technologies such as electronics, aeroacoustics, compression, heat transfer, refrigerant alternatives, and indoor air quality.

SERVING PEOPLE AND BUSINESSES WORLDWIDE

Carrier Corporation is one of six businesses under the United Technologies Corporation parent umbrella, which also includes Pratt & Whitney, Otis, Sikorsky, Hamilton Standard, and UT Automotive. Carrier Corporation, employing nearly 30,000 people throughout more than 130 countries, reports approximately $4.9 billion in annual sales.

Carrier's Residential Products Group, headquartered in Indianapolis since 1950, employs 2,700 people and operates manufacturing plants in Indianapolis and in Collierville, Tennessee.

More than 100 engineers and technicians are employed at Carrier's unique research and development center in Indianapolis, which includes facilities for environmental

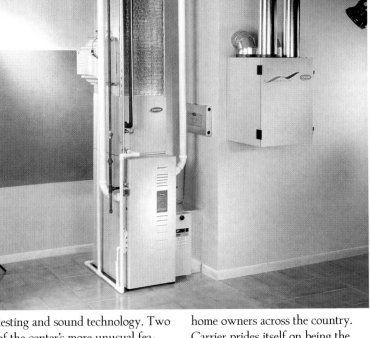

testing and sound technology. Two of the center's more unusual features are its ability to create snow, simulating arctic weather conditions with temperatures well below zero degrees Fahrenheit, and to create desertlike conditions at 125 degrees Fahrenheit. Another unique feature offered by the center is a sound room where heating and cooling systems are tested for consistently quiet operation.

Carrier manufactures and markets complete heating and cooling comfort systems within the Residential Products Group, including gas furnaces, air conditioners, fan coils, heat pumps, electronic air cleaners, humidifiers, thermostats, heat recovery ventilators, and zoning systems. The company's four brands are Carrier, Bryant, Day & Night, and Payne—each with its own complete line of systems. Products are distributed within a two-step distribution system that includes the sale of goods by the manufacturer to more than 100 distributors nationwide. The distributors then sell to 30,000 dealers who market the products to

◀ TOD MARTENS

home owners across the country. Carrier prides itself on being the only manufacturer that produces and sells complete heating and cooling systems.

THE TEAM APPROACH

Carrier applies a cross-functional team approach to product design. Input from home owners is an integral part of the design process, and other information is obtained through focus groups, by representatives in the field, and via phone and mail surveys.

"By working in teams and combining the expertise of our functional areas, we've seen remarkable results," says Frank Hartman, vice president and general manager of the Residential Products Group. "We've been able to accelerate our development process and bring new home-comfort products to consumers more quickly."

In a move to increase manufacturing efficiency, Carrier introduced its Lean Production System in 1991. Since that time, manufac-

CARRIER CORPORATION MANUFACTURES AND MARKETS COMPLETE HOME-COMFORT SYSTEMS (RIGHT).

TEAMS OF CARRIER PROFESSIONALS COMBINE THEIR EXPERTISE TO DELIVER ENERGY-EFFICIENT SOLUTIONS TO HOME OWNERS' HEATING AND COOLING NEEDS (BELOW).

EVERY GAS FURNACE MANUFAC-
TURED AT CARRIER'S INDIANAPOLIS
PLANT MUST PASS STRINGENT
QUALITY TESTS (LEFT).

turing floor space has been reduced by 32 percent and the number of units produced per employee has increased by 44 percent.

LEADER IN ENVIRONMENTAL STEWARDSHIP

Carrier is an environmental leader in Indianapolis and within the industry, reducing air emissions at the Indianapolis plant by 99 percent and hazardous waste generation by 89 percent between 1988 and 1993. The company received many awards, including the Clean Air Award from the Indianapolis Clean Air Committee in 1991, the Pollution Prevention Award from the Central Indiana Technical Environmental Society (CITIES) in 1993, and the Governor's Award for Excellence in Pollution Prevention in 1994 for success in reducing toxic air emissions.

"We're extremely proud of the strides we've made in environmental leadership in this community and within the heating and cooling industry," says Hartman. "Our achievements in air emission reduction are a step in the right direction toward maintaining the quality of life that we all enjoy in the Indianapolis area."

COMMUNITY INVOLVEMENT

Carrier is also actively involved in the community, making significant annual contributions to local charitable organizations. "We believe that it's important for us to give back to the community in which we live and work," adds Hartman.

In 1995 the company marked its 30th anniversary as a sponsor of the Indy 500, the longest nonautomotive sponsorship in the history of the race. The result has been in-

creased awareness of the Bryant name, in addition to bringing more than 1,000 dealers into the Indianapolis community throughout each May to attend the race. Since 1993 the company has been involved in the local Brickyard 400 NASCAR race as well.

As for the future, Carrier will continue to meet and exceed the expectations of its customers. The company plans to maintain its leadership in the heating and cooling industry while providing creative solutions for home owners' needs.

"Our future success and continued industry leadership will depend on our ability to listen to our customers and deliver the comfort and quality that they expect," says Hartman. "Our investments in research, technology, and people will make the difference."

CARRIER CORPORATION'S BRYANT
BRAND HAS A LONG-STANDING
TRADITION WITH THE INDIANAPOLIS
500 AS THE LONGEST-RUNNING
NONAUTOMOTIVE SPONSOR IN THE
HISTORY OF THE RACE (ABOVE).

CARRIER CORPORATION RIGOR-
OUSLY TESTS ITS EQUIPMENT AT THE
INDIANAPOLIS RESEARCH AND DEVEL-
OPMENT CENTER TO ENSURE TOP PER-
FORMANCE IN EXTREME WEATHER
CONDITIONS (LEFT).

he Dow Chemical Company, founded in 1897 and head-quartered in Midland, Michigan, is the fifth-largest chemical company in the world, with annual sales of more than $20 billion. Dow provides chemicals, plastics, energy, agricultural products, consumer goods, and environmental services to customers around the world. The company operates 94 manufacturing sites in 30 countries and employs about 39,500 people.

"Our vision is to be the best company in the world at applying chemistry to benefit customers, employees, shareholders, and society," says Frank Popoff, chairman of the board of Dow.

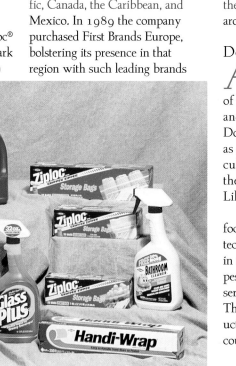

DowElanco's Indianapolis world headquarters, completed in 1993, houses approximately 1,100 administrative, scientific, technical, and service employees (right).

DowBrands

Indianapolis-based DowBrands is the consumer products affiliate of The Dow Chemical Company. Established in 1953, DowBrands is recognized worldwide as a leader in the development, manufacture, and distribution of quality household products. DowBrands employs approximately 2,000 people worldwide at its Indianapolis headquarters and at manufacturing facilities in Urbana, Ohio; Bay City, Michigan; Fresno, California; and several European locations. The company is comprised of two business units: Home Food Management and Home Care Products.

Popular brands include Ziploc® plastic bags, Saran Wrap (trademark of The Dow Chemical Company) and Handi-Wrap® plastic film, Dow Bathroom Cleaner with Scrubbing Bubbles®, Spray'n Wash® tough laundry stain remover, Fantastic® all-purpose cleaner, Glass Plus® multisurface cleaner, Ultra Yes® laundry detergent, and Vivid® color-safe bleach.

DowBrands has increased its international business to include opportunities in Europe, the Pacific, Canada, the Caribbean, and Mexico. In 1989 the company purchased First Brands Europe, bolstering its presence in that region with such leading brands as Albal™ in France and Domopak™ in Italy. In addition, DowBrands acquired Japan's Reed/Ziploc in 1990 and Canada's Baggies brand bags in 1991.

The company's commitment to total quality management targets continuous improvement and excellence both in the marketplace and within the organization. Employees are focused on making DowBrands the "Consumers' First Choice around the World."

DowBrands is recognized worldwide as a leader in the development, manufacture, and distribution of quality home food management and home care products.

DowElanco

Also headquartered in Indianapolis, DowElanco is one of the world's largest agricultural and specialty chemical companies. DowElanco was formed in 1989 as a joint venture of Dow's Agricultural Products Department and the Plant Science business of Eli Lilly and Company.

DowElanco is a customer-focused, global organization with technology and associated services in crop production and specialty pest management products that serve a variety of needs worldwide. The company manufactures products in 19 cities in 15 different countries.

DowElanco employs 3,200 people around the world. More than 1,000 employees work at

DowElanco's Indianapolis headquarters, which was completed in 1993. In addition to the Corporate Center and the Employee Development Center, the Research and Development Building contains more than 612,000 square feet, and 16 individual greenhouses comprise more than 66,000 square feet. Together, they form the world's largest plant-breeding and agricultural research center under one roof. Major research stations are also maintained in 19 other areas worldwide.

One of DowElanco's most important endeavors is the management of pests that destroy food, clothing fibers, timber resources, and personal property. Today's food producers and urban and suburban pest management experts rely on agricultural and specialty pest management products that are formulated to help control more than 1 million insect species; 1,500 known plant diseases; hundreds of weed species; 1,000 species of nematodes (microscopic wormlike organisms); and innumerable rodents, mites, and other parasites that interfere with harvesting.

DowElanco enjoys one of the broadest product portfolios in the industry. Dursban™ and Lorsban™ are the world's largest-selling insecti-cides and continue to gain market share. Newer products, such as Starane™ herbicide, have grown dramatically. Lorsban 15G is the number one product in the U.S. corn market, the world's largest market for insect management products.

With the development and manufacture of pest management products comes the responsibility of product and environmental stewardship. DowElanco engages in years of rigorous testing when evaluating and developing new products. To ensure that a product will not present unreasonable health or environmental risks, it is subjected to more than 120 separate tests. The company's criteria include environmentally friendly profiles, pest-specific characteristics, quickness to degrade, use of smaller quantities, and emphasis on responsible use.

COMMITMENT TO COMMUNITY

In addition to its commitment to quality and environmental stewardship, Dow recognizes its responsibilities as a corporate citizen. In August 1995 the parent company and its Indianapolis affiliates announced a $1 million

gift to the Children's Museum of Indianapolis to help fund the construction of the new Dow Science Center. Scheduled to open in June 1996, the center will occupy an entire gallery of the museum with hands-on, interactive experiences created for children from six to 10 years of age. The center is designed to generate interest and to educate children about the principles of basic science.

An active supporter of health and human services, education, the arts, and the environment, DowBrands also recognizes the efforts of its employees through annual community service awards. The company has been recognized for its contributions to Second Harvest, the nation's largest charitable food program, which supports a network of 180 food banks. Employees support the United Way and a host of other local service agencies.

In addition to its local commitments as a responsible corporate citizen, the Dow family of companies honors its global commitment. Responsible Care®—the chemical industry's worldwide initiative to improve environmental, health, and safety performance and to broaden communication with the public—emphasizes continuous improvement in pollution prevention, employee health and safety, distribution, process safety, product stewardship, community awareness, and emergency response. The Dow Chemical Company and its affiliates practice these principles where their products are manufactured throughout the world.

THE RESEARCH AND DEVELOPMENT CENTER INCLUDES 16 INDIVIDUAL GREENHOUSES CONTAINING MORE THAN 66,000 SQUARE FEET DEDICATED TO RESEARCH ON WEED, INSECT, AND PLANT DISEASE MANAGEMENT AS WELL AS BIOTECHNOLOGY.

THE DOW CHEMICAL COMPANY IS ONE OF THE SAFEST COMPANIES IN ANY INDUSTRY (LEFT). ITS LOW DAYS-AWAY-FROM-WORK ACCIDENT RATE TRANSLATES INTO AN ANNUAL ESTIMATED $10 MILLION COST ADVANTAGE OVER THE CHEMICAL INDUSTRY AVERAGE.

Responsible Care®
A Public Commitment

RESPONSIBLE CARE® IS THE CHEMICAL INDUSTRY'S WORLDWIDE INITIATIVE TO IMPROVE ITS ENVIRONMENTAL, HEALTH, AND SAFETY PERFORMANCE AND TO BROADEN ITS DIALOGUE WITH THE PUBLIC.

N THE SUMMER MONTHS, INDIANA SWEET CORN, HOMEGROWN melons, bright red tomatoes, and other farm-fresh fruits and vegetables are piled high in grocery bins. Nearby, colorful displays of more than 400 exotic, imported produce items from more than 50 countries provide a feast for the senses. In any season, Marsh Supermarkets, Inc. lives up to its slogan, "Gonna Make You Smile," by offering its customers the freshest and finest foods from around the world.

Marsh was created as a family enterprise in 1931 with only one store in Muncie, Indiana. In 1953 the company went public with 16 stores. Headquartered in Indianapolis, Marsh is one of the largest regional grocery chains in the United States. Through its three major divisions, the company operates 90 Marsh® Supermarkets, 179 Village Pantry convenience stores in Indiana and Ohio, and CSDC® (Convenience Store Distributing Company), a distribution company serving unrelated convenience stores in eight states. Marsh employs 13,000 people in its two-state service area.

INNOVATION AND NEW TECHNOLOGY

Increasingly, computerization is central to Marsh operations—in targeted marketing, improved inventory control, and storage of timely information about consumer preferences, both in product choices and media used to learn about them. Marsh pharmacies also rely heavily on computers to alert customers to potentially dangerous drug interactions. Another Marsh innovation is LoBill Foods, serving price-conscious consumers in smaller communities. These stores average 25,000 square feet and offer everyday low prices complemented by weekly specials.

Marsh customers can take advantage of a "News around the World" display, which offers newspapers from London, New Delhi, Washington, New York, and other major metropolitan areas. Marsh's full-service shopping experience also includes video rental, shoe repair, and film processing.

In 1994 Marsh expanded its retail square footage by 9.7 percent, nearly three times the company's historical average. To achieve that level of growth, six new supermarkets were opened, including three replacement stores. A major Indianapolis store was expanded and remodeled.

QUALITY, CONVENIENCE, AND CATERING

Customers entering Marsh's Village Pantry convenience stores are welcomed by the aroma of fresh-brewed coffee, freshly baked cookies, fat-free muffins, croissants, bagels, and made-to-order sandwiches. Driven by these new food offerings, the company's Village Pantry locations have experienced a marked increase in sales. The stores also offer fuel service under large,

MARSH'S VILLAGE PANTRY CONVENIENCE STORES OFFER FUEL SERVICE UNDER LARGE, ATTRACTIVE CANOPIES AND GAS PUMPS THAT ARE EQUIPPED WITH CREDIT CARD READERS (RIGHT).

CREATED AS A FAMILY ENTERPRISE IN 1931 WITH ONLY ONE STORE IN MUNCIE, INDIANA, THE COMPANY IS TODAY ONE OF THE LARGEST REGIONAL GROCERY CHAINS IN THE UNITED STATES, WITH 90 MARSH® SUPERMARKETS (BELOW).

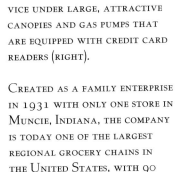

▼ MCGUIRE PHOTOGRAPHY

attractive canopies and gas pumps that are equipped with credit card readers.

Thanks, in part, to broad recognition of Marsh's expertise in the convenience store market, more than 1,300 unaffiliated convenience stores rely on CSDC for product knowledge, management services, and prompt product delivery. CSDC is headquartered in Richmond, Indiana, and serves customers in eight states.

In 1994 Marsh launched its newest division, ALLtimate Catering, which was awarded a multimillion-dollar, 10-year contract with the Indianapolis Zoo and became a major caterer at the Indianapolis Motor Speedway. The company's management recognized two emerging trends: Half of consumers' food-purchasing decisions were for food prepared outside the home, and the demand for catering by Marsh was growing.

ALLtimate acquired Crystal Catering in 1994 and the following year purchased Martz & Associates Food Services, Inc. and its affiliate, Carefree Catering, Inc., creating one of the largest food service operations in Indiana. Renamed Crystal Food Services in early 1996, the combined operation is now comprised of three divisions—cafeteria management, vending, and catering. "We now have the opportunity to serve customers as a total food retailer/distributor with the development of the varied capabilities represented in this new dimension of our business," says Don E. Marsh, chairman and CEO of total Marsh operations.

THE PAST AS A BRIDGE TO THE FUTURE

On June 26, 1974, Marsh became the first supermarket in the industry to install and use a laser scanner—the original "Model A"—when a 10-pack of Juicy Fruit gum was scanned using the universally accepted UPC bar code. Marsh store No. 59 in Troy, Ohio, was chosen as the test site for six scanners.

Twenty years later to the month, the scanner was donated to the Smithsonian Museum of American History by Spectra-Physics, the initial developer of laser scanners

for groceries. "From the moment the technology was presented to us, we knew that scanning was the wave of the future," says Marsh. "We moved on it right away, and we've never looked back."

In late 1995 Marsh embarked on another new venture, joining with National City Bank, Indiana, to issue a co-branded credit card— the first of its kind in Indiana. The new Marsh Fresh IDEA VISA card combined the benefits of Marsh's existing Fresh IDEA customer loyalty card with all the uses of a VISA card, plus providing a 1 percent rebate check for all card purchases, regardless of vendor, that is redeemable for free groceries at Marsh.

COMMUNITY INVOLVEMENT

Marsh Supermarkets plays a major philanthropic role in the city of Indianapolis, with generous gifts, countless sponsorships, numerous contributions, and many programs for youth. Some of the Marsh-sponsored youth programs include Computers for Education, We Value Youth, Marsh Symphony on the Prairie, the Children's Museum Haunted House, and Boy Scouts of America-Cookout on the Circle.

In 1994 Don Marsh spoke to the World Economic Forum in Switzerland regarding new developments and techniques in retail sales and merchandising. Although this busy CEO is in high demand nationally and internationally, his heart remains in Indiana, where his family business began, where his home is, and where Marsh Supermarkets has made a difference in the industry, for its employees, and for the city of Indianapolis.

IN ANY SEASON, MARSH LIVES UP TO ITS SLOGAN, "GONNA MAKE YOU SMILE," BY OFFERING ITS CUSTOMERS THE FRESHEST AND FINEST FOODS FROM AROUND THE WORLD.

OR THE LATEST IN BREAKING NEWS, CENTRAL INDIANA residents have learned to rely on WTHR, Channel 13, the NBC affiliate in Indianapolis, for the best local coverage. The station has carved a niche for itself by devoting more broadcast time and resources to news than any other local station. ◆ Founded locally in 1957, WTHR is part of the Dispatch Media Group, which is based in Columbus, Ohio. The Dispatch Media Group includes the *Columbus Dispatch*, Dispatch Consumer Services, The Bag Company, *Ohio Magazine*, This Week Newspapers, WBNS-TV, WBNS AM & FM, Ohio News Network, Radio Sound Network, WTHR-TV, and 27Alive, as well as Dispatch Interactive Television in Indianapolis and in Columbus, Ohio.

A NEW LOOK

The station's commitment to the community has been renewed through a multimillion-dollar expansion program that includes new technical equipment and a sharply expanded news staff. In May of 1995 *Channel 13 Eyewitness News* debuted a revolutionary new studio complex, the first of its kind in local television. The rich wood grains and colors of the main set were selected from the landscape of central Indiana. Behind the anchor desk spans an artistic compilation of the Circle City's famed architecture. And throughout the set complex are decorative railings featuring a graphic representation of Monument Circle as seen from the air.

There is also a new on-set weather office used by the SkyTrak Weather Team under the leadership of Weather Director Bob Gregory, Channel 13's weather director for nearly a quarter century. This state-of-the art weather center has sophisticated Doppler Plus radar, as well as other technologies that allow the team to accurately report such statistics as the number of lightning strikes during a thunderstorm and the measure of intensity of ultraviolet rays.

"COVERAGE YOU CAN COUNT ON"

Channel 13 Eyewitness News is distinguished by the fact that it is the only local television news operation with a helicopter. Chopper 13 allows reporters to travel to the scene of breaking news faster than any other station in the city. Viewed as one of the most important news-gathering tools, Chopper 13 has covered numerous compelling stories from the air, including Mike Tyson's release from prison, the Denny's

IN MAY OF 1995 *CHANNEL 13 EYEWITNESS NEWS* DEBUTED A REVOLUTIONARY NEW STUDIO COMPLEX, THE FIRST OF ITS KIND IN LOCAL TELEVISION (RIGHT).

WITH A NEW LOOK AND THE LATEST TECHNOLOGICAL INNOVATIONS AVAILABLE, WTHR CONTINUES TO PROVIDE RESIDENTS IN INDIANAPOLIS AND THE SURROUNDING AREA WITH SUPERLATIVE NEWSCASTS, COMMUNITY INVOLVEMENT, AND PROGRAMMING (BELOW).

Restaurant hostage crisis, and the North College neighborhood disturbances in the summer of 1995. Each morning, Chopper 13 is used to provide traffic information to viewers of *Eyewitness News Sunrise*. WTHR has also purchased a new, state-of-the-art satellite truck, which allows the *Eyewitness News* team to broadcast from any part of the state, and any part of the continent.

WTHR's commitment to local news can easily be seen in its newscast's title and slogan: *Channel 13 Eyewitness News* is Coverage You Can Count On. The team's bold investigative reporting offers further evidence of its commitment to providing the best news coverage possible to its viewers. John Stehr, a former CBS news anchor, and Anne Ryder form the coanchor team for *Eyewitness News*. They are joined by Gregory and Sports Anchor Dave Calabro.

Channel 13 has a rich history of winning prestigious television awards. The station received a national Emmy in 1992 for its documentary on the Ku Klux Klan. In 1995 WTHR was honored with the Radio and Television News Directors Association Edward R. Murrow Award for Investigative Reporting, which it received for the series *You Paid for It*. This series of reports exposed the misuse of tax dollars by legislators who were supposed to be attending seminars in New Orleans, but were instead finding entertainment elsewhere.

WTHR also operates a low-powered television station, 27Alive, which made its debut in January of 1994. Its signal reaches the northern portion of Marion County, southern Hamilton County, and southern Boone County. It can also be seen via cable systems in several central Indiana cities. Programming on 27Alive ranges from news and information to talk shows and entertainment programming.

Located at 1000 North Meridian, WTHR's broadcast facility was officially opened in May of 1982. It was one of the first buildings to become part of Mayor William H. Hudnut's revitalized North Meridian Street corridor. The building has an Indiana limestone facade, and the

lobby features a two-story mural by the late James Cunningham, an Indianapolis artist.

COMMUNITY ANCHOR

In addition to keeping the community apprised of important happenings, WTHR likes to highlight positive community events. *Eyewitness News* at 5 p.m. features a daily segment called "Positively Indiana" in which Anchor Lis Daily reports live from various community events. WTHR also airs an extensive schedule of community calendars, keeping viewers updated on a wide variety of community happenings.

WTHR has set a goal to become the leader in community events. Each June, the station hosts the "Children's Miracle Network Telethon" to benefit Riley Hospital for Children in Indianapolis. In the fall, WTHR presents Bob Gregory's Coats for Kids, a campaign to collect coats for the needy. Gregory also hosts the high school quiz show *The Brain Game*.

Each spring, the station salutes academic excellence in central Indiana's high schools through the Top of the Class. Valedictorians from high schools in Channel 13's viewing area are invited to a luncheon in their honor, and 30-second vignettes are produced to recognize their achievement.

WTHR continues to increase its involvement in the community. Viewers can be a part of many

Channel 13 events, from Sky-Concert, a spectacular fireworks show on the banks of the White River, to Holiday Express, a free tour of downtown holiday lights and decorations.

"WATCH US GROW"

With a new look and the latest technological innovations available, WTHR continues to provide residents in Indianapolis and the surrounding area with superlative newscasts, community involvement, and programming. It is this level of high-quality broadcasting for which the station has become known, and its reputation will continue to grow for each new generation of viewers.

CHOPPER 13 ALLOWS REPORTERS TO TRAVEL TO THE SCENE OF BREAKING NEWS FASTER THAN ANY OTHER STATION IN THE CITY (TOP).

WTHR's STATE-OF-THE-ART SATELLITE TRUCK ALLOWS THE *EYEWITNESS NEWS* TEAM TO BROADCAST FROM ANY PART OF THE STATE, AND ANY PART OF THE CONTINENT (BOTTOM).

OR MORE THAN 35 YEARS, MSE CORPORATION'S SUCCESS has been intertwined with the city of Indianapolis. Whether it's a roadway redesign to improve safety or a surveying project for a new school, this locally based company contributes to the quality of life in central Indiana. With annual sales exceeding $15 million, no one can take this firm for granted.

MSE ENGINEERS INCORPORATE A VARIETY OF TOOLS INCLUDING TRADITIONAL DRAFTING IMPLEMENTS, COMPUTER TECHNOLOGY, AND THE TEAM APPROACH.

MSE IS HEADQUARTERED AT 941 N. MERIDIAN STREET.

IN THE BEGINNING

In 1960, the year of the company's founding, Sol C. Miller and two other partners were the only employees. Formed as a surveying company on an operating budget that was expected to last no more than six weeks, Miller and his partners were determined that their vision, energy, and aspirations would be successful. Just as their money began to run out, the City of Indianapolis approached the firm about a major surveying project on the city's northeast side in an area that is now a thriving retail center. This important first contract allowed MSE to begin hiring other skilled surveyors and engineers.

But surveying and engineering are just two of the services offered by the firm today. Utility coordination, construction inspection, construction coordination, topographic mapping, data conversion, and digital mapping are integral parts of MSE projects, many of which have become landmarks on the Indianapolis skyline.

COMMUNITY COMMITMENT

Miller never forgot the fortuitous break given to MSE by the city. Throughout its history, the company's involvement in major civic projects has helped turn "India-no-place" into the midwestern gem it is today. MSE's involvement in public works projects has included the RCA Dome, Market Square Arena, Monument Circle beautification, Indiana State Office Building Complex expansion and renovation, West 38th Street/ Lafayette Road intersection redesign, downtown corridor beautification, and Union Station. Other important contributions to the city have included the Indianapolis Indians AAA ballpark, Capital Landing at White River State Park, and IMAGIS (Indianapolis Mapping and Geographic Infrastructure System).

MSE's commitment to the city is also a philanthropic one. Dozens of not-for-profit agencies benefit from the company's corporate contributions. The Indianapolis Chamber of Commerce, Purdue University, and Indiana University also receive generous contributions. In fact, an important part of Miller's vision includes improving the quality of life for the citizens of Indianapolis. "Our employees see the public projects we work on, and they know that their tax dollars are being spent in a good way," he explains. "We all benefit from these assets. I am proud that MSE has been a part of almost all of them since 1960."

MODERN TECHNOLOGY AND ANCIENT METHODS

The science of surveying is a very old one, relying on principles that have remained virtually unchanged since the Middle Ages. But the advent of the space age and the plethora of

satellites now orbiting the earth have brought advanced technology to modern surveying capabilities. GPS (global positioning satellite) receivers accept location coordinates from signals beamed down from satellites millions of miles away, with an accuracy greater than that achieved by conventional equipment. MSE was one of the first firms to utilize GPS equipment—a technology that still benefits clients today.

The infant science of digital cartography was born out of mating photogrammetric technology and advancing computer capability. Miller recognized the power of GIS (geographic information systems) and made the decision to position MSE as a major player in that industry. He purchased equipment, hired experts, and built the relationships that would allow the firm to become one of the world's largest data conversion companies. As a leader in the AM/FM/GIS industry, MSE has assisted utility and government clients from Canada to New Zealand and Hawaii to Europe with the design, development, and implementation of these systems. This kind of vision coupled with quality production has

been a hallmark of MSE's service to the industry.

THE PARTNERSHIP APPROACH

For MSE, the concept of partnership means never having to say "it's not my problem." In many of the firm's long-term relationships, the battle cry is "let's solve this thing together." Knowledge of the client's needs and an innovative approach to business are two keys to MSE's partnership with its clients. According to the company's experts, every project has room for an artistic sensibility manifested as creative or innovative design work.

"Sometimes realizing a client's vision means applying the basic principles of engineering standards in an innovative way," says Miller. "We make an effort to align ourselves with companies that are open to the reciprocal nature of a true partnership. Partnership doesn't mean that we agree to negotiate a contract without wading through the proposal process. In many cases, it means that the trust and bond between our company and our client are such that we will proceed with the project without a signed contract in place. There is a revolution going on in American business, and the partnership approach is a big part of that."

Adds Miller, "In the beginning we provided surveyors, engineers, and mappers to our customers. In order to grow and succeed in the future, we supply solutions—whether it's a professional service or data or a computer or our meeting rooms and clerical staff. There is no room for average service, no room for partial solutions. If the client wants it, we provide it all."

CLOCKWISE FROM TOP: MSE's FIELD SURVEY EQUIPMENT IN ACTION

FORMER INDIANAPOLIS MAYOR WILLIAM HUDNUT ACCEPTS DELIVERY OF THE FINAL IMAGIS MAP FROM MSE CEO SOL MILLER IN 1989.

IN THE FIRM'S GIS DEPARTMENT, A TYPICAL WORKSTATION SHOWS A PORTION OF THE IMAGIS LANDBASE AROUND MONUMENT CIRCLE.

HERE IS MUCH MORE TO R.W. ARMSTRONG ASSOCIATES THAN meets the eye. This full-service architectural and engineering firm, headquartered on Pennsylvania Street, blends quietly into the southside Indianapolis neighborhood where it has grown for more than 30 years. But there is nothing quiet about its competitiveness in the environmental industry, its outstanding architec-

tural projects, its national reputation for expertise in airport design, and its contributions in transportation and site design.

When the U.S. Postal Service needed a new national hub to accommodate the tremendous growth in Express Mail volume, the organization invited 30 airports in Indiana, Kentucky, Illinois, and Ohio to submit bids for a permanent hub. Development and construction of the mail-sorting center—named the Eagle Network Postal Hub—was awarded to Indianapolis International Airport in October 1991, based on a joint proposal by the Indianapolis Airport Authority; Armstrong; DeMars Haka Development, Inc.; Geupel DeMars, Inc.; and Geupel Construction of Ohio.

"Armstrong's participation in the proposal was invaluable," says Ann Walker, vice president of DeMars Haka Development. "They devoted their top people to the process and worked with the development and construction companies,

the airport, and other consultants in bringing together the winning proposal that, I'm told, weighed 180 pounds and was 48 inches tall!"

Armstrong was responsible for the design of the architectural and sitework elements. Teams within the firm had an edge because they had previously designed all the infrastructure associated with the 100-acre hub site, including improvements to taxiways, road-

ways, drainage, rough grading, and utilities. Each Armstrong team designed particular features of the Eagle Network facility: The airport team designed the air side, the architectural team designed the 290,000-square-foot sort building and offices, the transportation team designed the land side of the infrastructure, and the environmental team designed the sanitary sewer.

The real challenge, however, was the 365-day time frame. Archi-

A CHILD ENJOYS HIS OWN LEARNING ENVIRONMENT THROUGH THE GLASS BLOCK WINDOW AT THE 9,000-SQUARE-FOOT, 1.5-STORY FAMILY SERVICE CENTER IN MADISON, INDIANA (RIGHT).

AT THE EAGLE NETWORK POSTAL HUB, 44 ACRES OF CONCRETE APRON ARE HOME TO 29 BOEING 727S SIX NIGHTS A WEEK FROM MIDNIGHT TO 4 A.M. AS THEIR CARGO IS UNLOADED, SORTED, AND RELOADED (BELOW).

tect Tony Boschenko and Project Manager Dexter Jones used the firm's multidisciplinary expertise to plan and coordinate the $62 million project and to bring it in on time and within budget. The architectural team, for example, proposed a steel-frame building with precast concrete panels on the outside to allow quick construction.

The facility received a 1993 Excellence in Architecture Honor Award from the Indianapolis chapter of the American Institute of Architects—the only unanimous winner. "Our pride in the Eagle Network Postal Hub comes not only from the many awards it has won, but also from the process itself," says Armstrong President James A. Wade. "This project demonstrated a complete effort among the architects, the engineers, and the contractors."

Although the firm has built a reputation for excellence on its airport expertise, this talented group has by no means limited its scope. "Our growth in all areas—airports, architectural, environmental, and transportation services—has happened through people who have worked together and done a great job," says Vice President Susan M. Schalk. "As a result, over 90 percent of our workload is repeat business and we're growing: In fact, we're providing services on a wider basis—literally moving across America. In late 1995 we opened a new southern office in Atlanta."

Another example of Armstrong's diversified expertise is the $3.1 million Laurel Oaks Agriculture Center in Wilmington, Ohio. This vocational school building was designed to accommodate a meat-processing school, an agricultural engineering and mechanics program, and a natural resources science program. The cost-effective structural system includes flexible spaces for classrooms, a lecture facility, and a media and computer center to serve students and the local farming community. "Working within the constraints of the budget is a common thread among clients," says Wade. "They are looking for value in terms of durability, form, and function. We uphold our

promise to stay within their budget. There are no last-minute surprises."

Willing to take on a variety of challenges, Armstrong recently embarked on a highly creative endeavor in the architecture and interior design of a 9,000-square-foot, 1.5-story family service center in Madison, Indiana. Completed in 1994, the facility houses family services—including day care, Head Start, Step Ahead, developmental services, and special services—for children from low- to moderate-income families. The facility, named "A River Runs through It," features winding passageways colored in blues and greens. Windows—positioned at an appropriate height for children—offer different perspectives of the outside world through three unique panes of glass: bubbled, colored, and clear. In this environment, creativity soars.

Most of the firm's projects are not child's play. For instance, Armstrong handled a culverts inventory/GIS (geographic information systems) assignment for the Indianapolis Department of Capital Asset Management. The field inventory for the project, which covered 3,000 miles, was completed in November 1994 and clears the way for future planning of detailed city infrastructure. According to Administrator Mark Jacob, "Armstrong had a tremendous amount of experience doing bridge inspections, and

had specific experience on culverts inventory. They also had specific experience from a GIS perspective, enabling them to effectively respond to the demands of our project."

As these and other design challenges continue to arise, R.W. Armstrong Associates and its award-winning staff of more than 100 specialists will maintain the firm's longtime dedication to meeting diverse client needs in Indianapolis and beyond.

Because Indianapolis is roughly the geographic center, timewise, of the entire country, it is ideally suited for the Eagle Network Postal Hub.

R.W. Armstrong Associates created an affordable design that projects a modern image for the Laurel Oaks Agricultural Center in Wilmington, Ohio.

LL FINE ARCHITECTURE VALUES ARE HUMAN VALUES, ELSE THEY are not valuable," said famed architect Frank Lloyd Wright in *The Living City,* published in 1958. ◆ Indeed, choosing architects, engineers, and interior designers can be a daunting task, with a successful choice often resting in how well the values of the client and provider coincide. A belief in values is what makes CSO

▼ MARK PLATT

CSO's FOUR-STORY, 65,000-SQUARE-FOOT ADDITION TO MERIDIAN INSURANCE COMPANY'S 135,000-SQUARE-FOOT FACILITY ENHANCES AN ESTABLISHED INDIANAPOLIS CORPORATION (TOP RIGHT).

THE FIRM PROVIDED THE LEAD ROLE IN THE ARCHITECTURAL DESIGN FOR THE INDIANA GOVERNMENT CENTER'S NEW, 1 MILLION-SQUARE-FOOT NORTH TOWER, LOCATED WEST OF THE INDIANA STATE HOUSE (BELOW).

Architects Engineers & Interiors so refreshingly different.

As a reflective, philosophical group of well-educated professionals, CSO sets forth its work ethics and values in *Essays on Values,* an artistic and creative document designed for its clients. CSO discusses values such as knowledge and integrity, respect, creativity, discipline, passion, and perseverance. This focus has resulted in more than 500 projects a year and repeat client business at an impressive rate of 80 percent.

CSO, founded in Indianapolis in 1961, has built its reputation on providing thorough and comprehen-

▼ GREGORY MURPHEY

sive services in architecture, engineering, and interior design. Every facet of a CSO project—from programming and site selection to construction and the finishing touches of interior designers—involves the hands-on participation of a project manager and a principal in charge. The 9100 Building at Keystone at the Crossing houses this architectural "solution center" where 80 experts work together to design signature buildings that represent the personalities and needs of each client.

MAKING ITS MARK
ON INDIANAPOLIS

CSO specializes in more than 12 building types, including corporate, educational, aviation, criminal justice, health care/medical, hotel, industrial, institutional/governmental, laboratory, religious, retail, and residential/multifamily. Project teams work from a practical, cost-effective perspective while bringing fresh, creative ideas to the firm's diverse projects.

CSO most recently provided services for the new Circle Centre Mall, a 970,000-square-foot, multi-level complex of retail, hotel, parking, and entertainment facilities in downtown Indianapolis. CSO worked with another Indianapolis

architectural firm to lead the redevelopment of three and a half city blocks, integrating both existing and new buildings. The project required the demolition, renovation, and rehabilitation of historic exteriors and interiors, while incorporating existing structures into the construction of three- and four-story coveredmall buildings. Parking facilities provide more than 3,000 spaces for mall patrons. A series of second- and third-level walkways cross streets and provide uninterrupted pedestrian flow between all blocks of the mall.

Another significant project CSO recently completed is the beautiful corporate addition for Meridian Insurance Company. The new, four-story, 65,000-square-foot addition to Meridian's existing 135,000-square-foot facility enhances an established Indianapolis corporation. The company has been located at 2955 North Meridian Street since 1950, and its history and commitment to the city significantly influenced the project's design. CSO's concept was to create a corporate campus for this prestigious company. To achieve that goal, Pennsylvania Street, which ran along the east side of the property, was closed to public traffic, and the main building entry was moved from Meridian

Street to the Pennsylvania Street corridor. The adjacent block of parking was transformed into a "parking garden" and new main entry. A conference center within the building links the original architecture with the new, richly detailed addition and organizes the architectural pieces of this stone, concrete, brick, and glass corporate structure. The design addresses the changing needs of a dynamic corporation while unifying its campus with the architectural fabric of the Meridian Street corridor.

COMMITTED TO DOWNTOWN

CSO has a long-standing commitment to downtown revitalization, which is demonstrated by the variety of projects the firm has completed in downtown Indianapolis. One such project is the Claypool Center Embassy Suites, completed in 1985 for Melvin Simon and Associates, Inc. The hotel is constructed of precast concrete and green glass. Its spacious atrium captures the sunlight, which streams from the extensive, clear-glass sky roof. The unique postmodern character of this magnificent hotel exterior adds a new, interesting dimension to the city's skyline.

Another project exemplifying CSO's commitment to downtown is the renovation of the Indiana Government Center. The firm provided the lead role in the architectural design for the new, 1 million-square-foot North Tower, located west of the Indiana State House. CSO led a team of architects, engineers, interior designers, and other consultants in renovations and additions to an older structure to create an architectural solution more aesthetically compatible with the historic character of the Indiana State House. A significant feature is an elegant stone loggia, spanning 500 feet, which links the North Tower to the new South Tower addition and provides a graceful pedestrian entry to the government complex. The entire design and construction was accomplished over a five-year period and was completed without moving any of the occupants from the building. The new limestone, granite, and glass structure is a tribute to the grandeur of the state capitol.

The list of successful design projects continues to grow at CSO. For more than three decades, the firm's contributions to the community have helped transform Indianapolis into a progressive city achieving its dreams at the cross-

roads. With a dedication to preserving the best of the past and a determined vision for the future, CSO will continue its strong architectural, engineering, and interior design presence in the Indianapolis community.

As CSO President Les Olds, AIA, states, "The strength of Indianapolis is based on its historic and enduring public/private partnership that has transformed the city from a small town into a thriving metropolis. CSO's ability to recognize values and interests from both sides of the partnership has been the cornerstone of our success."

THE FIRM'S INTERIOR DESIGN WORK INCLUDES THE RECEPTION AREA AND CONFERENCE ROOM FOR LONDON WITTE & COMPANY (ABOVE).

CSO RECENTLY PROVIDED SERVICES FOR THE NEW CIRCLE CENTRE MALL, A 970,000-SQUARE-FOOT, MULTILEVEL COMPLEX OF RETAIL, HOTEL, PARKING, AND ENTERTAINMENT FACILITIES IN DOWNTOWN INDIANAPOLIS (BOTTOM LEFT).

BOTH RESIDENTS AND BUSINESSES IN CENTRAL INDIANA HAVE benefited from the diverse curricula of Ivy Tech State College, Central Indiana Region. Tracing its local roots to 1963, the college offers more than 22 programs that culminate in the associate of applied science or associate of science degree, or that lead to technical certificates. ◆ Areas of study available at Ivy Tech include accounting technology, business administration, associate of science nursing, medical assistant, design technology, computer integrated manufacturing, and applied fire science, to name a few.

TRAINING FOR TODAY'S WORKFORCE

Contrary to popular belief, Ivy Tech offers more than automotive programs. "That is one of the greatest misconceptions. We have an automotive program that is a co-op with Toyota, GM, and Ford," says Dr. Meredith Carter, vice president/chancellor. "These are really highly technical programs, but they are among our smallest programs."

Instruction is based on practicality so that students can readily use what they learn in the classroom as soon as they enter the workforce. There are 104 full-time instructors and 300 part-time instructors, all of whom have excellent academic credentials that have been supplemented by solid experience in the workforce.

Classes are offered seven days a week, and programs are divided into three instructional divisions: business and technology, health and human services, and general education. "Our courses are meant to be much more practical than theoretical so that someone who comes out of either a course they took for skills improvement or a program in which they earned a two-year degree would be ready to go to the job site. That's really our direction," says Carter, adding that Ivy Tech boasts a 95 percent placement rate for graduates.

The college also offers the Business and Industry Training program, which provides Indiana businesses with customized training and retraining programs either on-site or on the Ivy Tech campus. Programs range from specialized software training to robotics equipment training, customer service, or even basic writing skills. Partnerships have been formed between the college and a number of Indiana businesses, including Bank One, Columbia House, Raybestos Products Company, and LTV Steel.

PART OF A STATEWIDE NETWORK

Ivy Tech's central Indiana regional campus enrolls approximately 6,500 students annually. As part of the Ivy Tech State College network, which covers 13 regions with 22 delivery sites and serves more than 50,000 students statewide, Ivy Tech is the state's third-largest college after Indiana University and Purdue University.

"We're getting more and more students who come here and take college courses that will then transfer to a residential college," says Carter. Those students—whether transferring within Indiana or around the country—find in most cases that a significant number of their course credits are transferable.

The Indianapolis campus is situated north of downtown at the corner of Fall Creek Parkway and North Meridian. This convenient location offers students easy accessibility and forges an important link between Indianapolis businesses and the city's incoming workforce.

By serving residents and businesses in central Indiana with outstanding training and preparation for today's work environment, Ivy Tech State College will remain one of the area's most valuable resources.

IVY TECH CULINARY ARTS GRADUATES ARE WORKING IN THE AREA'S FINEST RESTAURANTS AND CATERING BUSINESSES (RIGHT).

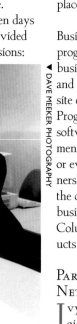

IVY TECH IS A CERTIFIED NOVELL SITE AND OFFERS A VARIETY OF SPECIALIZED TRAINING OPPORTUNITIES IN COMPUTERS (BELOW).

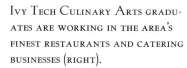

◀ DAVE MEEKER PHOTOGRAPHY

Hoosier Orthopaedics and Sports Medicine, P.C.

ANCERS WITH TORN LIGAMENTS, ATHLETES AND WEEKEND warriors with "blown-out" knees, elderly people with bad hips, and race car drivers suffering from crash injuries—all can find the high-quality care they need for a speedy recovery at Hoosier Orthopaedics and Sports Medicine, P. C. ♦ Founded in 1969, the practice has grown to seven staff physicians, each with train-

ing and expertise in a variety of subspecialty areas. These include total hip, knee, and shoulder replacement; sports medicine and arthroscopic treatment of shoulder and knee injuries; fracture and trauma care; foot and ankle treatment; pediatric and adolescent orthopaedics; and reconstructive surgery of the hand, wrist, and elbow.

Hoosier Orthopaedics is a part of the St. Vincent Health Network and maintains satellite offices in Greencastle, Brownsburg, Greensburg, and Kokomo, and on the west side of Indianapolis. The practice has established its main office on the north side of Indianapolis, located just north of I-465 on Meridian Street. This orthopaedic center is replete with state-of-the-art equipment and focuses on providing one-stop, comprehensive orthopaedic care. Within the center, patients can undergo cost-effective, same-day surgery, often at half the cost of inpatient hospital surgery. Also, all treatment, education, physical therapy, and rehabilitation services are offered under the same roof, which provides an added convenience to patients.

Occupational Medicine Services

Workers' compensation cases are an area of expertise for Hoosier Orthopaedics. The surgeons and staff work diligently to ensure that injured employees return to the workforce as quickly as possible. The practice employs case managers who act as direct liaisons between the employer, insurance company, doctor, and patient. This provides everyone involved in the process with a complete understanding of the treatment and the patient's progress during the healing process.

General Motors, Chrysler, Delco Electronics, Thomson Consumer Electronics, and Eli Lilly and Company are just a few of the local companies that take advantage of the center's occupational medicine services. The practice fosters a close-knit relationship with employers and their insurance companies to determine what is in the best interest for both employers and injured workers.

Sports Medicine Specialists

Hoosier Orthopaedics provides expertise and sports medicine services for local colleges, high schools, and athletic organizations. The team of physicians and athletic trainers works closely with dancers in Butler University's Ballet Department and Jordan College of Dance, recreational athletes at the Midwest Softball and Recreational Park, and a variety of student athletes across the Indianapolis area.

Sports injury patients range from professional athletes to amateur enthusiasts, from fitness buffs to weekend competitors. They rely on the Hoosier Orthopaedics team to evaluate and treat all sports-related injuries and help minimize the risk of future injuries.

Total Joint Replacement

Hoosier Orthopaedics is committed to improving the quality of life of the elderly and those people suffering from hip and knee arthritis. Artificial joint replacement stands out as one of the major advances in medicine over the past 25 years. For a patient with arthritis in the hip or knee, a successful joint replacement often results in dramatic improvement in the patient's quality of life, function, and ability

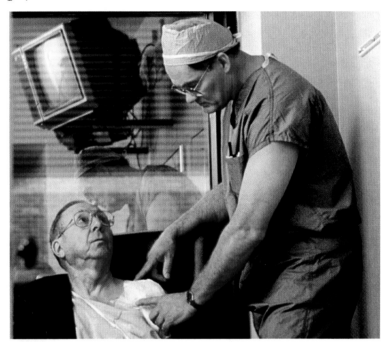

to maintain an independent lifestyle.

Surgeons at Hoosier Orthopaedics perform hundreds of joint replacements each year at St. Vincent Hospital, where the patient enjoys a short and comfortable stay.

Hoosier Orthopaedics and Sports Medicine continues to serve the Indianapolis community by providing the best technology and expertise in the treatment of orthopaedic problems.

DURING ROUNDS AT ST. VINCENT INDIANAPOLIS HOSPITAL, DR. THOMAS TRAINER CHECKS ON A PATIENT FOLLOWING TOTAL SHOULDER ARTHROPLASTY (TOP).

HOOSIER ORTHOPAEDICS AND SPORTS MEDICINE PROVIDES SPORTS MEDICINE EXPERTISE AND GAME COVERAGE FOR VARIOUS HIGH SCHOOLS AND AMATEUR ATHLETIC ORGANIZATIONS IN THE GREATER INDIANAPOLIS AREA (BOTTOM).

THE BOEHRINGER MANNHEIM GROUP, ONE OF THE LEADING HEALTH care companies in the world, is, nevertheless, a company that maintains a low profile. ◆ Within the medical community—in hospitals across the country, by physicians' organizations and other health care organizations—the company is known for its high-quality products. But among members of the community

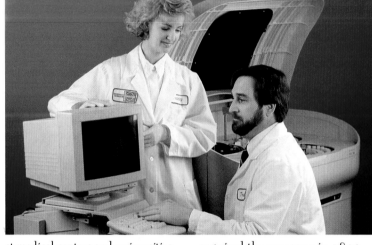

at large, the company may be somewhat of a mystery.

This is true even in Indianapolis, home of the company's U.S. and North American headquarters. The Indianapolis company is identified as Boehringer Mannheim Corporation (BMC) and comprises the diagnostics and biochemicals business focuses. A sister company, Boehringer Mannheim Pharmaceuticals Corporation (BMPC) is headquartered in Gaithersburg, Maryland.

The worldwide Boehringer Mannheim Group is privately held by Corange Limited. Annual sales for the parent company in 1994 were $3.5 billion. BMC's sales for the same period were nearly $700 million.

Boehringer Mannheim Corporation has a diverse portfolio of in vitro diagnostic tests and related automated instrumentation, and a wide range of biochemicals for life science research and the health care industry. BMC is well known for its high-end biochemical products, which are made from both natural and synthetic components, and are used as raw materials in a number of health care products. Medical research scientists—who conduct some of the most advanced research

at medical centers and universities— also value Boehringer's biochemicals because of their consistency and reliability.

BEGINNINGS

Throughout its history, the company has remained family owned. It was originally formed by Christian Friederich Boehringer and his sons in Stuttgart in 1859. The name of the company links the family name with the city of Mannheim, Germany, where BMC's worldwide operations have been headquartered since the late 1800s. Dr. Friedrich Engelhorn, the company's first research scientist,

acquired the company in 1892 when Ernst Boehringer died without heirs. Members of the third generation of the Engelhorn family are currently at the helm. In the early 1980s, Curt Engelhorn formed Corange Limited, a holding company, which provides long-term financial management for the Boehringer Mannheim family of companies around the world. "Corange" is the Engelhorn name translated into French.

Boehringer Mannheim first came to the United States in 1964 when a sales office was opened in New York City. The company established its presence in Indianapolis in 1974 by acquiring Bio-

BOEHRINGER MANNHEIM'S AUTOMATED CLINICAL LABORATORY ANALYZER SYSTEMS HELP HOSPITALS AND LARGE LABS PROVIDE ACCURATE RESULTS RAPIDLY AND EFFICIENTLY (RIGHT).

BELOW, FROM LEFT:
THE ACCUCHECK® ADVANTAGE BLOOD GLUCOSE MONITORING SYSTEM APPLIES ADVANCED, HIGHLY ACCURATE SENSOR TECHNOLOGY TO DIABETES TESTING.

THE CARDIAC T™ RAPID ASSAY ENABLES PHYSICIANS TO DIAGNOSE ACUTE MYOCARDIAL INFARCTION WITH GREATER SPEED AND GREATER CERTAINTY THAN OTHER EXISTING TEST SYSTEMS.

WITH THE ACCUSPORT® LACTATE MONITOR, ATHLETES CAN ADEQUATELY MONITOR THEIR BODY'S USE OF ESSENTIAL CHEMICALS AND MAINTAIN MUSCLE OXYGENATION.

CHEMSTRIP® URINE ANALYZER SYSTEMS MAKE RAPID, ACCURATE DRY CHEMISTRY TESTING PRACTICAL IN CLINICS AND PHYSICIANS' OFFICES.

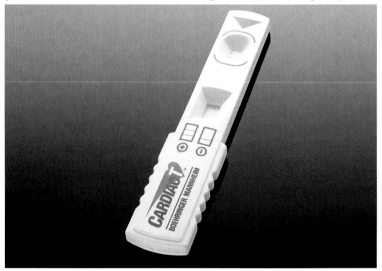

Dynamics, which was founded there in 1964 by Bill Eason, a former chemical engineer with Ford Motor Company. The number of people working at the Indianapolis facilities has grown from about 200 in 1974 to more than 1,500 in 1995. The company's campus-style headquarters continues to grow as well, encompassing more than 120 acres, 13 buildings, an employee park, and beautifully landscaped grounds that include ponds, picnic areas, and sports fields. BMC also has facilities in California and Puerto Rico. Total employment in the United States is approximately 3,000.

A WEALTH OF PRODUCTS

The company has been a leader in diabetes monitoring systems for many years. These at-home testing systems are just one of the various simple-to-use, self-testing kits produced by BMC.

The company also manufactures desktop analyzers suitable for clinics, doctors' offices, and other professional settings. This range of products includes blood analysis, urinalysis, and coagulation testing systems. Currently BMC's new diagnostic test for heart attack (acute myocardial infarction) is undergoing trials in the United States in preparation for FDA approval. This test is already in use in Europe and has had remarkable results at hospitals throughout the United States.

Boehringer also leads in the field of high- and medium-volume automated analyzer systems. These large, multifunction analyzers are the backbone of accurate, rapid

service in central reference laboratories and hospitals. Manufactured by Hitachi in California and Japan, these instruments represent one of BMC's first international alliances, linking Japanese technology with Boehringer's knowledge in the chemical diagnostic field. Also held by Corange Limited is DePuy, Inc., a worldwide orthopedic company based in Warsaw, Indiana. DePuy produces orthopedic implant devices and other orthopedic products.

INDIANAPOLIS REMAINS HOME

Despite BMC's frequent offers to relocate, Indianapolis remains the North American base for the organization, as it has for the past 30 years. This global company has chosen to be in Indianapolis because the city has been supportive, corporate executives say. BMC believes Indianapolis is a good city to work in, and its culture matches the company's culture. Likewise, the midwestern environment seems to be compatible with the family-owned company.

BMC and its employees also enjoy the cultural and higher educational opportunities that Indianapolis offers. The company maintains strong, valuable relationships with local colleges and universities, particularly with the state universities—from a research angle, from a recruiting standpoint, and from a partnership standpoint. The city provides a number of educational opportunities for Boehringer's employees to continue their education.

Indianapolis has all the offer-

ings of a larger metropolitan area, but with a small-town feel that appeals to BMC. The opera, symphony, and theater at a variety of levels—from professional to community and experimental—are definite advantages when it comes to recruiting top-notch professionals.

Through many decision points over the years, the company has chosen to stay in Indianapolis and to grow here. By producing a wealth of products both for in-home diagnostic use and to further research in a professional setting, Boehringer Mannheim Corporation will continue to be a positive force in Indianapolis' corporate community.

LOCATED ON A BEAUTIFUL, 120-ACRE CAMPUS IN NORTHEAST INDIANAPOLIS, BMC IS THE NORTH AMERICAN HEADQUARTERS OF A GLOBAL DIAGNOSTICS AND BIO-CHEMICALS HEALTH CARE COMPANY. EXCELLENCE IN BIOTECHNOLOGY, BIOCHEMISTRY, AND WORLD-CLASS CUSTOMER SERVICE IS THE HALL-MARK OF BOEHRINGER MANNHEIM (BELOW).

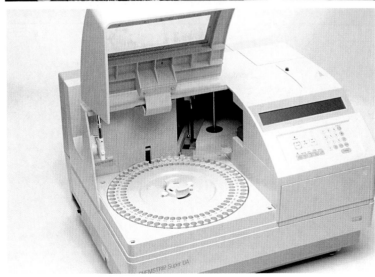

ERVICE GRAPHICS INC. (SGI), ESTABLISHED IN INDIANAPOLIS in 1967 as a pharmaceutical sample distribution company, is now an industry leader in systems-based warehousing and distribution of literature and support materials. The company provides fully integrated marketing communications services, including database development and management, promotion-al material warehousing and fulfillment, assembly, and printing.

OUTSOURCING SERVICES

In partnering with its customers, SGI commits to meeting or exceeding their needs. The company's customers are typically Fortune 500 firms looking for cost-effective ways to outsource marketing service functions that have limited strategic relationship to their core competencies.

"More and more companies are looking to partner with firms that can help them better control costs," says President Michael Burks. "However, a focus on service remains critical. We wouldn't be successful if our employees didn't deliver superior service every day."

Service Graphics has assisted major corporations such as Allison, Firestone, and Eli Lilly with functions unrelated to their primary business to help enhance their productivity and cut expenses.

TRACKING VITAL INFORMATION

One example of outsourcing is literature fulfillment. Using its expertise in systems and data tracking, SGI can collect indi-vidual item inventory and ordering information, provide reports in a user-friendly format, and track items that have been under- or overproduced. To improve a company's turnaround time, Service Graphics can fill orders within 24 to 48 hours, even when special handling is required. To provide further expertise and service, the company's logistics operations can check order fulfillment accuracy, manage inventory, provide cycle counting, and calculate safety stock levels and reorder points. In addition, SGI offers storage space for any size project, security storage for cost-sensitive items, premium material storage and handling, and a complete mail room facility for handling large mailings.

"Currently, we are expanding our customer base nationally," says Director of Sales and Marketing Buckley D. Beranek. "We've done an excellent job in this region and have benefited from the references provided by current clients."

Management information systems is another area of expertise for Service Graphics. The company provides database management services with its professional staff of programmers who successfully design targeted, customized programs for customers. As SGI develops a database through its information systems group, the company can implement targeted mailings and associated replies, and can help evaluate the effectiveness of promotional materials for its clients. According to Beranek, "It's an extremely valuable approach to maximizing our clients' marketing dollars."

A technical support staff is available to ensure that programs run smoothly and efficiently. Some of these programs include inventory status and tracking, item history, shipping activities, sales incentive programs, lead tracking, reporting, lead generation, cost allocation, and invoicing. "For example," says Beranek, "we can collect individual survey responses to compile a cus-

SGI's LEADERSHIP INCLUDES (FROM LEFT) VICE PRESIDENT TOM DEAN, PRESIDENT MICHAEL BURKS, AND CHIEF FINANCIAL OFFICER BERNIE WEITEKAMP.

THE COMPANY'S EFFICIENT LOGISTICAL OPERATIONS ARE A KEY FACTOR IN REDUCING OPERATING COSTS.

◀ HAROLD LEE MILLER

tomer profile for our clients. This helps target the customer's needs specifically so that marketing efforts can be focused in that direction."

TWENTY-FIVE YEARS OF SERVICE

For more than 25 years, SGI has provided marketing communication support to Fortune 500 companies. These services include production of promotional or training materials, direct mailings, meeting materials preparation and distribution, product launch materials and distribution, warehousing and distribution of marketing materials, and custom programming and reporting. The company also provides interactive customer service through toll-free 800 numbers, cost allocation by personnel or departments, chargeback usage and freight fees to other budgets, and invoicing for materials.

Service Graphics employs more than 130 people at its 200,000-square-foot headquarters facility in Indianapolis. "The company's strength comes from employees who commit to doing a better job," says Burks. "Our people don't want to rely on management to direct all of their activity. We all want to be responsible for our own actions."

To further this objective, the company has established the "I Power System," a popular employee suggestion program. Employees carry a small pad with them during the workday, jotting down ideas and then depositing them in a box in the vice president's office. The ideas are read by management and noted as "A," "B," or "let's talk about it." The A ideas are published and copied to all employees. "The program has been very successful," says Vice President Tom Dean. "It's the little ideas, each building

upon the previous ones, that create the journey of continuous improvement."

The growth of Service Graphics has led to its diversification of services. "If our customers ask us to do something, we'll perform," says Burks. "We have their trust. That has allowed us to move into new areas of business. We will continue to be client-focused, rather than services-focused. That's how we can add value to our partners over the long term."

COMMITTED PEOPLE ARE THE STRENGTH OF SGI.

EADQUARTERED ON THE NORTH SIDE OF INDIANAPOLIS, ITT Educational Services, Inc. (ITT/ESI) has been actively involved in the country's higher education community for nearly three decades. In 1966 ITT Corporation acquired Indianapolis-based Howard W. Sams, a textbook publishing company that owned three proprietary schools in the Midwest. Two years later, the corporation established ITT/ESI, with plans to expand the network of campuses. Today, through its 58 ITT Technical Institutes in 26 states, ITT/ESI continues to provide high-quality postsecondary education to more than 20,000 students across the nation.

ITT/ESI is currently one of the largest publicly traded higher education systems in the United States. Two million shares (16.7 percent of the company's stock) are currently traded on the New York Stock Exchange under the symbol ESI, with parent company ITT Corporation owning the remaining stock.

PREPARING A WORKFORCE FOR THE FUTURE

The ITT Technical Institute system offers programs of study in high-technology fields such as electronics engineering, computer-aided drafting, and automated manufacturing. These diverse, in-depth programs—which primarily lead to a bachelor's or associate's degree—focus on the development of critical thinking, communication techniques, and teamwork skills. In 1995 ITT/ESI announced the development of three new programs of study to help meet industry needs: a master's degree in project management, a bachelor's degree in computer visualization technology, and an associate's degree in chemical technology. All programs of study are reviewed by advisory committees comprised of business and industry leaders. In addition, ITT Technical Institutes are accredited by (or are seeking accreditation from) an association recognized by the U.S. Department of Education.

Classes are generally offered five days a week in four-hour sessions that meet in the morning, afternoon, or evening. This flexible scheduling system allows bachelor's degree students to complete their course requirements and enter the workforce within three years. Students take courses year-round during four 12-week sessions.

"We believe our educational system better prepares our graduates for the complexities of the future," says Rene Champagne, chairman, president, and CEO of ITT/ESI. "We emphasize experiential teaching techniques, which develop practical knowledge and skill sets sought by employers."

Programs of study at ITT Technical Institutes blend traditional academic content with applied learning

HEADQUARTERED ON THE NORTH SIDE OF INDIANAPOLIS, ITT EDUCATIONAL SERVICES, INC. HAS BEEN ACTIVELY INVOLVED IN THE COUNTRY'S HIGHER EDUCATION COMMUNITY FOR NEARLY THREE DECADES.

concepts. This is accomplished through class sessions with 60 percent of class time devoted to theory exploration and the remainder to practical study in a laboratory environment. The result of this unique, hands-on approach is that students spend about as much time with experiential learning as they do listening to theory lectures.

ITT Technical Institute's innovative system of instruction is designed to equip graduates with the skills they will need in a rapidly and constantly changing economic and technological environment. In addition, all disciplines are periodically updated to reflect technological advances and to respond to the changing requirements of American industry. Graduates of ITT Technical Institutes have gone on to assume careers with such powerhouse companies as Thomson Consumer Electronics, Apple Computer, The Boeing Company, Intel Corporation, Microsoft Corporation, and Motorola, to name a few.

FOSTERING INDIVIDUAL GROWTH

The mission of ITT/ESI is to promote an educational environment that fosters professional growth while encouraging each person to reach his or her highest potential. Also included in the mission statement is the organization's commitment to fostering

ethical responsibility and individual creativity within the framework of equal opportunity and affirmative action.

"Hard work is attractive when you're attempting to accomplish a goal," says Champagne. "Our students are building a sense of value while working toward a rewarding and enjoyable career."

Conceptual thinking is in demand in today's workplace, especially abilities that can be applied to solving complex, often technical problems without significant supervision from managers. Students at ITT Technical Institutes learn to solve such problems by exploring innovative and creative solutions. In the classroom, students present their solutions in written and oral format, which fosters confidence and helps them acquire the communication skills necessary for success in today's work environment. The vast majority of ITT Technical Institute students find the rigorous curriculum to be a challenging opportunity.

Placement of graduates is a high priority at ITT Technical Institutes, and students are encouraged to prepare for the job market well in advance of graduation. ITT Technical Institutes offer courses on career success as well as assistance with preparing résumés and coaching on how to handle interview situations with confidence. The placement

departments on each campus remain in contact with students and graduates as well as employers within the community who have job openings. In turn, the placement offices forward appropriate résumés and assist students and graduates in arranging interviews at the school or at an employer's place of business.

REACHING THE COMMUNITY

Because the ITT/ESI system is composed of individual, community-based campuses, each ITT Technical Institute is actively involved in its respective neighborhood. Staff, faculty members, and students often take part in local civic affairs and charitable events.

The individual campuses also assist the community's secondary school system. ITT/ESI provides a critical service to students, to the communities where its campuses are located, to the employers who hire its graduates, and to the nation's economy as a whole.

"If America is to reach the next century strong enough to compete globally, we must have the technically skilled labor force to do the job," says Champagne. "ITT Technical Institutes are committed to meeting that challenge by providing an education designed to meet the needs of today's workplace."

THE ITT TECHNICAL INSTITUTE SYSTEM OFFERS PROGRAMS OF STUDY IN HIGH-TECHNOLOGY FIELDS SUCH AS ELECTRONICS ENGINEERING, COMPUTER-AIDED DRAFTING, AND AUTOMATED MANUFACTURING.

ITT/ESI's UNIQUE, HANDS-ON APPROACH ALLOWS STUDENTS TO SPEND ABOUT AS MUCH TIME WITH EXPERIENTIAL LEARNING AS THEY DO LISTENING TO THEORY LECTURES.

VISIT TO INDIANA UNIVERSITY-PURDUE UNIVERSITY INDIANAPOLIS quickly impresses you with this fact: IUPUI offers more of what students seek in higher education. Whether they're just graduating from high school or are returning to or starting college after working and beginning a family, IUPUI offers students more programs, more class scheduling options, and—most important—more of the quality they want for their next step in life.

IUPUI offers a distinctive combination of the best of Indiana's two major universities. Marked by the academic excellence and professional prestige that have earned Indiana University and Purdue University international reputations, IUPUI offers more than 180 complete degree programs. From certificates and associate degrees through doctoral studies, the array of programs at IUPUI is the most comprehensive in the state.

The campus, forged in 1969, offers flexibility and convenience in courses and programs to residents throughout central Indiana and serves the area as its fourth-largest employer. IUPUI is an urban campus, offering the dynamic spirit that characterizes a metropolitan city. As a 21st-century model for American public higher education, the campus thrives on a fast pace and connections with the city and its people. There are no isolated, out-of-touch ivory towers; rather, the people of IUPUI are in partnership with the city, moving towards the brightest possible horizons for urban and academic life.

The campus has maintained a strong connection with the community since its formative years. The professional health programs help provide care to those in Indianapolis, as well as high-quality education and hands-on experience to students. Other programs foster connections to the political, social, business, and cultural arenas, and provide students with strong links to internship and employment opportunities.

IUPUI students come from many walks of life and head in many directions. They wear faded jeans and tailored suits, drive vans and sedans, and study every topic from archaeology to zoology, plus a thousand subjects in between. Three out of four of IUPUI's 27,000 students are undergraduates, and each year some 4,000 earn their Indiana University or Purdue University degrees at IUPUI.

As one of five colleges and universities in Indianapolis, IUPUI is located just west of downtown, with easy access to the state centers of government, business, arts, and education. The cultural treasures of Indianapolis—outstanding museums, parks, and performing arts—combine with IUPUI programs in music, art, and theater to give students the extras so essential to a well-rounded education.

One of the characteristics that sets IUPUI apart from smaller, narrowly focused schools is the great diversity on campus. Under-graduate students, for example, have access to a rich mix of faculty experts, graduate students, labs, libraries, and lectures because IUPUI offers so many professional and graduate programs.

Indiana's only medical and dental schools are at IUPUI. So are the state's largest law school and the nation's largest nursing school. Several state, county, and federal hospitals and dozens of clinics at the IU Medical Center contribute to campus programs in health care.

The IUPUI campus encompasses 60 buildings and has won numerous awards for its contemporary architecture and design. The University Library is furnished with the most up-to-date electronic research system available, which makes researching materials both in-house and across the globe simple

THE UNIVERSITY'S 285-ACRE CAMPUS IS LOCATED NEAR THE STATE'S GOVERNMENT CENTER AND IS THE FOURTH-LARGEST EMPLOYER IN CENTRAL INDIANA (RIGHT).

THE IU MEDICAL CENTER LIBRARY IS A FOCAL POINT FOR ONE OF THE NATION'S LARGEST SCHOOLS OF MEDICINE (BELOW).

through various computer workstations. Study carrels are individually wired with data connections so patrons can use laptop computers throughout the facility. The libraries on campus also serve the community through public access to vast numbers of government documents, legal resources, and other materials available on-site and via the Internet.

The 285-acre downtown campus boasts outstanding athletic facilities within the IUPUI Sport Complex that help make Indianapolis known as the "Amateur Sports Capital of the World." These include a 50-meter competition pool and an 18-foot diving well housed in the IU Natatorium; 18 outdoor and six indoor tennis courts at the Indianapolis Tennis Center; and a 400-meter, nine-lane oval track at the Track & Field Stadium, which has been the site of several world records. All have been used for national and international events, such as Olympic trials and RCA tennis championships.

Another focal point that brings the world to IUPUI's front door is the University Place Conference Center and Hotel, where meetings of government leaders, academic researchers, Fortune 500 companies, and community organizations take place. The facility, which includes a 278-room, AAA Four Diamond hotel, is the only central Indiana member of the International Association of Conference Centers.

Access, connection, and networks are key words in today's learning environment. At IUPUI students can enhance their studies in the state-of-the-art electronic lecture hall, at the computerized conference center, or in computer classes. In the learning centers on campus, students have access to microcomputers, laser printers, and hundreds of software applications. IUPUI takes great care to serve fully all members of its community, and is on the cutting edge of technology.

IUPUI is a center for advanced studies. Faculty working with students in graduate and professional programs are expanding the knowledge base in numerous fields of inquiry. Collaborative research and cross-disciplinary teaching among schools and departments are encouraged to help share talent and bring full insight for a unique synergy.

IUPUI also offers courses at sites within the neighborhoods and corporations throughout the city. Because many IUPUI students work full-time, having classes at convenient times and locations helps ensure IUPUI is best serving its community.

CLOCKWISE FROM BOTTOM RIGHT: TRIALS FOR THE U.S. OLYMPIC SWIMMING AND DIVING TEAMS HAVE BEEN HELD AT THE IU NATATORIUM AT IUPUI SINCE THE FACILITY OPENED IN 1982.

THE UNIVERSITY LIBRARY BRINGS IUPUI'S 27,000 STUDENTS ELECTRONIC ACCESS TO RESEARCH MATERIALS FROM THROUGHOUT THE WORLD.

IUPUI OFFERS MORE THAN 180 DEGREE PROGRAMS FROM ASSOCIATE THROUGH DOCTORAL LEVELS, AND HAS BECOME INDIANA'S MOST COMPREHENSIVE UNIVERSITY CAMPUS.

THE 278-ROOM UNIVERSITY PLACE CONFERENCE CENTER AND HOTEL, RATED AS A AAA FOUR DIAMOND HOTEL, IS HOST TO THOUSANDS EACH YEAR WHO TAKE PART IN CORPORATE, ACADEMIC, AND COMMUNITY CONFERENCES, WORKSHOPS, AND EVENTS.

▶ PETER H. BICK

1970-1996

1971	THE INDIANA HAND CENTER
1972	BROWNING-FERRIS INDUSTRIES OF INDIANA, INC.
1972	VASA BROUGHER, INC.
1973	CROSSMANN COMMUNITIES, INC.
1973	REI INVESTMENTS, INC.
1975	BSA DESIGN
1977	MARTIN UNIVERSITY
1977	NORTHSIDE CARDIOLOGY, P.C.
1979	CONSECO, INC.
1980	IBJ CORPORATION
1980	MAYS CHEMICAL COMPANY, INC.
1981	MACMILLAN PUBLISHING USA
1982	CROWE CHIZEK
1982	MANSUR GROUP
1983	YOUNG & LARAMORE
1984	BATES USA / MIDWEST
1984	SOFTWARE SYNERGY, INC.
1984	TELAMON CORPORATION
1986	KeyBank NATIONAL ASSOCIATION
1987	THOMSON CONSUMER ELECTRONICS
1988	FedEx®
1988	QUANTUM HEALTH RESOURCES, INC.
1988	RE/MAX OF INDIANA
1989	BRIGHTPOINT, INC.
1989	MyStar COMMUNICATIONS CORPORATION
1992	THE MORLEY GROUP INC.
1993	BLAISING ST. CLAIRE ASSOCIATES
1994	CHAUTAUQUA AIRLINES, INC./USAir EXPRESS
1994	GUIDANT CORPORATION

HE INDIANA HAND CENTER, FOUNDED IN 1971, IS KNOWN throughout the world as a leader in the care and treatment of the entire upper extremity: hand, wrist, elbow, and shoulder. As pioneers in the diagnosis, treatment, and rehabilitation of the upper extremity, the center's surgeons are committed to providing the highest level of cost-effective care, all

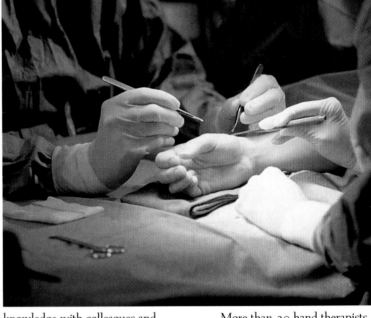

while focusing on returning their patients to active lives as quickly as possible.

Located on the St. Vincent Hospital campus on the north side of Indianapolis, The Indiana Hand Center houses 18 patient examination rooms, an outpatient surgery center, and occupational therapy services. In order to meet the needs of its patients, the center has developed more than 20 satellite locations throughout the state. Each day, more than 500 patients are treated by The Indiana Hand Center. As part of this expanded reach throughout the state, the center's surgeons are on staff at many hospitals in Indianapolis, including St. Vincent, Methodist, and Indiana University Medical Center.

Many of the center's physicians lead national and international professional societies. All Indiana Hand Center surgeons are active lecturers, and several have developed the tools used in surgery by physicians throughout the world.

Indiana Hand Center physicians share their expertise and

knowledge with colleagues and have developed a fellowship program whereby annually six orthopedic surgeons receive advanced specialty training in hand and microvascular surgery. This year-long training program is provided at The Indiana Hand Center's Indianapolis location.

More than 30 hand therapists provide rehabilitation services to patients throughout Indiana. Most of the therapists are certified hand therapists who have completed required advanced training on the hand and upper extremity.

In addition to the hand surgeons, the center provides occupational medicine treatment. The needs of workers' compensation patients are addressed through the Return to Work Program where injured patients gain the strength and endurance needed to return to the workplace.

Housed at the center is the Ruth Lilly Hand Surgery Library— an extensive collection of books, journals, and papers on the upper extremity. Also sponsored by The Indiana Hand Center is the Foundation for Hand Research and Education, which funds research on conditions of the upper extremity.

This innovative organization is dedicated to providing its hand and upper extremity patients with a complete continuum of the best care available.

BSA DESIGN

INCE OPENING ITS DOORS IN 1975, BSA DESIGN HAS BEEN dedicated to architectural and engineering expertise, providing innovative design solutions for complex technical environments. After years of specializing in the health care field, BSA is currently expanding its customer base in keeping with its market diversification plans for the future. Resting solidly on its strong reputation,

BSA enjoys a unique niche in the health care field, having worked on projects for all major Indianapolis hospitals.

A full-service architecture and engineering design firm, BSA tackles the challenges of increasingly complex health care, health science, and higher education facilities by using effective planning solutions that reflect an understanding of the design/function relationship. The Indianapolis-based firm offers a comprehensive range of services, including facility planning, facility management, architectural services, mechanical engineering, electrical engineering, civil engineering, structural engineering, energy conservation, interior design, and construction project management. A prime example of BSA's planning expertise is the Riley Children's Cancer Center in Indianapolis, one of three children's cancer centers in the United States offering stem cell transplants.

EFFECTIVE PLANNING FOR CLIENTS

Modern Health Care magazine ranks BSA as the 21st-largest health care planning and design firm in the nation, while Engineering News-Record ranks BSA among the top 500

design firms nationally. The company's broadening client base includes physicians, multihospital systems, rural health care providers, university teaching hospitals, research laboratories, and colleges and universities. While the firm will continue its acclaimed work on health care and research facilities, BSA is also planning for a more diverse future. "We anticipate maintaining our dollar volume in the health care market while growing further into other markets—primarily corporate, institutional, and higher education," says President Monte L. Hoover.

Success is no stranger to BSA—85 percent of its workload comes from repeat business. Methodist Hospital of Indiana, Inc.; St. Vincent Hospital and Health Care Center; Indiana University Hospitals; and Community Hospitals Indianapolis are just some of the repeat clients served by BSA's 98 employees. Each project is managed by one of the firm's 18 principals who act as "Client Champions," serving the individual needs of the client and ensuring long-term relationships. During its 20-year history, the firm's planners, designers, and engineers have provided services nationally for more than 600 successful projects, including

9 million square feet of space with construction costs of more than $1.2 billion.

BSA's comprehensive, long-range approach to planning allows clients to identify, develop, and implement their goals. Sensitive, cost-effective facility planning that exceeds client expectations is a critical element in the philosophy the company applies to every new project. "We are a dynamic, high-energy, hard-working firm," says Don Altemeyer, chairman of the board. "I like to think that we are surprising—offering fresh, new ideas to clients."

As BSA approaches the new century, its sense of renewal and commitment carries the firm toward a future ripe with diverse architectural opportunities.

THE MEDICAL SCIENCE LIBRARY AT METHODIST HOSPITAL OF INDIANA REPRESENTS A NEW IMAGE FOR HEALTH CARE FACILITIES.

EMPLOYING ITS EXPERTISE IN HEALTH CARE PLANNING AND DESIGN, BSA WORKED WITH INDIANA UNIVERSITY TO CREATE ONE OF THE PREMIER CANCER RESEARCH AND TREATMENT CENTERS IN THE UNITED STATES.

ARBAGE ISN'T JUST GARBAGE ANYMORE. IN FACT, MORE THAN 70 percent of the waste stream in the United States can be recycled. Today, the term is "materials management," and it is a big business. ◆ Browning-Ferris Industries, Inc. (BFI), with a presence in Indianapolis since 1972, is one of North America's largest publicly held waste-service companies. Its subsidiaries and affiliates collect, process for recycling, transport, and dispose of a wide range of commercial, industrial, medical, and residential solid wastes.

Headquartered in Houston, BFI employs approximately 40,000 people worldwide, serving commercial, industrial, governmental, and residential customers throughout North America, the United Kingdom, and the Middle East.

Through its commercial and industrial collection services, BFI serves hospitals, retail shops, apartments, airports, restaurants, manufacturing plants, shopping centers, schools, and others with waste collection systems using on-site containers. Container types and sizes, as well as frequency of collection, are tailored to each customer's needs.

In creating a residential solid waste collection program, BFI matches labor and equipment to the population, geography, and waste-generating characteristics of the area. Curbside collection and back door pickup are two services frequently provided under contracts with municipal governments, subdivisions, and/or individual home owners.

A Recycling Pioneer

As an industry leader in waste collection and disposal, and as a pioneer in America's efforts to recycle, BFI has developed four successful RecycleNOW® programs encompassing industrial, commercial, and residential collection, as well as materials processing. The purpose of these programs is to recover a range of valuable commodities, from office paper and corrugated cardboard to newspaper and beverage containers.

BFI has hands-on experience in designing and implementing successful, neighborhood-oriented recycling activities through its multimaterial curbside program and the yard waste curbside program. The company helps communities across the world recover yard and food wastes, sludge, and wood and coal ash through organic waste recycling programs. The BFI Tire Recyclers™ group provides scrap

AN INDUSTRY LEADER IN WASTE COLLECTION AND DISPOSAL, BFI HAS ALSO ESTABLISHED ITSELF AS A PIONEER IN AMERICA'S EFFORTS TO RECYCLE.

tire collection, stockpile abatement, and processing programs customized to meet local tire recycling goals. The company also assists communities in implementing a combination of three types of recycling centers: RecycleNOW Buy-Back Centers, RecycleNOW Drop-Off Centers, and the BFI Recyclery™.

DIVERSE SERVICES WITH AN ENVIRONMENTAL FOCUS

Millions of tons of waste are disposed of annually by BFI at company-owned and -operated sanitary landfills around the globe. The sanitary landfill method, pioneered by BFI, is the most environmentally compatible and economically feasible alternative for solid waste disposal. Uniquely engineered, sanitary landfills are valuable assets to areas served during their operation. Upon completion, they can be converted to recreational or other types of public areas.

BFI is in the forefront of developing technologies for the recovery of energy and reusable resources from wastes. In January 1984 BFI teamed with Air Products and Chemicals, Inc. to market waste-to-energy plants. This joint venture operates as the American Ref-Fuel® Company.

BFI also operates the nation's largest network of medical waste disposal facilities. The company specializes in the collection, treatment, and disposal of medical waste from health care facilities by steam sterilization or incineration. In Indianapolis, BFI serves all of the city's major hospitals.

THE HEARTLAND DIVISION

In June 1993 the Heartland Division was formed to help BFI get closer to the Midwest marketplace and to its customers in Indiana and Illinois. The division's organization is team driven. "We solve problems through the use of breakthrough teams made up of representatives from all sectors of the company," says Ron Ackerman, vice president of the Heartland Division. "We identify a problem; then, during an eight-week process, the team works out solutions."

The Heartland Division takes

its people orientation a step further by supporting local and national charitable organizations. In 1995 BFI instituted the Indiana Neighborhood Watch Program, using trucks and drivers to monitor and report any suspicious activity to local police departments. Several BFI drivers around the country have received awards for their involvement in similar programs.

A COMMITMENT TO GROWTH

BFI has a real commitment to growth," says Ackerman. The Heartland Division will experience double-digit growth again and continue to be sustained by continuous improvement initiatives, personal development programs, and the implementation of more efficient equipment service and capacity investments.

Displaying a bright blue T-shirt inscribed with the words "Big Hairy Audacious Goal," Ackerman says with a smile, "We have a vision. In 1995 we achieved 19 percent growth in sales. We expect to reach 20 percent top-line growth in 1996. The big, hairy, audacious goal is to grow by 300 percent by 1998."

To achieve that level of growth, BFI has formulated a series of action strategies. One is to decrease the cost of service per unit by 2 percent by the end of 1996. "Companies that can de-

crease costs while adding value lead in their industry," says Ackerman. "We are the largest solid waste management company in the United States. We take our market leadership role seriously."

BFI's SUBSIDIARIES AND AFFILIATES COLLECT, PROCESS FOR RECYCLING, TRANSPORT, AND DISPOSE OF A WIDE RANGE OF COMMERCIAL, INDUSTRIAL, MEDICAL, AND RESIDENTIAL SOLID WASTE.

VASA BROUGHER, INC.

ODAY MORE THAN TWO-THIRDS OF U.S. BUSINESSES OF NEARLY every size put self-funding—a popular method of group medical coverage—to work for their employees. In order for a self-funded insurance plan to work, these companies must take additional measures to protect themselves from excessive expenditures and catastrophic losses. ◆ Indianapolis-based VASA Brougher, Inc.

serves as an underwriting administrator of medical excess-loss, or stop-loss, coverage for self-insured employers. The company determines risk, issues policies, and pays claims on behalf of the carriers it represents.

ADVANTAGES OF SELF-FUNDING

There are numerous advantages to self-funding over traditional, fully insured plans. Self-funded plans can be customized to fit specific group needs, giving employers the freedom to select only those benefits of value to employees. These flexible plans also offer independent cost-containment measures. Leftover funds in the claim account may be reconciled against future contributions, while interest earned on these accounts creates additional income for the fund. In addition, stop-loss coverage provides simplified budgeting because the

stop-loss carrier safeguards a company's limit for maximum expenditures on health care.

"We believe the option of employers to self-insure their employees' health benefits needs to be a part of any new reform plan adopted by Congress," says Eric Olson, president of VASA Brougher. "Self-insurance is more cost-effective, flexible, and user-friendly than standard forms of insurance. Employers are able to adapt the plan to their own employees' needs." Olson also notes that employers who use self-insurance have a greater incentive to make the programs cost-effective and to encourage wellness and prevention programs in the workplace.

VASA Brougher continues to work energetically to preserve employer choice and true market competition in the insurance industry. The company believes in responsibly educating and informing U.S. policy makers about the value

and importance of self-insurance, as well as about employer responsibility in health care reform.

AN INTERNATIONAL COMPANY WITH A LOCAL PRESENCE

Established locally in 1972, VASA Brougher is a subsidiary of Seaboard Insurance Group, a group of companies doing business in the life insurance and employee benefits markets. Seaboard's parent company, Eureko B.V., is the hub of more than a dozen companies located in Europe, Australia, and North America. The Amsterdam-based Eureko has total assets exceeding $3 billion.

The Brougher Building in downtown Indianapolis houses VASA Brougher's corporate headquarters. The 100-year-old structure was the original Manual Training High School and later Harry E. Wood High School. In October 1988 the renovated red-brick building received awards of excellence for design and development from the Commission for Downtown Indianapolis and the Metropolitan Development Commission.

From its Indianapolis base, VASA Brougher maintains working relationships with more than 350 third-party administrators (TPAs) nationwide. The company also does business with reputable independent brokers and agents.

In terms of premium volume, VASA Brougher is the largest producer of stop-loss coverage in the United States. The company serves as an underwriting administrator for several carriers that offer stop-loss coverage, and represents them in the placement of this coverage. Among these carriers are Seaboard Life Insurance Company (USA) and VASA North Atlantic Insurance Company, affiliates under

DEAN HERSHMAN

the Seaboard Insurance Group umbrella. VASA Brougher also shows businesses how to coordinate an entire gamut of employee benefits, as well as how to monitor and control the cost of their benefit plans.

A Great Place to Work

One of VASA Brougher's goals is to be an employer of choice. In an effort to reach that goal, the company offers customized employee benefits, an employee gain-sharing program, a casual dress policy, and flexible hours.

VASA Brougher has also developed several unique programs that demonstrate the degree to which the company values its employees. For example, the company employs a full-time fitness director to manage its wellness program. In addition to a full-court gym and weight room at the Indianapolis headquarters, locker rooms and a sauna are available. Basketball leagues, open volleyball, and health screenings represent a few of the program's offerings.

"I want people in the organization to be self-actualized, to speak their mind within the organization, and to be the best people they can be," says Olson. "I want people who are so certain of their own marketability and value that they will speak their mind. We'd compete for people like that."

In 1992 VASA Brougher received the Indiana Family Life Enhancement award presented by Methodist Hospital of Indiana, Inc. In 1992 and 1993 Methodist issued this award to five Hoosier companies. Charitable contributions in large numbers are also on VASA Brougher's agenda, with more than 60 local organizations supported by its generosity.

For more than two decades in the Indianapolis area, the company's evolution has kept it on a successful path, creating dynamic growth and a synergistic corporate culture. VASA Brougher works from a win-win philosophy, empowering the company's employees to find solutions.

With the help of VASA Brougher, companies of all sizes now have the option of providing their own self-insurance plans to employees. By eliminating the risk of devastating medical expenditures, VASA Brougher not only has assisted its client companies, but also has provided a model for the future of health care reform.

EMPLOYEES PARTICIPATE IN A GROUP STRETCH BEFORE THE COMPANY'S FITNESS WALK ON NATIONAL EMPLOYEE HEALTH AND FITNESS DAY (TOP).

THE 100-YEAR-OLD BROUGHER BUILDING IN DOWNTOWN INDIANAPOLIS—ORIGINALLY MANUAL TRAINING HIGH SCHOOL AND LATER HARRY E. WOOD HIGH SCHOOL—TODAY HOUSES VASA BROUGHER'S CORPORATE HEADQUARTERS (BOTTOM LEFT AND RIGHT).

MOST FIRST-TIME HOME BUYERS ONLY DREAM OF FINDING A NEW home that is affordable and quality built. Since its beginnings in 1973, Crossmann Communities, Inc. has helped thousands of families realize their dream. Ranked as the largest new home builder in Indianapolis, Crossmann's two building divisions— Deluxe Homes and Trimark Homes—offer affordably priced entry-level and first-move-up homes. In recent years, Crossmann has delivered more new homes in Indianapolis, Lafayette, and Fort Wayne than any other builder in Indiana.

The success of the company rests on a targeted approach to building. Crossmann concentrates its efforts in areas where there is significant and long-term demand for its homes. Standardized products and high volume help create efficiencies in the company's construction processes that result in quality at the most affordable prices.

KEYS TO SUCCESS

Part of being successful stems from the people with whom you surround yourself," says President and Chief Operating Officer Richard H. Crosser. "Our contractors and suppliers are long-term loyal partners. Many contractors work exclusively for our company and have been doing so for years."

Crossmann stands behind the quality of its homes and is committed to customer service. Buyers are encouraged to visit their home during the construction process. Inspections are conducted before buyers take possession and again at periodic intervals after they have lived in the home. Included with each new Crossmann home is a 10-year warranty from an independent warranty company. Crossmann customer service vans can be seen all around the Indianapolis metropolitan area. When a new home owner needs help, the vans are ready to roll at the ring of the phone.

Realizing many buyers have financial concerns, Crossmann offers its customers several unique programs. The Buy & Save Plan gives the customer up to six months to save the down payment for a new home—just like putting a new home on layaway. Also, the Guaranteed Sale Plan provides families a way to begin building a new home before selling their current home by putting their existing equity to work.

Sales consultants for both Deluxe Homes and Trimark Homes are top professionals who work closely with each customer. Flexible financing through Crossmann's own mortgage company means consultants always have the most current information and can help find the right financing program for each family.

GROWTH PLANNING POINTS TO SUCCESS

In 1993 Crossmann Communities became publicly owned with a stock offering of 2.22 million shares, the sale of which netted nearly $22 million. Designed

SINCE ITS BEGINNINGS IN 1973, CROSSMANN COMMUNITIES HAS HELPED THOUSANDS OF FAMILIES REALIZE THEIR DREAM OF AN AFFORDABLE, QUALITY-BUILT HOME. IN ITS LAND ACQUISITION AND DEVELOPMENT ACTIVITIES, THE COMPANY'S OBJECTIVE IS ALWAYS TO BUILD A COMMUNITY NEIGHBORHOOD. CROSSMANN'S OFFERINGS INCLUDE THE LARGER TRIMARK LINE (BELOW LEFT), WHICH IS AVAILABLE IN ONE- AND TWO-STORY PLANS, AND THE DELUXE LINE (BELOW RIGHT), WHICH IS BEST KNOWN FOR ITS RANCH-STYLE HOMES.

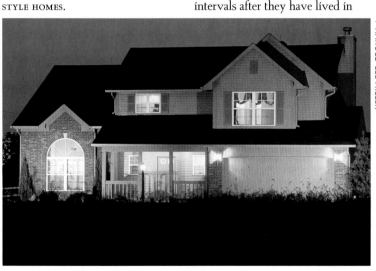

◀ HAROLD LEE MILLER

to increase growth potential, the stock offering ultimately gave Crossmann an opportunity to launch major expansion efforts. The company has successfully expanded in the Midwest, targeting cities with strong similarities and characteristics that make them attractive to new employers, which in turn creates demand for housing. Crossmann currently offers its homes in Indianapolis, Lafayette, Fort Wayne, and Bloomington, plus several more cities in southern Indiana. The company also builds homes in Dayton, Columbus, and Cincinnati, Ohio, and in Louisville, Kentucky.

DELUXE HOMES AND TRIMARK HOMES

Two distinct Crossmann product lines are aimed at entry-level and first-move-up buyers, who are often pleasantly surprised by the quality and value of these homes. "Features that probably would have been found only in a custom home 15 years ago are today standard in our first-time buyer homes," says Chairman and CEO John B. Scheumann.

The Deluxe Homes American Dream Builder line, available in all Crossmann markets, has a variety of floor plans. Although two-story homes are available, Deluxe is best known for building its ranch-style homes. Prices vary by location, with average prices in the mid $90s, which always includes three or four bedrooms and two baths with double garage. Deluxe's newest line of homes, the New American series, is available in selected areas. These somewhat smaller homes are ideal for families or singles just starting out, with very affordable prices in the $70s and $80s including homesite.

Trimark's Mark of Excellence homes, offered in the Flair Series or the more upscale Prestige Series, are available in both one- and two-story plans. Nearly all Trimark locations have natural settings with lakes, trees, and parks. New home buyers have the option of choosing from any of its functional floor plans or of modifying an existing plan. Thus, the size of a Trimark home ranges from 1,400 to 2,000 square feet, while the price varies from $99,000 up.

LAND ACQUISITION AND DEVELOPMENT

Crossmann also acquires raw land for future building. Once land has been purchased, the company begins development activities, including site planning and engineering as well as construction of roads; sewer, water, and drainage facilities; and other amenities. Crossmann's objective is always to build a community neighborhood. And the company's management team strives to maintain an inventory of developed lots sufficient for a building period months in advance.

SUCCESS—A TEAM EFFORT

Successful companies are built from the bottom up," says Crosser. "A lot of planning and teamwork are keys to Crossmann Communities' success. The input of the sales force, as well as many of the 200-plus employees, is always valued by management. Major marketing programs are usually on the drawing board months in advance."

Crossmann was ranked by *Builder* magazine as the 50th-largest home builder in the United States in 1994. Of Indianapolis, Crosser notes, "City government is extremely cooperative and has provided encouragement to new companies relocating to this city. As a result of this positive attitude by government, we have experienced tremendous job growth. Thus, the real estate industry has benefited substantially. We think our corporate home of Indianapolis is the greatest city in the United States."

CROSSMANN CUSTOMER SERVICE VANS CAN BE SEEN ALL AROUND THE INDIANAPOLIS METROPOLITAN AREA.

EI INVESTMENTS, INC. IS RIGHT ON THE MARK WHEN IT COMES to understanding real estate development of Indianapolis. As a locally owned company, REI has kept pace with the growth of the city's business community by developing, leasing, and managing more than 2 million square feet of downtown and suburban office space. ◆ "We're proud of the fact that

we have been able to play a major role in Class A office building development over the past decade and look forward to continuing to serve the needs of our customers by providing a first-class office environment for them," says Michael W. Wells, president of REI Investments. "We are in the best position to meet the needs of our customers because we own and manage our properties. In addition, we provide expertise in development, leasing, property management, construction, and landscape services."

A MISSION OF ENHANCING PROPERTY INVESTMENTS

REI Investments owns properties in downtown Indianapolis, on the west side, and in Carmel. Much of this space is Class A office space; however, the company offers retail, industrial, and warehouse space as well as numerous building sites located within its office parks. In particular, REI's Meridian at 465 office park, which is the home of Thomson Consumer Electronics' corporate headquarters, offers several excellent office building sites with visibility and access to the interstate and Meridian Street.

REI's office properties include such well-known landmarks as 300 North Meridian, Gateway Plaza, Fidelity Plaza-Tower I and II, Landmark Center, Science & Technology Park, 11711 North Pennsylvania Street, and several properties on Congressional Boulevard. The firm is also developing new projects at Meridian Mark III, Fidelity Plaza IV, Meridian at 465, Meridian Technology Center, and Airport Technology Center.

NEW VENTURES FOR BETTER SERVICE

In January 1995 Browning Real Estate, Inc. was renamed REI Investments, Inc. Providing vibrant enthusiasm for the new venture, Michael W. Wells—a former real estate attorney who also served six years as director of development at Browning Investments—assumed the helm as president of REI Investments at its inception.

REI Investments retained REI Real Estate Services, Inc., formerly known as Browning Management, to manage its properties. REI Real Estate Services provides property management, accounting, financial reporting, human resources assistance, and computer support, as well as other services for REI Investments.

Building maintenance also falls under the direction of REI Real Estate Services. Tailored to fit the

REI'S OFFICE PROPERTIES INCLUDE SUCH WELL-KNOWN INDIANAPOLIS LANDMARKS AS (CLOCKWISE FROM BELOW) GATEWAY PLAZA, 111 CONGRESSIONAL BOULEVARD, AND 11711 NORTH PENNSYLVANIA STREET.

◀ WM PHOTOGRAPHIC SERVICES

needs of clients, these services include 24-hour emergency response, fire and life safety programs, Americans with Disabilities Act (ADA) compliance, and preventive maintenance.

BMI Construction Services, a branch of REI Real Estate Services, offers high-quality general contracting, construction management, and

other construction-related services. BMI Landscape Services provides complete landscape and irrigation services.

LEADING THE COMMUNITY

Wells is an active community leader. He serves as president of the Indianapolis Airport Authority and participates

in other local organizations including the Volunteers of America, the Steve Goldsmith Committee, and the Indiana Recreational Development Commission. He also serves on the boards of a number of organizations, including the Indianapolis Project, Indianapolis Zoo, YMCA of Greater Indianapolis, and Indianapolis Economic Development Corporation.

"Real estate is a local business," Wells says. "You have to know the community very well, which we strive to do. We plan to develop our extensive land holdings into build-to-suit offices and warehouse space. We're in the process of revitalizing our real estate portfolio to enhance the value of our holdings in addition to developing new real estate properties. This is an important step in further enhancing the relationship between REI, its customers, and the community."

OTHER REI PROPERTIES INCLUDE 300 NORTH MERIDIAN (ABOVE LEFT) AND SCIENCE & TECHNOLOGY PARK (ABOVE RIGHT).

ALSO LOCATED IN INDIANAPOLIS ARE REI'S LANDMARK CENTER (LEFT) AND FIDELITY PLAZA (BELOW).

N MANY REGARDS, MARTIN UNIVERSITY IS SIMILAR TO OTHER liberal arts schools in that it offers a wide variety of courses in numerous fields and has high academic expectations for its students. However, the university's focus on its unique student body sets Martin apart from other schools. By offering a creative approach to learning, Martin gives adult, low-income,

and minority students a chance to expand their horizons through their desire to learn. The university is also unique in offering students credit for life learning that is college level and can be documented.

Martin has created a multicultural curriculum with bachelor of arts and science degrees in 26 different majors, including religious studies, business, marketing, behavioral sciences, chemistry, biology, and addictions. Graduate degrees in

REVEREND FATHER BONIFACE HARDIN IS THE FOUNDER AND PRESIDENT OF MARTIN UNIVERSITY (RIGHT).

THE MARTIN UNIVERSITY PERFORMING ARTS CENTER (BELOW) HOSTS MANY CAMPUS AND COMMUNITY EVENTS. ADJACENT TO THE CENTER IS THE BERNICE FRACTION FINE ARTS BUILDING.

community psychology and urban ministry studies are also available.

FOUNDED ON CARING PRINCIPLES

Martin University was founded in 1977 by Reverend Father Boniface Hardin, O.S.B., who also serves as president. Hardin named the university in memory of Dr. Martin Luther King Jr. and St. Martin de Porres, both of whom cared about serving the physical, spiritual, mental, and intellectual needs of people—especially the poor.

The university was incorporated in 1979, and in 1980 it received candidacy status with the North Central Association of Colleges and Schools. Regional accreditation was granted in 1987, and the name was changed to Martin University in 1990, the same year the school received permission from the North Central Association to offer its master's programs.

The main nine-building campus is today located on Avondale Place in the inner-city neighbor-

hood of Brightwood. Many of the buildings were once occupied by St. Francis de Sales Catholic parish. The original campus, located at 35th Street and College Avenue, is still used for outreach initiatives, such as an educational AIDS program targeted at the African-American community. In addition, the university runs health clinics for staff, students, and Indianapolis citizens.

PROVIDING HIGHER EDUCATION FOR ALL

The philosophy of Martin University is that higher education should be made available to all who can benefit from it. Hardin says that many believe the poor are powerless, but this is not true at Martin. "We don't believe that. We believe that if you're free in mind, you're free. If you can't read and write and figure, then you're in bondage," he maintains.

More than 600 graduates have passed through Martin's doors. Some have gone on to pursue advanced degrees, including seven who have completed doctoral degrees and one who has completed his doctoral studies at Oxford University. Approximately 550 students attend classes each semester, with an average age of 40. Fifty percent of the student body are women.

In addition to offering traditional academic courses, Martin opens its doors to seniors and children who wish to attend computer courses and summer school programs. Economic- and political-empowerment seminars are open to the public. Martin also reaches out to the inmates at the Indiana Women's Prison. As of May 1995, a total of 17 students have graduated from the university's Lady Elizabeth campus at the prison.

MYNELLE GARDNER AND SISTER JANE SCHILLING CONFER BEFORE TEAM-TEACHING A CLASS ON URBAN EDUCATION (LEFT).

While the university does not have a sports program, it does excel in its dramatic and musical productions. Since 1993 Martin has put on an annual theatrical production on the life of Frederick Douglass, a former slave whose work as an abolitionist led to his appointment as U.S. minister to Haiti. Other programs include productions of operas; plays by Shakespeare and Nobel Prize-winning Nigerian playwright Wole Soyinka, among others; and the appearance of the Carmel Symphony Orchestra with Martin faculty member Andrea Lacy Perry as soloist.

Although students are encouraged to remember the history of their forefathers and foremothers, Martin urges them to look to the future and to expand their horizons globally. Hardin, for example, promotes student participation in the language programs, which include some travel abroad.

Many staff and faculty members have global ties, representing Afghanistan, South Africa, Nigeria, Japan, and China, as well as a variety of religions, including Judaism, Christianity, and Islam. Of the 36 faculty members on staff, 18 hold a Ph.D. or J.D. and the remainder hold master's degrees. An additional 38 people serve as full- or part-time support staff.

LEADING COMMUNITIES INTO THE FUTURE

Hardin is actively involved with many city committees and organizations, including GIPC (the Greater Indianapolis Progress Committee), the Indianapolis Salvation Army, the President Benjamin Harrison Home, and the Sickle Cell Center. "We try to be a part of the mainstream, yet, at the same time, touch the lives of those who have been rejected," Hardin says.

Hardin believes the university will continue to play an important role in minority and lower-income communities of Indianapolis. He

hopes to see Martin develop programs in early childhood development and parenting, programs for underlearners—those who have not continued their education—and programs to prepare high school students to enter college or the business world.

Hardin foresees the development of doctoral programs in urban ministry studies and community psychology so that more professionals will be available to assist in healing the community. The founding president's dream also includes building the World Cultural Center, which has already been designed and will ultimately enhance a global exchange program.

"We're always in the state of becoming, always meeting unmet needs," says Hardin. "If we're not willing to change, then we have no business existing. We have to really be ready to meet the needs of the times and of the future."

KAMIA JACKSON SHOWS BARBARA CARTER A NEW SWEATSHIRT IN THE MARTIN UNIVERSITY BOOKSTORE (ABOVE).

MARTIN UNIVERSITY STAFF MEMBERS KENT BUELL AND PHYLLIS CARR GREET ONE ANOTHER ON CAMPUS (LEFT).

ORTHSIDE CARDIOLOGY, P.C. HAS MADE A CONTINUING COMMIT-
ment to the care and treatment of heart disease and has responded
with a legacy of leadership and innovation that is unparalleled in
Indiana. Northside is dedicated to providing appropriate utilization
of cardiovascular services, quality clinical outcomes, and cost-
effective care. ◆ Northside was founded in Indianapolis in 1977

by Edward F. Steinmetz, M.D.,
J Stanley Hillis, M.D., and
Donald A. Rothbaum, M.D.,
and has grown over two decades
to achieve international prominence. For the people of Indiana,
Northside provides the resources,
technology, and benefits of a large
practice with a focus on one-to-
one patient relationships.

RIGHT: DR. CLIFFORD HALLAM
(LEFT) ASSISTS DR. MARTIN SEE
DURING A CARDIAC CATHETERIZA-
TION IN THE NORTHSIDE CARDIAC
CATHETERIZATION LABORATORY.

EXPANDING COMMUNITY ACCESS

With its established net-
work of cardiovascular
specialists, Northside advances
medical knowledge in the field
of cardiovascular medicine and
enhances cardiovascular care
throughout the state. "We're
unique in that we started in Indianapolis at St. Vincent and have
grown by taking our services to
other cities and smaller communities," says Managing Physician
Clifford C. Hallam, M.D.

The Northside Cardiology
offices are located at the Indiana
Heart Institute Professional Office
Building, adjacent to the Cardiovascular Center at St. Vincent
Hospital. The practice also has
offices throughout central Indiana,
including facilities in Columbus,
Greenfield, Greenwood, Lafayette,

BELOW: DR. MICHAEL BALL (LEFT)
AND DR. RONALD LANDIN DISCUSS
THE RESULTS OF A NUCLEAR STUDY.

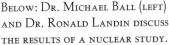

Anderson, Carmel, and Kokomo.
Outreach clinics are held in Green-
castle, South Bend, Connersville,
Rushville, Logansport, Winamac,
Elwood, Peru, and Knox.

CARDIOVASCULAR EXPERTISE

Northside has among its medical staff some of the most
respected cardiologists in the
United States. All cardiologists
affiliated with Northside are
board-certified or board-eligible
in cardiovascular medicine.

Northside is making a significant and lasting contribution in
cardiovascular care by providing
daily clinical training to medical
students and by offering advanced
fellowship programs for specific
areas of cardiology. Annual conferences are held for primary care
physicians. Other courses and
seminars are offered throughout
the year for physicians and nurses
on a variety of topics related to
the field.

◄ WILBUR MONTGOMERY

Whether through an innovative interventional procedure or
pharmacologic therapy, Northside
is leading the way in the care of
cardiovascular patients. The physicians are involved in several areas
of medical research, allowing them
to evaluate and make available to
patients the latest advances in the
treatment of heart disease. "Because

we are on the cutting edge of cardiovascular care, we are often called
upon to evaluate new products in
view of the volume of experience
we have," says Hallam.

THE RESOURCES BEHIND NORTHSIDE CARDIOLOGY

As a comprehensive resource,
Northside is committed to
meeting the needs of cardiovascular patients throughout the state,
including education, prevention,
diagnosis, treatment, and rehabilitation. To ensure that patients
receive the most appropriate,
cost-effective, high-quality care
available, Northside developed
a primary care network in 1992.
This network includes 32 primary care physicians and sub-
specialists in addition to its
37 cardiologists providing care
within 27 offices and clinics
throughout Indiana.

A COMMITMENT TO CARING

Northside is dedicated to uti-
lizing the finest methods to
produce the best possible results
for its patients. This dedication
to innovation by the entire organization guarantees that Northside
Cardiology and all affiliated facilities will remain a leader in cardiac
and primary care for years to
come.

_I_NDIANAPOLIS _BUSINESS JOURNAL_ PLAYS AN ESSENTIAL ROLE in the city's news reporting by covering the local business community. The niche was a natural, and it provided the key to success for the weekly, which is targeted to upper and middle management, CEOs, professionals, and business owners. "The newspaper has been extremely well received," says Chris Katterjohn, president of IBJ Corporation, the newspaper's parent company.

On April 15, 1995, _Indianapolis Business Journal_ celebrated its 15th anniversary at the Indiana Roof Ballroom with 750 people in attendance. "It was a real testimony for the paper and for its standing as an institution in the business community," says Katterjohn.

ROOTS OF A PUBLISHING COMPANY

Local businessmen and primary shareholders Michael S. Maurer and Robert Schloss purchased IBJ Corporation from its out-of-state owners in 1990. The company now owns three local newspapers: _Indianapolis Business Journal_, with a circulation of 15,000; _The Indiana Lawyer_, a biweekly statewide newspaper for attorneys with a circulation of 6,500; and the _Court & Commercial Record_, a legal notice publication that is published five days each week for its 800 central Indiana subscribers.

Over the years, _Indianapolis Business Journal_ has honed its focus on the local business community. "The daily newspaper and the mass media in general do not report on the local business community the way businesspeople like to read about it. The daily newspaper can't afford to give 50 pages to the business community alone, although the community was craving that kind of coverage," says Katterjohn. "Our focus hasn't changed; we've just gotten better at what we do."

Indianapolis Business Journal also publishes its popular _Book of Lists_, a comprehensive annual listing of the area's top 25 companies in different categories. The _Book of Lists_ has been expanded to include industry information and demo-

graphics, and is used as a resource by local businesses for sales leads, research, fund-raising, and job searches. It is sold in print format as well as on computer disks designed for mass marketing. "The _Book of Lists_ has become one of the most used and most popular reference tools for Indianapolis businesspeople," says Katterjohn.

Also published by IBJ Corporation are _Who's Who_, _Small Business Monthly_, _Not-for-Profits of Note_, and Indy 500 and Brickyard 400 festival programs, among other publications. In December 1995 the company published _Business in Indianapolis_, a 912-page book that includes an overview of the city and more than 850 individual company profiles.

TRUE TO THE INDIANAPOLIS COMMUNITY

IBJ Corporation remains actively involved in the community while maintaining its status as an independent, credible news source. The company sponsors a number of local events in addition to donating advertising space and manpower in support of the city's not-for-profit community.

A new venture is in the making in which IBJ Corporation will serve as a continuing legal education (CLE) provider for Indiana attorneys needing credit hours to maintain their licenses. The company will provide classes, management, and materials for an accredited curriculum approved by the CLE Commission. "It's going to be a good opportunity for our _Indiana Lawyer_ newspaper and for attorneys," says Katterjohn.

The future looks bright for IBJ Corporation. Plans call for further expansion into contract publishing, as well as involvement in other book projects and electronic publishing. In addition to _Indianapolis Business Journal_, the broad array of publications offered by the company is not only an indispensable resource for the business community, but also a great asset to the city of Indianapolis.

THE IBJ MANAGEMENT TEAM INCLUDES (TOP, FROM LEFT) CHRIS KATTERJOHN, PRESIDENT AND PUBLISHER; GLENDA RUSSELL, PUBLISHER; SHERI LINDSAY, CIRCULATION; GREG MORRIS, ADVERTISING; TOM HARTON, EDITOR; CHRIS BANGUIS, EDITOR; KIM HARLOW, MARKETING; AND PATRICIA KEIFFNER, PRODUCTION.

IBJ CORPORATION CURRENTLY OWNS _INDIANAPOLIS BUSINESS JOURNAL_, _THE INDIANA LAWYER_, AND THE _COURT & COMMERCIAL RECORD_.

CONSECO, INC.

ONSECO, INC., HEADQUARTERED JUST NORTH OF INDIANAPOLIS in Carmel, is a financial services holding company with more than $17 billion in assets. Through centralized management, the company acquires life insurance companies and builds their value. Stephen C. Hilbert, Conseco's founder, believes that consolidation will greatly reduce the number of life insurance companies in the 21st century.

BUILDING A VISION

Hilbert—who is also Conseco's chairman, president, and CEO—formed the company in 1979. His goal was to build a holding company that acquires existing insurance companies, and improves their efficiency and overall performance by consolidating administrative functions and refocusing marketing efforts.

"I think we really are operators who understand the workings of the life insurance industry about as well as anyone. We also have the entrepreneurial strength of going out and seeing opportunities, then quickly acting on the opportunities that create value," says Hilbert. "Being financial people is the nature of the beast, but our real strengths are our unique operating capabilities and our entrepreneurial spirit."

Hilbert's entrepreneurial spirit emerged from humble beginnings. As a student at Indiana State University, he once sold encyclopedias door-to-door as a summer job, and soon decided his aptitude for sales far exceeded his interest in college. After accumulating $19,000 at that job, Hilbert was drafted into the army. Upon discharge, drawing on his earlier success in sales, Hilbert became an insurance salesman. He held positions with United Home Life Insurance Co. and Aetna Life & Casualty, only to decide he had his own ideas about the insurance industry.

Hilbert borrowed $10,000 from his father to establish a start-up life insurance organization in 1979. By 1980 the company had found enough investors to reach its goal of $3 million in financing. Conseco went public in 1985. In 1990 the company formed Conseco Capital Partners L.P., which acquired Great American Reserve, Jefferson National, Beneficial Standard Life, and Bankers Life. A second acquisition partnership in 1994 raised $624 million of capital commitments from 35 outside investors. The company's stock has increased 30-fold in value since the initial public offering.

FROM START-UP TO LEADERSHIP

Conseco's strengths have propelled the company into a position of industry leadership. In 1982, its first year of actual operation, the company made $30,000; by 1995 earnings had reached $220 million. Conseco's strategy for profitability is based on knowing its products and eliminating unprofitable ones.

The company's conservative business philosophy encompasses three major principles: maintaining an efficient operation, carefully managing investments, and focusing resources on profitable products. Conseco is among the most effective in the industry at operating efficiently, which has been measured by comparing the company's operational expenses to the percentage of managed assets. In managing its portfolio, Conseco has avoided problem investments like junk bonds and derivatives. The company has also placed its greatest emphasis on products that return its invested cash quickly, such as those that bring in substantial revenues within their first year of availability.

Conseco also applies its operating principles to its internal opera-

CONSECO IS HEADQUARTERED JUST NORTH OF INDIANAPOLIS IN CARMEL.

CONSECO EMPLOYS MORE THAN
3,000 PEOPLE, INCLUDING 1,000
WHO ARE BASED IN CARMEL.

tions. "If we're straying away from what got us here, we snap ourselves back to reality," says Hilbert. "We've taken commonsense business principles and applied them to the company and to the industry."

CHANGING WITH THE TIMES

Conseco moves and thrives with change. When times and prices are favorable, the company focuses on acquisitions. When prices for acquisitions are too high, the company seizes the opportunity to pursue internal growth. "From 1986 through 1989, there were numerous

acquisition opportunities," says Hilbert. "Today's prices are out of whack, so we will grow internally."

The process of determining what makes a successful acquisition involves in-depth analysis and a clear focus. "When we're looking at a company, we send teams from each of our departments. We take the company apart," says Hilbert. Four to six months are usually required to complete an acquisition; Conseco makes use of that time by continuing its analysis. "We want to understand exactly what we're buying," adds Hilbert. "It's not

rocket science. The truth is, it's very simple stuff. We just don't get sidetracked."

Conseco employs more than 3,000 people, including 1,000 who are based at its headquarters in Carmel. The company's four executive vice presidents are Rollin M. Dick, Ngaire E. Cuneo, Donald F. Gongaware, and Lawrence W. Inlow.

"Indianapolis is our home," says Hilbert. "We want to promote the business climate and support the city, Hamilton County, and the state." To that end, Conseco contributes generously to the United Way, Junior Achievement, the arts, sports, education, and municipal projects like Circle Centre Mall. Likewise, employees are encouraged to volunteer for local community service projects.

One company observer concludes, "Stephen Hilbert had a vision—not of what the company was going to be, but what the company needed to be. His genius lies in simple business principles that are practiced at Conseco with careful attention to detail. He understands how these principles can work, and he doesn't make it any more complicated than that."

THE COMPANY'S CONSERVATIVE
BUSINESS PHILOSOPHY ENCOMPASSES
THREE MAJOR PRINCIPLES: MAINTAINING AN EFFICIENT OPERATION, CAREFULLY MANAGING INVESTMENTS, AND
FOCUSING RESOURCES ON PROFITABLE
PRODUCTS.

AS A VISIONARY LEADER, WILLIAM MAYS TOOK MAYS Chemical Company, Inc. from ground zero to $50 million in revenues after a decade in business. Today, the company's revenues soar beyond $100 million annually with consistent growth and earnings. ♦ Mays Chemical, headquartered in Indianapolis, is a full-line chemical distributor that serves the food, pharmaceutical,

and automotive industries. A bulk terminal facility is located in Indianapolis, and additional facilities are located in Chicago and in Taylor, Michigan.

CLIMBING THE CORPORATE LADDER

Mays, who serves as president of the company, graduated from Indiana University with a degree in chemistry. He left his first job as a lubricant tester in Indianapolis with Link Belt to become a sales representative for Procter & Gamble in

southern Indiana. Mays soon took charge of major accounts, such as L.S. Ayres, Woolco, Topps, and G.C. Murphy. "I was really pretty good," says Mays. "I was on my way to becoming the youngest black sales manager in the country."

After three successful years at Procter & Gamble, Mays accepted a fellowship that led to an MBA from Indiana University. During the fellowship period, he worked in market planning at Eli Lilly and Company in Indianapolis. "There was such an underrepresentation of qualified blacks in the business environment. I had 10 or 12 job offers just after finishing my MBA," recalls Mays. "I chose the least glamorous job, and one that didn't pay the most."

Mays accepted an offer to be the assistant to the president at Cummins Engine Company in Columbus, Indiana, which moved him into an excellent position to learn the business. After nine months, he moved to a middle management position in corporate planning, which gave him responsibilities for worldwide coordination of forecasting for engine demand.

"Cummins is where I really learned and understood planning. All of that experience was first-rate in knowing how to deal with a

billion-dollar company. I made the most of every opportunity," says Mays.

IN TRANSITION

Mays left Cummins after four years to become president of Specialty Chemical, a small subsidiary chemical distributorship owned by Chemical Investors in Indianapolis. During the three years under his leadership, sales increased from $300,000 to $5 million. "The attraction was being in control, testing whether I could apply everything I'd learned to operate all the facets of a company. I actually took a 25 percent pay cut. I'm not sure I'd do that again," says Mays. In 1980 he left Specialty Chemical, refusing to market the company as a minority-run business when it wasn't.

Three days after his resignation, Mays founded Mays Chemical in Indianapolis. "There was no premeditated plan to start the company. I just needed a job," laughs Mays, now a self-made millionaire.

SUCCESS IN THE FAST LANE

Mays Chemical's year-to-year revenue growth averages about 25 percent. In 1993, based on revenues of $65 million, the company ranked 20th on a list

WILLIAM MAYS FOUNDED MAYS CHEMICAL IN 1980 (BELOW LEFT). SINCE THEN, THE COMPANY'S REVENUES HAVE SOARED BEYOND $100 MILLION ANNUALLY WITH CONSISTENT GROWTH AND EARNINGS.

HEADQUARTERED IN INDIANAPOLIS (BELOW RIGHT), MAYS HAS ADDITIONAL FACILITIES IN CHICAGO AND IN TAYLOR, MICHIGAN.

of the nation's 100 largest African-American-owned businesses compiled by *Black Enterprise* magazine. In 1994 the company ranked 14th on the list. Mays predicts revenues in 1995 will exceed $100 million, a figure he hopes eventually to double.

The building blocks of this extremely successful business have remained the same: price, quality, and service. "I started my business with a simple philosophy. If you are able to have excellent quality, competitive pricing, and outstanding service, it doesn't matter what color you are," says Mays.

"The company takes on my personality to some extent. Chemical companies don't have to be stale, stodgy, and conservative. They can be enthusiastic and outgoing. That's been part of our success. All of our vice presidents have been here 10 years or more, and the company is only 16 years old. It's not just a job; it's an experience," adds Mays.

COMMUNITY SERVICE: A PRIORITY

Community service is a top priority at Mays Chemical. Employees are encouraged to participate in community organizations of their choice and can do so on company time. Managers are often required to contribute time and money to a variety of community efforts. The company always matches such contributions, and company time and resources are made available when needed. In 1994, for example, Mays Chemical supported more than 300 community organizations with contributions in excess of $250,000.

From 1992 through 1995 Bill Mays served as the first African-American campaign chairman of the United Way of Central Indiana, leading one of the most successful campaigns in the country in 1992. Mays has also served as chairman of the Indiana Lottery and as cochairman of the Circle City Classic, and is a member of numerous boards throughout the city.

The company's managers have been active on boards of the Boys Club, Girls Club, Indiana Repertory Theatre, Red Cross of Central Indiana, Center for Leadership Development, YWCA, Big Sisters of Central Indiana, National Association of Black Accountants, and Indiana CPA Society.

Mays Chemical has also actively participated in the fund-raising and program development activities for many community organizations. Employees are active in churches and in grassroots organizations ranging from Little League to school organizations to Riley Hospital for Children.

"I've wondered how I could lead and make a difference for blacks coming after me," says Mays. "I've put African-Americans in places of leadership so that there would be representation at the Chamber of Commerce and the United Way for years to come. That presence will be there whether Bill Mays is there or not."

MAYS CHEMICAL IS A FULL-LINE CHEMICAL DISTRIBUTOR THAT SERVES THE FOOD, PHARMACEUTICAL, AND AUTOMOTIVE INDUSTRIES (TOP LEFT AND RIGHT).

THE COMPANY CELEBRATES THE GROUND BREAKING FOR A NEW CHICAGO FACILITY (BOTTOM).

ased in Indianapolis, Macmillan Publishing USA (MPU) is the reference division of Simon & Schuster, the publishing operation of Viacom Inc. MPU is the world's largest computer book publisher and a leader in the home and library reference markets. The Indianapolis company creates and distributes timely, authoritative, and entertaining information

in traditional media such as books, audiobooks, and videotapes, as well as in new media including CD-ROM and on-line formats.

Using the most advanced digital technology, Macmillan Publishing USA produces bound books within a matter of weeks, allowing for exploration of niche markets and alternative information delivery systems.

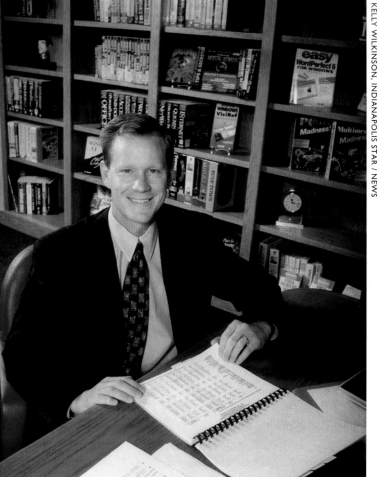

OF THE COMPANY'S 1,400 EMPLOYEES, 950 ARE BASED AT ITS HEADQUARTERS IN INDIANAPOLIS (ABOVE LEFT).

MACMILLAN PUBLISHING OPERATES UNDER THE DIRECTION OF SCOTT FLANDERS, WHO JOINED THE COMPANY IN 1982 AS DIRECTOR OF INTERNATIONAL SALES FOR QUE CORPORATION. HE WAS APPOINTED PRESIDENT IN 1994 (ABOVE RIGHT).

MPU comprises 1,400 employees, of which 950 are based in Indianapolis, with other locations in New York and California. The company's operating units are Macmillan Computer Publishing USA, Macmillan Reference USA, and Macmillan Online USA.

MACMILLAN COMPUTER PUBLISHING USA

The information revolution has created booming demand for computer reference and tutorial materials. Macmillan Computer Publishing (MCP), the world's largest computer book publisher, was founded in Indianapolis in 1981 as QUE Corporation, which produced the first book on using the IBM PC. In 1984 QUE published *Using 1-2-3*, the world's first microcomputer book to sell 1 million copies.

QUE was the beginning foundation of MCP, which eventually, through a series of mergers and acquisitions, became a division of Macmillan Publishing USA, created in 1994. MCP provides computer users of all abilities with the know-how to operate computer technology, and now has 11 separate publishing imprints. Tutorial and reference titles are published under the names QUE, Sams Publishing, sams.net, Borland Press, New Riders, Hayden, Adobe Press, BradyGAMES, Waite Group Press, Ziff-Davis Press, and Que Education and Training.

Among MCP's titles sold throughout the world are best-selling book series such as *Special Edition Using, Teach Yourself,*

Unleashed, Adobe Design Essentials, Starter Kits, Bible, How To, Inside, How It Works, and *PC Learning Labs* as well as video, PC, and arcade strategy game guides from BradyGAMES. Additionally, MCP publishes boxed and shrink-wrapped software under several of its imprints, as well as courseware materials at Que Education and Training.

MACMILLAN REFERENCE USA

Macmillan Reference USA publishes leading reference products for the scholarly and popular reference markets, with special emphasis on electronic media. In the popular reference market, Macmillan Reference

USA publishes world-renowned franchises including Betty Crocker, Burpee, Weight Watchers, Frommer's travel guides, J.K. Lasser tax guides, Webster's New World dictionaries, and ARCO academic and professional test preparations guides. Macmillan Reference USA also publishes language reference texts and general nonfiction titles in business, history, sports, health, and pet care, as well as a variety of general interest books, including the best-sellers *Politically Correct Bedtime Stories, Once Upon a More Enlightened Time,* and *Politically Correct Holiday Stories.*

A diverse list of encyclopedia, dictionary, atlas, and library reference sources is also published through Macmillan Reference USA's Schirmer, Scribner, and Twayne imprints. These books have won the Dartmouth Medal for editorial reference publishing five out of the last six years. Key titles include *Atlas of United States Environmental Issues, Encyclopedia of the Holocaust, Encyclopedia of American Social History, Encyclopedia of Sociology, Dictionary of the Middle Ages, Baker's Biographical Dictionary of Musicians,* and *Civilization of the Ancient Mediterranean: Greece and Rome.*

Within this division, Macmillan Digital USA publishes CD-ROM reference titles including *The War in Vietnam: A Multimedia Guide from CBS News and the New York Times, Politically Correct Bedtime Stories: Cyber-Sensitivity for Our Life & Times, Frommer's Interactive Travel Guides,* and *The Fighting Irish: The History of Notre Dame Football.*

MACMILLAN ONLINE

Macmillan Online is the company's Internet voice. Its award-winning Macmillan Information SuperLibrary Internet site digitally houses more than 6,000 titles for on-line preview and purchase, including world-famous brands like Betty Crocker cookbooks, Frommer's travel guides, *The Macmillan Baseball Encyclopedia,* and *Politically Correct Bedtime Stories.*

Macmillan Online provides millions of Internet users with access to the latest computer industry news, books, games, and software

as well as to industry experts and authors, and to Macmillan Publishing USA staff. It not only shows off the latest in technology and reference products, but gives users on-line catalogs and an electronic means of purchasing products.

THE FUTURE OF PUBLISHING

As the 21st century approaches, multiple-media publishing opportunities for reference and leisure-time information will continue to grow. The most successful publishers will be those with a rich content base, world-renowned brands, strong author relationships, and a deep institutional knowledge of what information people want and need and the formats they demand.

Both today and tomorrow, Macmillan Publishing USA brings a fountain of information to the world.

MCP HAS ITS OWN INTERNAL DESIGN DEPARTMENT, RESPONSIBLE FOR THE CREATION OF ALL BOOK COVERS FOR NINE OF THE 11 IMPRINTS. WITH APPROXIMATELY 15 GRAPHIC ARTISTS AND DESIGNERS, THE DESIGN DEPARTMENT PRODUCES MORE THAN 500 COVERS EACH YEAR.

THE MACMILLAN REFERENCE USA OPERATING UNIT PUBLISHES LEADING REFERENCE PRODUCTS FOR THE SCHOLARLY AND POPULAR REFERENCE MARKETS, AS WELL AS LANGUAGE REFERENCE TEXTS AND GENERAL NONFICTION TITLES IN BUSINESS, HISTORY, SPORTS, HEALTH, AND PET CARE (BELOW).

ROWE CHIZEK, THE NATION'S 10TH-LARGEST CERTIFIED PUBLIC accounting and consulting firm and the largest based in Indiana, opened its Indianapolis office in 1982. Since then, the office has grown from 20 to 120 employees, and from the 14th-largest to the fourth-largest accounting firm in the city. ♦ "When we entered the Indianapolis market, we had no clients, five partners,

and eight staff members," says Mark L. Hildebrand, partner-in-charge of the Systems Consulting Group. "We hung out our shingle and said, 'We're here; we're ready to compete.' "

Just two years later, Crowe Chizek was offered the opportunity to partner with Hewlett-Packard to develop an automated order-entry and inventory-control system for AT&T. "That project put us on the map," recalls Hildebrand. "The market was instantly made aware of our vast service capability." Today, Crowe Chizek's Systems Consulting Group is one of the largest of its kind in the Midwest.

The decision to combine its tax and audit capability with its systems consulting expertise in servicing its key business segments contributed immediately to Crowe Chizek's success. "The market was quick to accept a firm that was able to provide the breadth of service similar to that of national firms, but on a more localized basis. Indianapolis afforded us a unique opportunity to leverage our full-service capability," says J. Kevin McGrath, partner-in-charge of Crowe Chizek's Indianapolis office.

Headquartered in South Bend, Crowe Chizek maintains eight full-service offices in addition to two specialized offices. One specialty office, located in Fort Lauderdale, Florida, provides audit, tax, and consulting services to automobile dealerships. Crowe Chizek's other specialty office, in Redhill, England, markets and supports lending software utilized mainly by the financial institutions industry.

In Indianapolis, the firm's business strategies are administered by five primary groups: the Systems Consulting Group, which provides planning, implementation, and improvements for clients' business systems, processes, and information technologies; the Financial Institutions Group, which provides audit, tax, and consulting services to financial institutions; the Manufacturing Services Group, which provides comparable services for manufacturers; the Public Sector Group, which provides financial advisory and consulting services to municipalities and other government subdivisions; and the Emerging Specialties Group, which services a variety of other industries including not-for-profit, hospitality, health care, auto, and transportation.

SERVING INDIANAPOLIS

"We are diversified, yet focused," says Hildebrand. "We cultivate and pursue the industries we know how to serve best. We provide for their total enterprise needs." McGrath adds, "We maintain a high level of partner involvement, and this, coupled with our low levels of staff turnover, ensures a consistent, value-added level of service."

The firm's Indianapolis office has distinguished itself by its high level of involvement in shaping the city's future. For example, Crowe Chizek was extensively involved in the privatization efforts that later resulted in Indianapolis becoming a national model for privatization.

Crowe Chizek not only gives generously of its time and expertise to its clients, but to Indianapolis as well, participating in numerous civic projects and contributing to a wide array of charitable causes.

"We came to Indianapolis in 1982 with few people recognizing our name," laughs Hildebrand. "Now our reputation and ranking speak for themselves."

CROWE CHIZEK IS THE NATION'S 10TH-LARGEST CERTIFIED PUBLIC ACCOUNTING AND CONSULTING FIRM, AND THE LARGEST BASED IN INDIANA (RIGHT).

THE INDIANAPOLIS OFFICE MEASURES ITS SUCCESS BY THE SUCCESS OF ITS CLIENTS.

WE CREATE SUCCESS STORIES.℠

ELAMON, A GREEK WORD FOR "SUPPORT," APTLY DESCRIBES the nature of Telamon Corporation's role in the telecommunications industry. The Indianapolis-based firm supports telephone companies and original equipment manufacturers by providing a variety of products and services. ♦ In 1984 Albert Chen began his journey, as an entrepreneur, into the

telecommunications industry by founding Telamon. With only a general sense of direction and no specific services in mind, Chen set out to address the telecommunications problems of his new customers. In those early days, Telamon had only two employees—Albert and his wife, Margaret.

Today Telamon has grown into a diversified company that provides services to many areas of the telecommunications industry. It now employs more than 120 people and closed its 1995 fiscal year with sales of $108 million. Albert and Margaret are particularly proud of the fact that Telamon is a company of great ethnic diversity.

SERVICES AND PRODUCTS

Following the original vision, Telamon has evolved as a company that provides customized telecommunications products and services to meet specific customer needs. Albert has positioned the company as a place for one-stop shopping. Thus, he seldom needs to tell customers that they desire something Telamon cannot deliver. This can-do attitude often means that Telamon must invest heavily in new technologies and enter into areas where it has little experience.

The cornerstone of Telamon's success in growing into these new ventures has been its total commitment to quality and on-time delivery. No matter what it takes, Albert and his team will deliver what they have promised on schedule. In 1994 Telamon achieved ISO 9002 quality certification for three of its subsidiaries. This certification assures that customers can expect a consistently high level of quality.

Currently, Telamon's services include loaner phone programs for

many of the nation's largest phone companies. Under these programs, Telamon ships more than 16,000 phones each month to telephone company customers and provides the support services necessary to assure total customer satisfaction. Telamon also offers marketing support programs that help large companies get their products and services to market as rapidly as possible. Telamon's network infrastructure services are directed primarily at telephone companies nationwide. Telamon technicians build and assemble complex communications equipment for many of the regional Bell operating companies.

Most recently, Telamon has taken the one-stop shop approach to bring digital connectivity to the mass market. Under the "I Care" program, carriers and their customers have one place to call for expertise, equipment, and provisioning for ISDN service.

Albert believes that high-quality customer service is the key to Telamon's success. He also credits

his employees with the role they have played. "Everything I have achieved has come from the people who have helped me and the dedication of our staff," says Albert. In recognition of the contributions of employees, Telamon sets aside a significant portion of its annual profits for sharing with all employees. Because Albert recognizes the value of an employee's family, Telamon offers cash rewards for employees' children who demonstrate academic achievement and gives a monthly stipend for the purchase of educational materials to all employees with young children. Because of these and other similar programs, Telamon received the 1994 Family Life Enhancement Award from Methodist Hospital.

Living up to its name for more than a decade, Telamon continues to provide support services for its clients' evolving telecommunications needs. As people and businesses around the world adopt new ways to communicate, Telamon will continue to offer its expertise and support.

FOUNDED IN 1984 BY ALBERT CHEN, TELAMON CORPORATION HAS GROWN INTO A DIVERSIFIED COMPANY THAT PROVIDES SERVICES TO MANY AREAS OF THE TELECOMMUNICATIONS INDUSTRY.

WHEN ARCHITECTS HAROLD D. GARRISON AND CORNELIUS M. Alig combined their talents in 1982 to form Mansur Development Corporation, they carved a niche in the marketplace with a focus on redevelopment. Their highly successful business venture, today known as the Mansur Group, boasts a real estate portfolio with a development value of more than $500 million.

"The architecture business had been victimized by the recession," recalls Alig, vice chairman and COO. "Rather than wait for the phone to ring, we proceeded with our plans to develop, taking advantage of the availability of historic downtown Indianapolis property and the growing demand for office space."

FOUNDATIONS IN REDEVELOPMENT

Little downtown renovation had occurred by the early 1980s, as most Indianapolis developers were targeting new construction in the suburbs. Mansur's first project was the renovation of the Century Building, which was built in 1901 and is now listed on the National Register of Historic Places. Upon its completion in 1983, the

nucleus of a 180,000-square-foot, mixed-use complex. Completed in 1986, Lockerbie Marketplace provided a much-needed downtown grocery and convenience shopping complex in addition to more than 100,000 square feet of office space.

Mansur's renovation portfolio also features several other projects in the heart of the downtown business district, including the Omni Severin Hotel, the Illinois Building, and the MWA Building. Perhaps the group's most dramatic downtown project was the renovation of the old Indianapolis Rubber Company factory on South East Street for Farm Bureau Insurance. Mansur ambitiously assembled a 10-acre site with the renovated factory serving as a 350,000-square-foot headquarters building.

In October 1989 Mansur obtained $153 million in financing for Mansur Center, a downtown

mixed-use project that includes more than 1.2 million square feet of office and retail space in three buildings on or near Monument Circle. The complex is anchored by Market Tower, an impressive, 568,000-square-foot office building.

EXPANDING THE PORTFOLIO

With steady growth ahead and a firm foundation in office and mixed-use renovation and new construction, Mansur diversified its services in 1988 to include planned residential communities. Hamilton Proper—a 1,400-acre, master-planned community in nearby Fishers—allowed the company's entry into large, planned residential community projects. "Hamilton Proper is the state's largest self-contained village, with distinctive homesites and neighborhoods situated

Century Building was the largest privately funded renovation project in Indiana, launching Mansur's redevelopment opportunities as well as the renaissance of this historic wholesale district.

The group's next big project was Lockerbie Marketplace, formerly a Sears department store built in 1929. The building was renovated and combined with two new office structures, forming the

around a championship golf course and a private golf and country club," says Garrison, who serves as Mansur's chairman. In spring 1996 the group broke ground in Oakland County, Michigan, for the Villages of Oakhurst, an 800-acre community that features a private golf course. With the growth of its planned residential communities, Mansur is now focusing on diver-

of the city's urban core, while introducing new developments that contribute to downtown's ongoing resurgence as a city center. For example, the group has worked with the city and two local community development corporations (CDCs) in developing 500 Place and the Stewart Center, office projects in the historic Canal District in downtown Indianapolis.

sifying into home construction through a new housing division, with primary focus on urban and high-density suburban housing.

Mansur's continued success has led to greater diversity in the portfolio of services it offers. The company now provides a variety of services for commercial and residential real estate, in addition to an in-depth understanding of the financial requirements. In an effort to help growth in urban areas, Mansur has formed new alliances by providing consulting services to municipalities and community development corporations. Mansur also offers real estate financial planning and asset management services. The Mansur Group's affiliated partnerships and companies today employ more than 450 people.

A COMMITMENT TO DOWNTOWN

Cofounders Garrison and Alig have demonstrated a firm commitment to downtown Indianapolis not only by locating the Mansur Group's headquarters in the Market Tower, but also by participating in the preservation

In July 1995 work began on Watermark, a three-year project offering the first new home ownership opportunity on the canal itself. "We carefully researched this project, looking nationally for the best residential prototype for an urban environment," says Garrison. "We selected a traditionally southern architectural style for our home designs, which is easily accommodated on narrow lots while still allowing the occupant plenty of privacy." Scheduled for completion

in 1997, Watermark occupies one city block between North and Walnut streets.

THE MANSUR SUCCESS FORMULA

The way you succeed is by innovation and growth," explains Alig. Garrison agrees, adding that Mansur's "diversification is based on access to capital. We've built a strong base of business relationships and a process to access capital over the years. That and a strong management team have provided us with growth opportunities."

The company has grown far beyond its humble beginnings when Alig and Garrison were its only employees, answering their own phones while making plans for the future. Now, with steady growth and diversification, the Mansur Group has become a well-known regional company. "As long as the capital markets continue to respond favorably to our projects," smiles Alig, "there are no limits."

CLOCKWISE FROM ABOVE: MANSUR'S FIRST DEVELOPMENT PROJECT WAS THE CENTURY BUILDING RENOVATION, COMPLETED IN 1983.

COMPLETED IN 1986, THE 180,000-SQUARE-FOOT, MIXED-USE LOCKERBIE MARKETPLACE PROVIDED A MUCH-NEEDED DOWNTOWN GROCERY AND CONVENIECE SHOPPING COMPLEX IN ADDITION TO MORE THAN 100,000 SQUARE FEET OF OFFICE SPACE.

MANSUR'S VERMONT ROW TOWN HOMES ARE LOCATED ADJACENT TO HISTORIC LOCKERBIE SQUARE.

OUNG & LARAMORE IS A LITTLE BURDENED BY ITS REPUTATION AS the region's leading creative shop. "To a lot of people—businesspeople—'creative' means 'self-indulgent,'" says David Young, "and a lot of ad firms around the country have proven those businesspeople right with clever ads that do more to satisfy copywriters' urges to write comedy than to advance their clients' efforts to do

business successfully. So we spend a lot of time proving that our primary strength is strategic thinking and that creativity is not only compatible but a necessary companion to it in successful communication."

A Steak n Shake ad that asks "Why do we slice our pickles the long way?" may seem like comedy, but in fact builds the legend of Steak n Shake around real attributes of the restaurant. "If we use humor in an ad," says Young, "it is derived naturally out of the product, not out of an old *Saturday Night Live* skit."

In much of Young & Laramore's work, good, rational communication comes off as unbridled creativity. In each case, the agency has thought through the strategic position with an almost cold, rigorous objectivity. Red Gold cajoles consumers into understanding why a midwestern tomato is so flavorful. First Indiana Bank astonishes customers with the self-awareness of its slogan, "Because banking shouldn't take up a lot of space in your life." McNamara Florist doesn't give the public just another billboard; it turns a billboard into an artistic expression of the color and motion of flowers.

What is seen by the public as inspired creativity is, from the

Young & Laramore perspective, simply good professional practice. What was once a billboard that proffered standard-issue grocery and used car ads is now "Ossip's Eyes," a landmark in Broad Ripple, Indianapolis' cultural center. The billboard performs its advertising function in a way that goes beyond the usual strengths (and weaknesses) of the outdoor medium by becoming a piece of public sculpture—creating a kind of sponsored gift to the community. That's in large part Young & Laramore's philosophy: "Better to engage the public with an idea than to attack them."

FROM LONG-WAYS PICKLES AND BEAN CROCKS TO CHEEKY GRILL GUYS, THE LONG-RUNNING TV CAMPAIGN FOR STEAK N SHAKE TAKES ADVANTAGE OF THE UNIQUE ASPECTS OF THE RESTAURANT. THE COMPANY'S PARTNERSHIP WITH YOUNG & LARAMORE HAS HELPED CREATE SUSTAINED DOUBLE-DIGIT GROWTH FOR FIVE YEARS RUNNING.

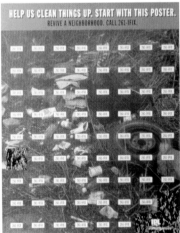

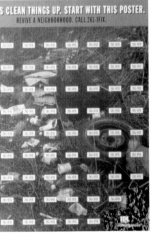

THIS INTERACTIVE POSTER FOR INDIANAPOLIS POWER & LIGHT'S REVIVE A NEIGHBORHOOD CAMPAIGN HELPS PEOPLE WHO WANT TO VOLUNTEER. AS INDIVIDUALS TAKE A PHONE NUMBER WITH THEM, THE IMAGE CHANGES FROM TRASH TO GRASS, A SEAMLESS ANALOGY FOR THE WORK THEY WILL VOLUNTEER TO DO.

Called the city's best public sculpture by one critic, this billboard for Ossip Optometry is not just art. Ossip's business has tripled, and the firm can track 90 percent of its client base to advertising.

TV ads gently persuade viewers about the geographic benefits of growing tomatoes in the Midwest as Red Gold does. Opening a can of Red Gold tomatoes proves it. Sales in the company's TV markets have overtaken big national brands.

Over the course of a few weeks, abstract flowers gradually appeared on McNamara Florist's billboard. In creating expressions of the color and motion of flowers, Young & Laramore invited the public to join in the interpretation.

BATES USA/MIDWEST

HISTORIC ADVERTISING EXCELLENCE THRIVES IN THE OFFICES OF Bates Midwest: Ted Bates, the advertising agency that first put a presidential candidate (Dwight Eisenhower) on television, that ingrained "melts in your mouth, not in your hands" in the public's mind, and that established the USP (unique selling proposition) concept . . . McCaffrey and McCall, the New York

STAYING COMPETITIVE REQUIRES MAXIMIZING INDIANA'S BUDGET DOLLARS AND POSITIONING THE STATE AS A SHORT-TRIP DESTI-NATION. INQUIRIES INCREASED DRAMATICALLY THROUGH BATES' CREATIVE APPROACH (ABOVE).

BATES CREATED MATERIALS LIKE THIS PRINT AD TO FEND OFF A HOSTILE TAKEOVER OF PSI ENERGY— NOW CINERGY—IN A CAMPAIGN THAT REQUIRED SPONTANEOUS ADVERTISING (CENTER).

IN CONTRAST, ARCHITECTURAL MATERIALS ARE SPECIFIED AS EARLY AS THREE YEARS AWAY FROM THE ACTUAL GROUND BREAKING. BUSI-NESS-TO-BUSINESS ADVERTISING IS USUALLY PRODUCT-SPECIFIC, BUT SOMETIMES ALLOWS FOR SOME AESTHETIC DREAMING (BOTTOM RIGHT).

advertising agency heralded for its cutting-edge commercials for Mercedes and Tiffany's . . . Backer and Spielvogel, the international advertising agency known for its worldwide branding capabilities.

From these well-established roots rises Bates Midwest, an energetic and flourishing advertising resource headquartered in the heart of the Midwest—Indianapolis.

The uptown Manhattan-like atmosphere of the Bates Midwest offices in Indianapolis sets the pace for the local advertising community. And there's more than a spiral staircase linking the 30,000 square feet of space. There's the spirit and the excitement of the people inside. It's the complexity and the joy of problem solving. Managing Director Daniel B. Roman has assembled some of the best creative minds in the business.

"I always point out that we're not just a local agency, but a regional/national force. We're part of Bates USA and Bates Worldwide, a $5 billion international resource for

creative excellence and marketing savvy," says Roman with justifiable pride. "Just look at our client roster. Names such as ITT Educational Services, Thomson Consumer Electronics (RCA, GE, ProScan), Wendy's International, Indiana Tourism, Cinergy, Huntington Bancshares, The Ohio State University Medical Center, Eli Lilly and Company, and the Associated Group."

Bates Midwest was established in Indianapolis in 1984 under the

Don't Take The Bait.

Indianapolis Power and Light has been trying to have you into believing their hostile takeover of PSI won't hurt you. But so the plan they filed with the Federal Government, they've admitted they will charge consumers an extra $900 million if their hostile takeover is successful. Don't get caught in their trap. Call 1(800)855-3839.

Pull the Plug on IP&L's Hostile Takeover. Call 1-800-855-3839.

psiEnergy

name of McCaffrey and McCall as an office to service ITT. But through the entrepreneurial spirit so alive in Indianapolis, it has become the city's largest advertising agency and the only such agency with global links.

"Through our network, we have a total unit dedicated to interactivity. We have an ongoing group of people who constantly research consumer trends and relationships—where people are going, what they're thinking about. And we publish our studies. These are the things you can't afford on a smaller level," says Roman. The Bates Interactive division has established homepages on the Internet for several clients and monitors consumer activity for international clients.

The staircase rotunda of Bates Midwest showcases the numerous creative awards from both local and national competitions, but Roman is quick to point out that garnering awards is not the agency's primary role or goal. "I think one thing our clients would say about us is that our focus is not on getting pats on

THE OBJECT OF ART IS TO GIVE LIFE SHAPE.
JEAN ANOUILH

Kawneer
The Mark Of Responsibility.

Firestone Building Products; Arthur G. James Cancer Hospital and Research Institute; and Combibloc.

Combined billings for both offices of Bates Midwest (including Columbus, Ohio) currently total $95 million.

"Bates Midwest has distinguished itself as one of the best-resourced agencies in the region with its ability to provide both quality local service and global reach," says Roman. "Our local position is one of great strength."

Roman and his associates would like to convert more local companies to this midwestern ad agency that thinks locally and acts globally. "There are too many companies who think they need to take their advertising dollars to Chicago or New York. We've established a strong presence here to serve the needs of major national advertisers," he maintains. "We have the resources and we have the people with the experience on a national level working with megadollar budgets. Why not here?"

THIS INTRODUCTION OF THE RCA DIGITAL SATELLITE SYSTEM IN SOUTH AMERICA ALLOWED BATES MIDWEST THE OPPORTUNITY TO "TECHNO-SPEAK" TO INTERNATIONAL AUDIENCES (FAR LEFT).

THIS COMMERCIAL FOR ITT EDUCATIONAL SERVICES CUTS THROUGH THE CLUTTER BY CUTTING THROUGH A CLOCK WITH A LASER, ILLUSTRATING THE POINT THAT LESS TIME IS NEEDED TO EARN A TECHNICAL DEGREE (NEAR LEFT).

the back from our peers or just being creative for the sake of it," he states. "We constantly assess all of our advertising programs. We're very marketing-driven, very strategically driven, and measurable. We believe in effectiveness and results, and in every program we do, there will be a measurement. We want to know that it's working."

He continues, "Campaigns can be funny, breakthrough creative, or visually stunning, but they're not worth paper or film if you can't link consumer ads to changes in shopping habits or changes in response. The days of doing advertising for image alone are long gone. No one has the money to keep pounding away at image. Today's advertising must be very results-oriented."

Regardless of the regional/national focus of the agency, Bates Midwest people never forget to pay back the community whenever and wherever their talents can be utilized. "We are extremely active in the community," says Group Account Director Charlie Larson. "Go through the agency after hours any night and you'll find people working for worthwhile community organizations. We're involved. Whether it's YouthLinks Indiana, Children's Museum of Indianapolis, Juvenile Court Volunteer Services, Family Service Association, Humane Society, or Riley Hospital for Children, our people willingly give their time and talent."

Among other clients on the Bates roster are the Indianapolis Ice; Indianapolis Downtown, Inc.; RCI (Resort Condominiums International); NBC affiliate WTHR-13; the *Indianapolis Business Journal*; Kawneer Architectural Products;

ENGINEERING THE WORLD'S FIRST 80" ProScan TV WAS A TALL ORDER.

ProScan

THE WORLD'S LARGEST TELEVISION— A PROSCAN 80" FROM THE MAKERS OF RCA—IS GIVEN WORLD-CLASS PROMOTION BY BATES MIDWEST (ABOVE).

THIS INFAMOUS SYMBOL OF EVIL WAS USED TO DEMONSTRATE THAT RACISM HAS NO BOUNDARIES AND CAN STILL FIND A WILLING AUDIENCE IF NOT RECOGNIZED AND COUNTERED (LEFT).

The last time racism took hold, it created a real führer.

A COMMERCIAL FOR INDIANAPOLIS' NBC AFFILIATE SHOWS HOW THE STATION'S NEWS TEAM LITERALLY COVERS THE TOWN TO PROVIDE IN-DEPTH REPORTING (BELOW).

HEN J. MICHAEL CUNNINGHAM, PRESIDENT AND OWNER OF Software Synergy, Inc. (SSI), first dreamed of an information systems consulting business, he never imagined that his company would create such a history of consistent, stable, and profitable growth. Today, SSI's extensive and diverse range of professional services helps rank the company as one of the largest providers

of information and contract services in the Midwest.

Cunningham knew that his company's mission statement—to provide "the highest level of quality service as perceived and directed by each individual customer"—had to become a working reality. Starting from a "corporate office" that also served as his daughter's toy room, Cunningham entered the competitive technology marketplace in 1984, differentiating SSI from competitors through a fervent belief in individual responsibility and accountability, and a strong emphasis on quality service to customers.

SSI's holding group today employs more than 400 people at its company-owned Indianapolis headquarters and at branch offices in Louisville, Kentucky; Kansas City, Missouri; Phoenix, Arizona; and Columbus, Cincinnati, and Cleveland, Ohio. The company provides professional contract service solutions to a diverse customer base of more than 200 companies ranging from the well-established Fortune

500 to evolving, fast-growing businesses. "Even though our growth rate appears aggressive, we actually maintain a controlled and strategic management approach that focuses more on quality than quantity," says Vice President Bill Rodenberg.

THE SERVICE APPROACH

We are really a people-oriented company. We believe our employees are our internal customers," says Corporate Director Employee Services Richard Getch. The primary goal of the company's business philosophy is to satisfy both the customer and those employees who successfully serve that customer.

In 1992 SSI debuted its Circle of Success dual-purpose service strategy that propagates employee understanding and personal commitment through a culture designed to generate motivation and inspire morale. This creates an ability to raise customer satisfaction through service differentiation as derived from SSI's Saturation Service™

program. This initiative is monitored and controlled through the company's Service Quality Objectives: concern, responsiveness, reliability, communication, courtesy, professionalism, competence, and confidentiality. Corporate Director Consulting Services Bruce Newcome says, "These measurement criteria keep us focused. We live by these guidelines."

To keep itself at top operating performance, SSI provides its trademarked Saturation Service™ through its consultants, management group, customer services group, and employee services group whose primary objectives are to listen, understand, and communicate. This vital customer information—coupled with quarterly service reviews, project reviews, and employee self-reviews—creates an environment of continuous improvement in efficiencies and effectiveness.

PROFILE OF SERVICES

SSI works with its clients from the inside out by examining a

THE SSI TEAM INCLUDES (STANDING, FROM LEFT) BRUCE NEWCOME, JOE HUFFINE, RICHARD GETCH, GARY GIBBONEY, (SEATED, FROM LEFT) BILL RODENBERG, AND J. MICHAEL CUNNINGHAM.

company's technology challenges, assessing the issues, formulating strategy, developing an action plan, and remaining on-site until the customer is comfortable with the solutions. In addition, customers can make custom requests from SSI's full-service offerings.

SSI offers a complete range of professional services through four specialty groups: consulting, development, support services, and outsourcing. All employees have expertise in their respective disciplines and are required to have at least three years of experience in information systems.

The Consulting Group provides business and technical solutions that include information systems (IS) planning, business evaluations, feasibility studies, strategic systems planning, new technology solutions, systems evaluations, project management, and hardware/software evaluations.

SSI's Development Group designs, develops, and implements IS solutions, including system design; analysis and programming; new technology utilization; system and program conversions; software evaluation, installation, and customization; software system maintenance and support; and system integration.

The Support Services Group offers custom-designed writing and training solutions aimed at improving performance, including IS methods and standards development, system maintenance guides and overviews, operations and business procedures, project management and system design documents, and user guides and tutorials.

Solutions for a wide range of outsourcing engagements are provided by the Outsourcing Group, including complete system or individual program outsourcing, systems planning and design, systems conversion, and IS and operations management.

MICROSOFT SOLUTION PROVIDER® PROGRAM

SSI's analysis of tools available to meet clients' growing desktop needs has resulted in the company becoming a Microsoft Solution Provider®. In addition to creating an environment to con-

duct joint marketing and support activities with Microsoft, the program provides access to Microsoft's full suite of technical information, beta copies of new software, and a direct link to Microsoft's technical support group. This partnership will allow SSI to focus on training resources on a tool set, which is expected to play an increasing role in clients' strategic systems plans. "We believe that carefully selected alliances will enhance our internal training and improve our service offerings," says Corporate Director Business Services Joe Huffine.

To ensure that employees are productive and satisfied in their work environment, SSI provides an extensive array of programs and benefits. The Career Enhancement Plan increases professional acumen and uniqueness through hard and soft skills education and development. Corporate Director Professional Services Gary Gibboney says, "Products are consumed, but services are 'experienced.' We want not only to provide technical proficiencies but also to be able to better manage our customers' own service experience." This customized strategy also provides career direction and emphasis based on marketplace needs and technology-based trends.

SSI fosters teamwork and company spirit though employee peer groups that study, discuss,

and recommend solutions that will facilitate service to customers and employees. In addition, a personal financial planner works with each employee to customize a 401(k) plan according to his or her long- and short-term goals. SSI further demonstrates its concern for employees through an employee assistance program, offering a confidential hot line for individuals who need help with counseling issues or other matters of a private nature.

Employees also participate on company volleyball and softball teams, and each SSI branch office holds quarterly meetings, including an annual summer picnic and a year-end party. In 1994 the Indianapolis branch office extravaganza, held at the Indianapolis Children's Museum, was a huge success. In return, employees volunteer their time after hours to participate in quality circle meetings. "There is a mutual commitment to grow the company and our employees with it," adds Getch.

Building on more than a decade of growth in Indianapolis, and now encompassing a regional marketplace and a national presence, SSI looks to the future with enthusiastic optimism. Michael Cunningham's vision remains the same—only the original corporate office has been replaced with one that can accommodate and support all of the employees who share that vision and are making it a reality.

SATURATION SERVICE™ AND A TEAM APPROACH ARE SSI TRADEMARKS.

USTOMERS NEED TO FEEL WELCOME WHEN DOING BUSINESS with today's financial institutions, especially as banks become larger. To that end, KeyBank National Association strives to build strong relationships with its customers and to operate as a community bank, while providing the strength and services of a major financial organization. ♦ Although KeyBank's Indiana history is intertwined with banks established locally in the 1800s, the organization is a subsidiary of KeyCorp, a bank holding company based in Cleveland, Ohio. KeyCorp was formed from the merger of Society Corporation in Cleveland and KeyBank in Albany, New York, in 1994. Today it ranks among the nation's largest bank holding companies, boasting nearly $68 billion in assets and $5 billion in equity capital. KeyCorp operates more than 1,400 branches and affiliate offices in 25 states from Maine to Alaska. There are 41 KeyBank branch offices in central Indiana, with approximately 600 employees.

THE KEYBANK TEAM INCLUDES (FROM LEFT) GARY HENTSCHEL, COMMERCIAL BANKING; LEONARD HESS, CENTRAL REGION PRESIDENT; ANTHONY HEYWORTH, INDIANA CHAIRMAN AND CEO; LOUIS DAUGHERTY, TRUST AND PRIVATE BANKING; TIM WRIGHT, PUBLIC FUNDS; AND LYNN WILSON, INDIANA MARKETING MANAGER.

Entering the Indianapolis Market

KeyBank's Indianapolis history began in 1986, when Cleveland-based Ameritrust Corporation began acquiring six banks in the state—one in Marion County and five in the surrounding counties—that formed Ameritrust, Central Indiana. In 1992 Society Corporation, prior to its merger with KeyCorp, merged with Ameritrust, a $10 billion bank holding company. The name of the Indiana banks was then changed to Society National Bank, Indiana.

In early 1996 the Society banks in Indiana and Michigan merged to become KeyBank National Association. The mid-1996 addition of the affiliate bank in Ohio creates KeyCorp's first regional bank—KeyBank—in preparation for interstate branching in 1997. Banks will then be able to do business across state lines, as most other businesses have been able to do for years.

KeyBank and its employees are known for their involvement in, and contributions to, the communities in which they work and live. Many organizations benefit from the bank's generosity and giving spirit, including United Way and numerous community, civic, arts, education, and human services groups.

The bank has received an "Outstanding" rating from the Office of the Comptroller of the Currency (OCC) for its community reinvestment. In addition, KeyCorp employees nationwide, including central Indiana, leave the office for an afternoon of community service work each year during Neighbors Make the Difference Day.

"Our employees are our most important asset," says Tony Heyworth, who heads up the bank's Indiana and Michigan operations. "They are the key to the excellent service we offer our customers, and they are the people who make a difference in our communities.

"We've enjoyed great success, but the future looks even brighter."

KeyBank offers a full range of financial services, including consumer banking, investment management and trust, commercial banking and finance, private banking, securities brokerage, and financial services for small businesses.

RIGHTPOINT, INC. IS A YOUNG ORGANIZATION THAT HAS MADE its presence known around the world in the field of wireless communications. The company, formerly known as Wholesale Cellular USA, Inc., puts efficiency at the top of its list of objectives when it comes to serving customers. ♦ "We're known for our efficiency," says CFO and Executive Vice President J. Mark Howell. "We are the low-cost, high-service provider that manufacturers depend on to get their products to their customers."

A YOUNG LEADER

Founded in Indianapolis in 1989, Brightpoint is one of the leading wholesale distributors of wireless telecommunication devices and related products, such as PCS phones; cellular phones; and other vehicle-mounted, transportable, and handheld portable devices. Major brand-name products offered by the company include Nokia, Motorola, Ericsson, Audiovox, NEC, Oki, and Pioneer, to name a few.

In addition to selling wireless communication systems and accessories, Brightpoint offers a number of value-added services, such as inventory management, warehousing, end-user fulfillment, and custom packaging. Its worldwide customer base includes BellSouth (both in the United States and around the world), AT&T Wireless, United States Cellular Corporation, Celcom in Israel, and Telcel in Venezuela, among others. Brightpoint has more than 6,000 accounts—a number that continues to rise monthly.

CHARACTERIZED BY GROWTH

In its relatively short history, the company has built a reputation for fast-paced growth. In fact, *Fortune* magazine ranked Brightpoint among America's Fastest-Growing Companies in 1994 (30th) and 1995 (41st).

When Chairman, President, and CEO Robert J. Laikin first opened the company's doors, Brightpoint employed only 10 people. Today it has more than 100 employees. In April 1994 Brightpoint went public—a strategic move that provided the foundation for its aggressive growth. The company experienced sales growth of approximately 95 percent annually in its first five years and continues to set profitability records.

Roughly 30 percent of the company's $269.4 million in 1995 sales was generated from its international market. Brightpoint anticipates that international sales could top 40 percent of total sales in the near future.

Further evidence of the company's growth are its announced merger with Allied Communications, Inc.; the acquisition of Hong Kong-based Technology Resources International; and a joint venture with Wholesale Cellular Latina in Lima, Peru. Brightpoint recently moved into a new headquarters facility on the northwest side of Indianapolis.

Despite this continuing expansion, Brightpoint has been able to keep costs in check. Because of its focus on efficiency, overhead expenses have remained very low, and the company has passed its savings on to customers.

Keeping its customers at the forefront of wireless communications, Brightpoint will continue to provide high-quality, cutting-edge products and services in an age of expanding information technologies.

HEADQUARTERED IN INDIANAPOLIS SINCE ITS FOUNDING IN 1989, BRIGHTPOINT IS ONE OF THE LEADING WHOLESALE DISTRIBUTORS OF WIRELESS TELECOMMUNICATION DEVICES AND RELATED PRODUCTS.

HE CREATIVE INNOVATIONS AT THOMSON CONSUMER Electronics in Indianapolis are bringing new, revolutionary products based on digital video technology to the international marketplace. Thomson now dominates the market with its RCA brand digital satellite dish and set-top decoder box. Looking ahead, the company has plans to seize an even larger market share of future digital products.

HOME IN INDIANAPOLIS

Thomson is the world's fourth-largest home electronics company, with worldwide headquarters in Paris, France. Established in 1987, the Indianapolis operation is the site of Thomson's corporate headquarters for North and South America. Worldwide, Thomson employs nearly 60,000 people, manufacturing and marketing nine brands of consumer electronics products, including the famous RCA, GE, and ProScan names. As the largest consumer electronics employer in the United States, Thomson is committed to maintaining its leadership position in the American marketplace. More than 2,000 people are employed at the company's Indianapolis facilities.

Thomson has two buildings at its North Meridian Street complex, which opened in 1994. Designed by Indianapolis native and world-renowned architect Michael Graves, the complex includes the company's Administration Building and Technical Center. A contemporary circular four-floor atrium welcomes Thomson's customers to the complex and serves as a primary meeting space. Product galleries on the fourth floor provide a museumlike showcase for the company's current and future RCA, GE, and ProScan home entertainment products.

With 240,000 square feet of space, the Administration Building is the home of Thomson's Americas Marketing and Sales operation. This division includes national advertising, merchandising, sales promotion, sales training, and product design. Additional corporate functions include finance, human resources, communications, information systems, legal services, and environmental health and safety.

Thomson's 320,000-square-foot Technical Center is the size of three stacked football fields. The building houses engineering labs, extensive corporate research facilities, an engineering library, and prototype product fabrication shops. The company's global component-sourcing operation is also based at the center.

Thomson's major manufacturing facilities in Indiana include the world's largest color television assembly plant in Bloomington; a color TV picture tube plant in Marion; and a plastic components plant in Indianapolis, which manufactures printed circuit boards for color televisions, as well as plastic cabinets and other component parts.

MAKING ITS WAY TO INDIANAPOLIS

Thomson made its way to Indianapolis through the Radio Corporation of America (RCA) and a small Westinghouse light-bulb factory that operated at the corner of LaSalle and Michigan streets during the early 1920s. Initially established to market GE and Westinghouse radio equipment, RCA acquired the manufacturing capability and assets of the Victor Talking Machine Company in Camden, New Jersey.

In the early 1930s RCA purchased the Indianapolis Westinghouse factory, which had previously been converted to radio tube production.

As talking motion pictures became more popular, the Indianapolis

NIPPER AND CHIPPER SHARE CENTER STAGE WITH THE RCA DIGITAL SATELLITE SYSTEM, WHICH WAS DEVELOPED IN THOMSON'S INDIANAPOLIS LABORATORIES AND IS THE FASTEST-SELLING CONSUMER ELECTRONICS PRODUCT EVER LAUNCHED IN THE UNITED STATES (TOP RIGHT).

RCA HOME THEATRE PRODUCTS ARE DESIGNED AND MARKETED FROM THOMSON'S AMERICAS HEADQUARTERS (BELOW).

plant began production of the RCA Photophone Sound System used for motion picture sound. Throughout the 1930s, the local plant made sound equipment, public address systems, radio tubes, and recording gear. The company also became involved in pressing phonograph records at the Indianapolis facility.

World War II brought industrial expansion, and the Indianapolis plant shifted to war production. After the war, the facility began building television components. By 1961, when RCA's consumer electronics headquarters was moved from New Jersey to Indianapolis, the local plant became the site of the home electronics division's design, engineering, research, marketing and sales, and administrative functions.

In the 1970s, as RCA experienced tremendous change, the Indianapolis operations targeted consumer electronics. In 1986 GE acquired RCA and moved its own consumer electronics division from Virginia to Indianapolis. GE announced plans in late 1987 to sell the unprofitable consumer electronics business to Thomson. The RCA and GE consumer electronics product lines are now branches of the Thomson family. A third brand, ProScan—a premier line of home entertainment products—has now joined the RCA and GE lines.

PRODUCTS FOR THE FUTURE

One of Thomson's newest products includes a receiver that decodes digital broadcasts sent by ground-based microwave transmitters. The receivers will be manufactured for TELE-TV Systems—a wireless cable venture of Bell Atlantic, NYNEX, and Pacific Telesis phone companies. This three-year contract represents a potential $1 billion in revenues.

Indianapolis engineers have also joined forces with Time Warner and Toshiba to produce a new generation of compact discs that are capable of holding hours of digitally recorded video. Digital Video Disc (DVD) players—a new technology that is expected to eventually replace the VCR—will revolutionize home entertainment. DVDs are similar to CD-ROMs,

but will hold seven times more data and will enhance home viewing with improved picture and sound quality.

Today Thomson enjoys an unprecedented leadership position in the field of digital consumer electronics. "As any Thomson employee can tell you, our move into this field wasn't a slow intrusion of

light onto our profit-and-loss statement, but more of a well-planned explosion," says Alain Prestat, chairman and CEO of Thomson multimedia. "By the year 2000, Thomson's worldwide presence, continued breakthroughs in digital technology, and sharpened focus on design will diminish our recent past to elementary first steps."

FEDEX®

edEx® IS THE LARGEST EXPRESS TRANSPORTATION COMPANY IN the world, handling millions of packages and documents nightly. With worldwide headquarters in Memphis, FedEx serves 204 countries and employs 113,880 people throughout the world. In a 24-hour period, the company's aircraft travel nearly half a million miles; couriers log 2.5 million miles daily or 100 trips around the earth.

The reputation and investments of Federal Express make the company an industry leader in the introduction of new and innovative customer services. It was the first company dedicated to overnight package delivery and the first air express company to introduce the overnight letter, to offer 10:30 a.m. next-day delivery, to offer Saturday delivery, and to offer time-definite service for freight. Federal Express was also the first in the industry with money-back guarantees and free proof of performance services that now extend to its worldwide network.

THE INDIANAPOLIS CONNECTION

Since 1988 the city of Indianapolis has been home to a major Federal Express package-sorting hub that employs more than 2,000 people who sort 300,000 packages daily. "We are in Indianapolis because the city is strategically located in the middle of the United States. You can actually hit better than 60 percent of the major business markets within a one-day truck run," says Bob Palmer, vice president of National HUB Operations for Federal Express. "This is a business-friendly community with an excellent labor market. The work ethic here is very high."

The remarkable growth of Federal Express worldwide goes hand in hand with its multi-million-dollar expansion project at the Indianapolis International Airport. In August 1994 Palmer announced plans for a $210 million expansion of the Indianapolis package-handling hub. When completed in June 1997, the project will nearly double the size of the complex and create approximately 1,000 new jobs.

"This Federal Express facility was already an important factor as an employer and as an attraction to other businesses and industries in central Indiana," said Governor Evan Bayh at 1994's expansion announcement. "With this major expansion, not only will there be more jobs directly generated for Hoosiers, but the excellent reputation and performance of Federal Express will provide even more tools for Indiana business." The expansion will increase the size of the Federal Express hub from 120 acres to 240 acres and will increase the number of gates for airplanes from 44 to 58. Total square footage will increase from 645,000 to 1.2 million. The new sorting system will be able to handle 350,000 parcels in a two-hour period.

OVERNIGHT BEGINNINGS

Federal Express Corporation was founded by Chairman, President, and Chief Executive Officer Frederick W. Smith, who conceived the idea of an overnight delivery service while an undergraduate student at Yale University. The company began operations in April 1973. A fleet of 14 Falcon jets took off with 186 packages the first night of operation. Following air cargo deregulation in 1977, Federal Express expanded its fleet with Boeing 727 and McDonnell Douglas DC-10 aircraft. In 1978 the company became publicly held, listing on the New York Stock Exchange as FDX. Ten years after start-up, Federal Express reached $1 billion in annual revenues, becoming the first U.S. business to achieve this status without mergers or acquisitions.

Overseas operations began in 1984 with service to Europe and Asia following the first of several international acquisitions. In 1985 the company marked its first regularly scheduled flight to Europe and

FedEx AT WORK: EACH DAY, 2.5 MILLION PACKAGES PASS THROUGH THE FedEx SYSTEM.

in 1988 initiated direct, scheduled cargo service to Japan. Federal Express acquired Tiger International, Inc. in 1989 and integrated its international network into the FedEx system.

Federal Express was among the first express transportation companies to realize the benefits of technology. As early as 1978, just five years after it began operations, the company pioneered the first automated customer service center. To provide real-time package tracking for each shipment, FedEx uses one of the world's largest computer and telecommunications networks. The company's couriers operate SuperTracker® handheld computers to record the transit of shipments through the company's integrated network. FedEx also offers businesses the opportunity to track the status of their packages at all possible locations along the delivery route with the use of either PowerShip® terminals or FedEx tracking software.

In 1990 Federal Express became the first company to win the prestigious Malcolm Baldrige National Quality Award in the service category. This award recognizes outstanding quality achievements and places Federal Express in the company of recent winners such as General Motors' Cadillac division and IBM.

In 1994 Federal Express updated its corporate identity and formally adopted its primary brand

name, FedEx. Consistent with its tradition of "firsts," the company received ISO 9001 registration that same year for all of its worldwide operations, making it the first global express transportation company to receive simultaneous systemwide certification. The company reported $9.4 billion in

revenues for fiscal 1995.

FedEx has a clear vision for its future in Indianapolis and beyond: growth. For a company that enjoys 49 percent of the industry's market share, that path has already been paved with success. Considering the company's growth, quality, and high standards of excellence, it's pretty much a package deal.

CLOCKWISE FROM TOP: FROM EXOTIC ANIMALS TO INDY RACE CARS, FEDEX IS EQUIPPED TO DELIVER VIRTUALLY ANY ITEM.

THIS AIRBUS 300 IS ONE OF MORE THAN 500 AIRCRAFT IN THE COMPANY'S FLEET.

IN 204 COUNTRIES AROUND THE WORLD, FEDEX DELIVERS.

Q UANTUM HEALTH RESOURCES, INC. SETS A FAST PACE IN THE delivery of alternate-site therapies and support services for people with chronic disorders. Founded in 1988, the company's growth has skyrocketed, with total revenues reaching $286 million in 1995. Quantum continues to be one of the fastest-growing alternate-site health care companies in the

United States. "The company has expanded its services gradually. Over 40 percent of our business is now generated by disorders other than hemophilia, our first focused disorder," says Doug Stickney, cofounder, chairman, and CEO.

Started by four cofounders in Riverside, California, the company opened its first branch in Indianapolis in 1988. This branch was established in response to the needs of treatment center programs at several large local hospitals. In August 1994 Quantum moved its corporate headquarters from Orange, California, to a temporary location in north side Indianapolis. Today Quantum employs more than

1,200 people throughout the country, including more than 130 at its Indianapolis branch and corporate locations.

"Since our initial public offering on April 30, 1991, we've definitely bred more competitors. I take it as a compliment that there are more companies out there talking about meeting the needs of families with chronic disorders," says Stickney. "But I don't believe there's anyone right now who has, on a national basis, the number of contacts and the credibility that we have."

A MODEL FOR HEALTH CARE DELIVERY

Quantum employs a unique philosophy that serves as

a model in the management of rare chronic health disorders like hemophilia, primary immunodeficiencies, autoimmune disorders, genetic emphysema, and others. The company's Chronicare™ model offers comprehensive, integrated support for the treatment of lifelong disorders through a circle of care that addresses the psychosocial, therapeutic, professional, and socioeconomic concerns of patients and their families.

Chronicare allows Quantum to bring cost-effectiveness to one of the most expensive segments of the health care market. Patients with chronic disorders represent approximately 5 percent of the total patient

IN AUGUST 1994 QUANTUM RELOCATED ITS CORPORATE HEADQUARTERS FROM ORANGE, CALIFORNIA. IN JANUARY 1996 THE COMPANY MOVED FROM TEMPORARY OFFICES INTO ITS NEW CORPORATE LOCATION IN NORTH SIDE INDIANAPOLIS (BELOW).

population in the United States, but account for more than 30 percent of the total cost of care. The Chronicare model sets a standard of excellence in the industry with its responsiveness to the rapid change inherent in today's managed health care environment. Alternate-site therapies, usually delivered in the home, have been shown to be less costly than inpatient hospital care.

"The Chronicare model is designed to improve the quality of life for the patient and to reduce the costs of care. These goals are in alignment with the goals of managed care," says William Reed, senior vice president, operations and information services. "With therapies being delivered at home, consumers lead active and relatively normal lives."

QUANTUM'S OPERATIONS

Patients throughout the United States are served by Quantum's four pharmacy-licensed regional centers, 21 pharmacy-licensed branches, and 14 service branches. Specialist physicians, managed care organizations, and payers are recognized by the company as primary referral sources.

The company also interfaces with pharmaceutical and biotechnology companies in monitoring the latest developments in leading-edge therapies. These advancements can then be applied to enhance Quantum's patient services and develop new markets.

In 1994 the company diversified its product offering with the addition of Quantum Disease Management. While Quantum Health Resources is focused on physician and payer referrals and the delivery of home care, Quantum Disease Management participates in case management, analyzes medical outcomes, and reviews and develops specialized provider networks for patients. Quantum Disease Management can also share some of the financial risk for the cost of

care, allowing insurance companies to benefit from Quantum's clinical expertise.

PROGRAMS FOR PEACE OF MIND

Quantum diligently looks for ways to empower the patients it serves, which, in turn, offers peace of mind to their families. One example of these efforts is the Lifestyle Plus™ program. Developed through discussions with Quantum's consumers, Lifestyle Plus makes the challenges of daily living easier, giving families the freedom to enjoy life outside the home. The program offers a variety of components, including a medical record keeping system, a personal medical information card, newsletters and educational materials, a travel assurance program, and emergency treatment guidelines.

"They're simple things, but if you have to take medications every day, maintain accurate records, or help a family member, they provide added convenience and can reduce the cost of care," says Reed.

A SPIRIT OF COMPASSION

Quantum is active at the grassroots level in its branch location communities, with employee participation in local walkathons, other special fundraising events, and support group activities. The company also makes charitable donations to help support the national foundations representing many chronic disorders. Quantum is particularly enthusiastic about participation in the corporate culture of Indianapolis and about giving back to the community it serves.

"We are viewed as a compassionate health care company," concludes Stickney. "We are doing well by doing good. If we constantly meet and understand the diverse needs of our customers, we will be successful."

To ensure that Quantum's Chronicare services are confidential and discreet, medical products are delivered to the patient's home, office, or physician in unmarked vehicles.

RE/MAX of Indiana

T TOOK ONLY EIGHT YEARS FOR RE/MAX OF INDIANA TO move toward the top of the real estate market in Indianapolis, and today, the company's phenomenal growth shows few signs of slowing down. ♦ "We're the fastest-growing real estate organization in the state of Indiana, without question," says Mitchell Cox, vice president and regional director for RE/MAX of Indiana. "When RE/MAX came into the marketplace in 1988, we completely turned the industry upside down."

According to Cox, the success of RE/MAX is a result of the company's top agents, who, for nearly a decade now, have outproduced their competitors in number of transactions, volume, and income. In fact, over the past seven years, the Indiana company has grown by 30 percent annually in terms of additional associates, transactions, volume, and commissions. In 1994 alone, RE/MAX of Indiana produced more than $1.5 billion in sales with more than 16,400 transactions. In 1995 the firm will have sold a projected $1.8 billion in residential and commercial real estate and helped nearly 70,000 Indiana families buy or sell their home.

PROFESSIONALS AT WORK

We've been 'professionalizing,' " says Cox. "We're not a company that generally accepts new licensees or part-time people. Our membership is made up of well-educated people who make themselves aware of up-and-coming changes in the industry, and, as a result, have learned how to better serve their customers. We're the best of the best, which is amazing considering we're in competition with companies that have been in Indianapolis for more than 75 years."

Currently, RE/MAX of Indiana has 60 offices and more than 770 associates throughout the state. In the Indianapolis metropolitan area, 19 RE/MAX offices represent approximately 350 associates, including more than 50 new associates who were added to the roster in 1995. That same year, the company's first commercial franchise for Indianapolis was signed. David Bickell, CCIM, heads the new RE/MAX Commercial Group, and company officials expect its endeavors to be just as successful as those in the residential sector.

The original franchise in Indiana, RE/MAX Real Estate Group, represents approximately 105 associates who conduct more than $250 million in business annually. Across Indiana, RE/MAX has a presence in 32 markets and

TETHERED BALLOON RIDES ARE A POPULAR ATTRACTION BEFORE THE ANNUAL DOWNTOWN INDIANAPOLIS SKY CONCERT. ALL PROCEEDS GO TO RILEY HOSPITAL FOR CHILDREN (RIGHT).

"WE'RE THE FASTEST-GROWING REAL ESTATE ORGANIZATION IN THE STATE OF INDIANA, WITHOUT QUESTION," SAYS MITCHELL COX, VICE PRESIDENT AND REGIONAL DIRECTOR FOR RE/MAX OF INDIANA (BELOW).

The RE/MAX name is prominent throughout Indiana.

ranks either first or second in 17 of those. These factors, along with an impressive number of sales, make RE/MAX the "Leading Real Estate Organization in the State of Indiana," according to Cox. In turn, its associates have been paid close to $200 million in commissions.

The top producers in the RE/MAX circle are also looked to as leaders by associates in other real estate companies. For example, in 1996 Norman McClain of the Greenwood office assumed the post of president of the Indiana Association of Realtors, and Gay Keys of RE/MAX Real Estate Group was named president of the Metropolitan Indianapolis Board of Realtors.

AN INTERNATIONAL ORGANIZATION

RE/MAX of Indiana is affiliated with Denver-based RE/MAX International (the acronym stands for "real estate maximums"). The company's founders, Dave and Gail Liniger, originally from Marion, Indiana, set out in 1973 to establish a firm whereby associates share in office overhead and management fees, but at the same time receive the highest possible compensation for their efforts. International in scope, the company also has offices in Canada, Mexico, Hong Kong, the Caribbean, South Africa, Italy, Israel, Spain, Germany, and Greece.

To keep associates on top of

changes in the business world and a step ahead of the competition, RE/MAX offices use the latest technology, including CD-ROM, CompuServe, and innovative software programs to improve customer service. In 1995 RE/MAX became the first real estate organization with an address on the Internet. Likewise, the RE/MAX Satellite Network provides interactive videoconferencing for sales associates and administrative personnel,

as well as a RE/MAX news program and other informative live and taped programming.

SHARING RESOURCES WITH THE COMMUNITY

In addition to selling homes, "RE/MAX associates work hard to give something back to the communities they represent," according to Michelle Thieme, communications director for

RE/MAX. In Indiana, the Miracle Home Program allows associates to donate a percentage of their commissions to the Riley Hospital for Children in Indianapolis. "In 1994 RE/MAX associates in Indiana raised more than $53,000 for the Children's Miracle Network [CMN]," says Thieme. As the local participating hospital of CMN, Riley Hospital for Children benefited greatly from those donations. RE/MAX International is the exclusive real estate sponsor of CMN, and the Indiana group ranked number six internationally for its fund-raising efforts in 1994.

RE/MAX's community consciousness is also evident in other sponsored activities. Many of the firm's offices host annual events, such as neighborhood picnics and Halloween pumpkin giveaways. The RE/MAX hot air balloon, purchased by RE/MAX in 1989, also makes 80 to 100 flights each year. In addition to flying at the Indiana State Fair, the balloon is a crowd favorite at a variety of other popular family functions, including the Conner Prairie Memorial Weekend Balloon Glow and the annual downtown Sky Concert held each Labor Day weekend.

"We would never have been able to achieve the success we have if it weren't for the type of people that make up the RE/MAX family," says Cox. "And we are a family."

RE/MAX ASSOCIATES HELP PROVIDE TOP-QUALITY CARE FOR THE YOUNG PATIENTS AT RILEY HOSPITAL FOR CHILDREN THROUGH THE COMPANY'S INVOLVEMENT IN THE CHILDREN'S MIRACLE NETWORK AND THE MIRACLE HOME PROGRAM.

HEN IT COMES TO SATISFYING THE LISTENING PLEASURES OF Indianapolis residents, MyStar Communications Corporation has just the ticket. As the owner of three local radio stations, which offer a variety of formats, MyStar provides something for everyone—even the most discriminating listener. ♦ MyStar Communications was founded in 1989 by Indianapolis

businessman Michael S. Maurer, who also has interests in several publications, including *Indianapolis Business Journal*, *The Indiana Lawyer*, and the *Commercial Statistics*. In addition, MyStar owns MySign Outdoor, a local billboard company established in 1995.

Something for Everyone

The company's radio stations fill several important niches in the Indianapolis market. WTPI, 107.9 on the FM dial, provides a mix of music and information designed to fit the busy lifestyles of listeners who range in age from 25 to 54 years. Steve Cooper and Kelly Vaughn start WTPI's day with a friendly "part of the family" approach to their morning show. WTPI, known as the city's listen-at-work station, offers a light, adult-contemporary format featuring music from the '80s and '90s during the workday. The evening program, *Nightbreeze*, offers listeners light favorites and smooth jazz to help them unwind from a busy day. And on Sunday, listeners are treated to a daylong jazz format. *Jazz Breakfast* and the *Sunday Morning Jazz Show* feature the music of classic and contemporary jazz artists, such as Kenny G, the Rippingtons, and David Sanborn. Chuck Workman, host of the *Sunday Morning Jazz Show*, also entertains and informs listeners with artist interviews and updates on the local jazz scene.

In 1994 MyStar purchased WCKN, formerly a country station that was once known as WIRE. The station, renamed WMyS 1430 AM, plays a menu of standards from the '40s, '50s, and '60s with performers such as Tony Bennett, Frank Sinatra, and Nat King Cole,

as well as more recent hits by such artists as Barbra Streisand, Neil Diamond, and Dionne Warwick. The station's format is designed to fill the gap between contemporary and big-band offerings. Dave Koffee is the station's morning personality, charming listeners with fresh conversation and important information to start the day.

As Indy's "newest" AM offering, WMyS is the fastest-growing station in the state, thriving beyond the expectations of owners and station managers. WMyS 1430 AM prides itself on being a full-service radio station, with hourly news updates from CNN and Bloomberg Business News. Listeners may also hear exclusive lap-by-lap coverage

of all Indy car races and follow the action of Indianapolis Ice hockey, Notre Dame football, and Butler University basketball.

MyStar Communications also owns WZPL 99.5 FM, known for playing "all the hits, all the time." The station's format includes the current music capturing the attention of adult listeners ranging in age from 18 to 34, as well as women in the 18- to 49-year-old age group.

WZPL's mainstream contemporary mix includes rock performers like John Mellencamp and Aerosmith; modern rock artists such as Hootie & the Blowfish and Melissa Etheridge; and top favorites from Boyz II Men, Mariah Carey, Janet

WZPL, known for playing "all the hits, all the time," sponsors Fourth Fest, which is considered to be one of the largest annual events in downtown Indianapolis.

Jackson, Prince, Madonna, and many others.

Community Celebration and Participation

Aiming to please the community, WZPL sponsors Fourth Fest on July 4, which is considered to be one of the largest annual events in downtown Indianapolis. The celebration features a full day of live music by local and national artists, as well as a food festival and, of course, a spectacular fireworks show.

On the corporate level, MyStar Communications has a firm commitment to serving the community through public service. The company's efforts have been duly recognized by the community through a number of awards, including the Community Appreciation for Service in Public Enlightenment and Relations award, the ART I award from the Arts Council of Indianapolis, and the Professionalism award from the American Women in Radio and Television.

The three MyStar stations support a wide variety of charitable organizations through activities that include a toy drive to benefit the Caring and Sharing Mission, a gelatin splash for the Leukemia Society, and a bike ride for the American

Diabetes Association. The stations also participate in other activities that benefit such organizations as the United Way, the St. Margaret's Hospital Guild, the Julian Center, the Susan G. Komen Center for Breast Cancer, and the United Christmas Service, to name a few.

MyStar recently consolidated all its operations to a single location at 9245 North Meridian Street. Previously, WTPI and WMyS

occupied space at 3135 North Meridian, while WZPL was located at the Pyramids on the city's north side.

The growing popularity experienced by these three stations has paralleled the growth of the metropolis they serve. Indianapolis continues to be a city on the move, and MyStar Communications responds to that pace, keeping to the beat of the city's dynamic pulse.

Dave Koffee starts the day at WMyS with the "Koffee Party." The station plays a menu of standards from the '40s, '50s, and '60s with performers such as Tony Bennett, Frank Sinatra, and Nat King Cole, as well as more recent hits by such artists as Barbra Streisand, Neil Diamond, and Dionne Warwick.

I'S HARD TO IMAGINE THAT A COMPANY AS YOUNG AS The Morley Group Inc. could have made it to the top as quickly as it has. The company's earnings have soared to more than $5 million in the four years since its creation. This kind of new-business growth in today's economy sounds like a fairy tale, but The Morley Group's success story continues, and there is no end in sight.

"Our mission is clear," says Michael A. Morley, president of the Indianapolis-based human resource management and consulting company. "We will clearly be among the top 1 percent of recruiting and personnel service firms in the United States in this decade."

A SUCCESSFUL BEGINNING

With years of experience in recruiting and human resource consulting behind them, Michael and Sharon Morley, his wife and business partner, were ready for a new challenge. In October of 1992 they founded The Morley Group to fulfill their vision for a cutting-edge human resource services company.

In just four years that vision has become a reality as this rapidly growing business has created a variety of diversified human-resource-related services, including professional and executive recruiting services, professional contract services, professional temporary services, compensation and benefits analysis, legal compliance, training, selection, assessment and testing, reference testing, and substance

A high-performance work team meets to establish performance targets (right).

abuse screening. The company ranks as the largest Indiana licensed employment service.

"The dream we started with was a company where all of our employees could share in creating the best company of its kind in the industry," says Michael.

"Our people feel this is their company. They are our greatest asset," adds Sharon, who serves as senior consultant and adviser for The Morley Group.

The thriving company's own employee base has grown from its initial two founders to a solid team of 52 people in 1996. Sharon adds,

"We recognize we will only be as strong as those who comprise the fabric of our company. We have been fortunate to be able to attract quality people who want to be a part of our vision." The Morleys spare no expense on their employees' well-being, in 1995 alone spending more than $70,000 on training and enhancement programs. "If we can't get up in the morning and be excited about what we are achieving, why get up?" questions Michael with a smile.

Employees certainly recognize the investment being made in them, and through high-performance

ATTENDING THE GROUNDBREAKING CEREMONY FOR THE COMPANY'S NEW HEADQUARTERS ARE (BELOW, FROM LEFT) MIKE AND SHARON MORLEY, RHEA SPEAR, AND ROGER BRUMMETT. UPON COMPLETION, THE 20,000-SQUARE-FOOT FACILITY (RIGHT) WILL HOUSE AN EXPANDED WORKFORCE OF APPROXIMATELY 100 PEOPLE.

work teams they take ownership of and accountability for their productivity, performance, and self-improvement on the job. Teams develop their own budgets, establish performance targets, and evaluate their fellow employees and colleagues, particularly in the areas of customer service and satisfaction. This peer system of checks and balances is harmonious with the work ethic and management philosophy at The Morley Group.

Growth Brings Expansion

The Morley Group's growth has resulted in the purchase of a 2.5-acre site at I-465 and West 71st Street in Corporate Park North, where a 20,000-square-foot facility will house an expanded workforce of approximately 100 people. The new facility is being designed for employee comfort, convenience, and productivity by an Indianapolis-based architectural firm, American Consulting Engineers.

The new building's brick facade will incorporate a significant amount of glass, allowing "genuine light" at Sharon's request. An open design concept will provide for ample workstations in tranquil colors with splashes of brighter, tasteful colors for added interest. Communal areas will be positioned in the middle of the building, allowing employees to enjoy windows in the work areas around the perimeter.

A pond, fountain, and attractive landscaping will add finishing exterior touches to what will be a

premier workplace for Morley Group employees. The facility's state-of-the-art telecommunications equipment will command a quarter-million-dollar investment. The new system will include headsets plugged directly into the computer system and Internet access, which will allow the company worldwide access to information on prospective clients and candidate resources.

Meeting Clients' Specific Needs

The Morley Group is dedicated to providing total human resource solutions for client companies and, in doing so, creating opportunities for candidates to enhance or dramatically alter their career paths. On behalf of its many clients, The Morley Group contacts nearly 2,000 candidates per day, and through the acquisition of these various candidate resources, the company

is able to effectively meet the human capital demands of its clients, whether permanent or interim. "We invest a tremendous effort in developing partnerships with both the client and the candidate in providing employment solutions. It is a commitment on all sides," says Michael.

The company targets specific industries including manufacturing, engineering, production, executive, and supervisory positions in the manufacturing industries; programmers, analysts, developers, administrators, technicians, and executives in the information service industry; chief executives, officers, managers, and specialists in the finance and banking industries; administrators, managers, executives, directors, technicians, and practitioners in the health care, physician, and rehabilitative health industries; and office support, clerical, office services, and administration in the secretarial and clerical professions.

"Our vision continues to be the cornerstone of all we are accomplishing," says Sharon. "This is not about money or power; it's knowing we have the ability to do something better than it has ever been done before. We are very fortunate to have this opportunity to achieve so much."

Michael adds, "We've built a great organization, and we're building a greater one. This is our opportunity to make an impact and create an exciting new model for our industry."

THE MORLEY GROUP UTILIZES A STATE-OF-THE-ART TELECOMMUNICATIONS SYSTEM WITH INTERNET ACCESS (LEFT).

THE COMPANY'S EMPLOYEES ARE ITS GREATEST ASSET.

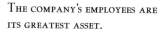

GROWTH
ONE HUNDRED

THE MORLEY GROUP WAS RECENTLY SELECTED AS A GROWTH ONE HUNDRED COMPANY BY INDIANA UNIVERSITY.

T HE WORLD HAS SEEN MANY CHANGES SINCE THE DAUGHTERS OF Charity began their health care. Yet the sick and poor have not disappeared, nor have the Daughters of Charity who continue to serve them. As part of the Daughters of Charity National Health System, St. Vincent is dedicated to providing quality, compassionate, and affordable health care services for everyone.

In 1633 Vincent de Paul and Louise de Marillac expanded their work with France's unfortunates by founding the Daughters of Charity. Through their faith and dedication to God, the Daughters devoted themselves to going wherever they were needed to nurse, feed, and comfort the sick and poor.

Generations later, on April 26, 1881, four Daughters of Charity arrived in Indianapolis. They brought with them hope; faith; a willingness to help the poor, sick, and injured; and $34.77. Their new home was an empty seminary where they opened the St. Vincent Infirmary. A short time later—when the infirmary was in full operation with 50 beds—the name was changed to St. Vincent Hospital. The hospital's subsequent accomplishments express a litany of faith and dedication to the city of Indianapolis and to the profession of medicine.

In 1913 the hospital was relocated on Fall Creek Parkway. In 1974 St. Vincent moved to its current main campus on West 86th Street. St. Vincent Hospitals now includes the 650-bed St. Vincent Indianapolis Hospital; the 104-bed Carmel Hospital in nearby Carmel,

Indiana; the 42-bed St. Vincent Mercy Hospital in Elwood, Indiana; the Stress Care Centers at St. Vincent, a specialty hospital offering programs in mental health and chemical dependency; and St. Vincent New Hope, which provides services for young adults with congenital or acquired disabilities.

Primary care is provided through a network of primary care physicians, as well as several family practice clinics, outpatient and occupational health centers, and a mobile mammography unit. Home care is also available. Specialties include one of the largest cardiovascular programs in the world, orthopaedics and sports medicine, cancer care, hospice, services for women and children, health promotion and wellness, microsurgery, advanced laser surgery, and neurology and neurosurgery. Today St. Vincent is one of the largest employers in central Indiana, with more than 6,100 associates and an operating budget of almost $380 million.

St. Vincent's medical staff roster encompasses graduates from the world's major medical schools. Because of the medical staff's reputation, St. Vincent's services are international and diverse in scope. St. Vincent physicians are prolific

writers, scientists, research analysts, and teachers.

As the largest local hospital network in the Daughters of Charity National Health System, St. Vincent continues the tradition of working in concert with the community. This enables the hospitals to remain responsive to community needs, including demands for more access to a continuum of services and more cost-effective care delivery.

Through all of the changes to come in health care, St. Vincent is committed to remaining focused on the philosophy, mission, and values of the Daughters of Charity: helping people achieve their highest potential through mental, physical, and spiritual health and access to appropriate high-value health care.

CLOCKWISE FROM TOP RIGHT: IN 1974 ST. VINCENT HOSPITAL MOVED TO ITS CURRENT MAIN CAMPUS LOCATION ON WEST 86TH STREET, WHICH INCLUDES THE 650-BED ST. VINCENT INDIANAPOLIS HOSPITAL.

THE 104-BED CARMEL HOSPITAL IN NEARBY CARMEL, INDIANA, IS PART OF TODAY'S ST. VINCENT HOSPITALS.

EARLY IN ST. VINCENT'S HISTORY, THE DAUGHTERS OF CHARITY REMODELED THE CHAPEL OF ST. JOSEPH'S CHURCH INTO A SMALLER CHAPEL AS WELL AS WAITING AND EXAMINING ROOMS.

OMMUNITY HOSPITALS INDIANAPOLIS IS THE CITY'S LARGEST health care system. With three hospitals, five MedCheck immediate care centers, and a variety of specialized services, Community serves thousands of area citizens every year. With its focus on access, cost efficiency, and quality, Community's patients have consistently rated the system "good," if not "excellent," on their patient surveys.

However, 40 years ago, Community was just a patch of land on which the residents of Indianapolis' growing east side placed their dreams for better, more accessible health care.

After World War II, Indianapolis grew toward the suburbs. Hospitals were crowded, and most were far from the citizens of the city's east side. To champion the cause of quality, accessible health care for the entire city, Edward Gallahue led a concerned civic group to form the Indianapolis Hospitals Development Association. Part of their challenge was to build a new east side hospital on land donated by Gallahue at 16th and Ritter Avenue.

As the first board of directors for the hospital was assembled, funds poured in from the entire community. Volunteers conducted house-to-house campaigns. Employees in several companies donated funds through payroll deduction. The *East Side Herald* dubbed it "the swiftest, most effective fund-raising campaign of our time." Today Community still serves patients who can proudly say they helped build the hospital.

Hundreds of Indianapolis citizens and then-Vice President Richard M. Nixon attended the ground breaking for the newly named Community Hospital. On August 6, 1956, with a full staff in place, Community Hospital opened its doors and admitted its first patient.

Since then, the hospital has expanded six times, has been renamed Community Hospital East, and has developed into part of a citywide health care system: Community Hospitals Indianapolis.

COMMUNITY HOSPITAL NORTH

In 1985, as the city's northeast side grew, the system built Community Hospital North, a full-service hospital at 82nd and Shadeland, to serve that area's expanding population. This was the first hospital in the city to offer labor, delivery, recovery, and postpartum (LDRP) rooms, now known as the Family Rooms. Also in the 1980s, Community began opening its widely recognized MedCheck centers for neighborhood residents' immediate medical care needs.

COMMUNITY HOSPITAL SOUTH

In 1989 the city's south side had become another area of growth and development, and Community again expanded into a growing population. On September 25, 1989, Community Hospitals acquired University Heights Hospital, now Community Hospital South, with a firm commitment to expand its services. This newest hospital—at 1402 East County Line Road South, near Greenwood Park Mall—now offers cardiology services in addition to the Family Rooms.

As Community Hospitals Indianapolis continues to grow, it offers solid acute medical and surgical services at each hospital and a variety of specialized health care programs. Some of these include cardiovascular services; inpatient and outpatient mental health services for all ages; the Regional Cancer Center; Hook Rehabilitation Center; older adult services; neurocare services; and women's and children's services, including maternity and pediatric care.

CLOCKWISE FROM BELOW: COMMUNITY HOSPITAL NORTH WAS ESTABLISHED IN 1985 TO SERVE RESIDENTS IN THE COMMUNITY SURROUNDING SHADELAND AVENUE AND 82ND STREET.

FOUNDED IN 1956, THE ORIGINAL COMMUNITY HOSPITAL WAS RENAMED COMMUNITY HOSPITAL EAST IN 1985.

IN 1989 COMMUNITY HOSPITAL SOUTH, FORMERLY KNOWN AS UNIVERSITY HEIGHTS HOSPITAL, JOINED THE COMMUNITY HOSPITALS ORGANIZATION.

OR TWO YOUNG ADVERTISING PROFESSIONALS, THE IDEA OF OPEN-
ing their own ad agency wasn't simply something to do for money.
It was something to do for adventure. As Stephen Blaising, the
agency's president, will tell you, quoting movie character Forrest
Gump, "Always be able to look back and say, 'At least I didn't lead
no humdrum life.'" ♦ And no one would ever accuse Blaising or

Bob St. Claire of leading a humdrum life. After helping open the
New York office of a large ad
agency in 1984, Blaising opened
the agency's Indianapolis office
in 1986. Three years later, St.
Claire, a Brooklyn native, joined
Blaising as a partner and executive vice president. St. Claire had

tions organizations in the region,
serving clients in the health care,
tourism, sporting goods, food, apparel, building products, and financial industries. In November
1992 they purchased the agency,
and in September 1993 they unveiled the new agency's name.

The new agency's mission is

3) Social responsibility. When
you have powerful tools of persua-
sion at your fingertips, be careful of
which buttons you push."

According to Blaising, "If
you're going to spend eight to 10
hours a day working, then it should
be for something that contributes to
society, rather than something with
a negative impact."

With one look at a Blaising St.
Claire Associates business card, one
can quickly appreciate the agency's
commitment to simplicity and creativity. Printed on the back are
three simple words, "Your idea
here." The inspiration for the
thought was the quote from a theatrical producer who once said, "If
you can't write your idea on the
back of my calling card, you don't
have a clear idea."

THINKING BIG AND GROWING FAST

Guests at the agency are
quickly drawn to the classic,
black-marble plaque that hangs
just inside the lobby entrance. At
the top are the words "What we
stand for and why." Below, it lists
the values and philosophies of
Blaising, St. Claire, and their associates. Included are philosophies
that sound as much like inspira-
tional thoughts for living as they
do ethics for working. Ideas like
"Altitude—Think big. Raise your
horizons. Take the 'what if' approach. Be a brainstretcher . . .
challenge our clients."

The agency's rapid growth
makes it obvious that the "Altitude"
philosophy is more than just a
message of inspiring words on a
fancy plaque. In just a short time,
the agency has managed to build
its business, adding clients like Fruit
of the Loom and Frigidaire to its
roster. The agency's creative efforts
have also proved to hold to the
philosophy of "brainstretching,"

BOB ST. CLAIRE (LEFT) AND
STEPHEN BLAISING (RIGHT) FOUNDED
THE AGENCY IN 1993.

"WE HAVE BEEN QUITE PLEASED
WITH THEIR ENTERPRISING CREATIV-
ITY. WE HAVE A VERY 'FRUITFUL'
RELATIONSHIP."
—ROGER BLANKSTEIN, SENIOR
VICE PRESIDENT OF MARKETING FOR
FRUIT OF THE LOOM.

"THEY HAVE AN EXCELLENT UNDER-
STANDING OF OUR BUSINESS, AND
HOW WE SHOULD BE INTERACTING
WITH OUR CUSTOMERS. WE'VE
FOUND THEIR EYES-FROM-OUTSIDE
VERY HELPFUL IN PLANNING BOTH
OUR BUSINESS STRATEGY AND CREAT-
ING OUR MARKETING PLANS."
—MALCOLM W. APPLEGATE,
PRESIDENT OF INDIANAPOLIS NEWS-
PAPERS, INC.

"THEIR CREATIVE IS EXCELLENT, AND
IT'S BASED ON A SOLID POSITIONING
STRATEGY."
—MARK WILTSE, VICE PRESI-
DENT OF MARKETING FOR SHROCK
CABINET BRAND (A DIVISION OF
FRIGIDAIRE).

"THEY'VE PROVIDED INVALUABLE
MARKETING AND COMMUNICATION
LEADERSHIP, AND THEIR CREATIVITY
AND MARKETING SAVVY HAVE BEEN
GREAT ASSETS TO US IN THESE IN-
TENSELY COMPETITIVE TIMES."
—WILLIAM J. LOVEDAY, PRESI-
DENT AND CEO OF METHODIST
HEALTH GROUP.

entered the advertising business
years earlier when he survived a
baptism of fire in the in-house ad
department of Macy's, where his
responsibilities included magazine
and broadcast supervision.

AN AGENCY BUILT ON PRINCIPLES

Together, Blaising and St.
Claire built one of the fastest-
growing marketing communica-

simply "to create marketing communications solutions, serving the
best interests of our stakeholders,
in accordance with three guiding
principles:

1) Simplicity. 'I love you.'
'Thou shalt not kill.' Clear, honest,
single-minded messages are the ones
people remember.

2) Creativity. New ideas don't
always work. But the lack of an idea
never does.

THERE'S NOTHING LIKE WAITING AN HOUR FOR THAT FIRST NIBBLE TO TEACH A KID THE VALUE OF PATIENCE.

Fishing is more than a sport. It's a passageway into life. So when we leave our favorite fishing hole, we go away with a lot more than a pole and tackle box. We take with us lessons in hope and persistence, as well as respect for the environment. For over forty years, Plano has been a part of this lifelong course in values.

PLANO.

Here's our club's idea of going through rush.

This program is supported by Subaru—The official car of the U.S. Ski Team.

having won many national awards for television, print advertising, and design, as well as radio.

BUILDING PARTNERSHIPS WITH EMPLOYEES AND CLIENTS

The clients of Blaising St. Claire look to the agency for guidance in building brands and protecting the integrity of a brand. "Branding is a long-term commitment," says St. Claire. "The concept of branding does not embrace schizophrenic marketing communications efforts, where one minute the brand's personality is warm and accessible, and the next minute the personality is that of a barra-cuda. Agency people, and clients too, need to remain aware of their responsibility as stewards of a product's brand."

As for the agency's management style, much can be discerned from the name itself. It's not Blaising St. Claire and Associates, because Blaising and St. Claire view themselves as associates. So do the employees, suppliers, and, most notably, the clients.

"Our continued growth is a result of helping our clients," says Blaising. "If we continue to deliver a creative product that helps our clients grow, then we'll enjoy continued growth ourselves. We haven't lost sight that we're in the 'selling' business for our clients."

EACH YEAR, BLAISING ST. CLAIRE ASSOCIATES CREATES PROMOTIONAL MATERIALS FOR THE CHILDREN FIRST BENEFIT BALL (BELOW), AN ANNUAL FUND-RAISING EVENT FOR THREE DIFFERENT CHILD ADVOCACY GROUPS. ENLISTING THE TALENT OF CELEBRITIES—INCLUDING MICHAEL BOLTON, TOM BROKAW, AMY GRANT,

THE CHILDREN FIRST

VAN HALEN, AND SALLY JESSY RAPHAEL—THE AGENCY'S PRO BONO EFFORTS HAVE HELPED RAISE MILLIONS OF DOLLARS FOR THE ABUSED AND DISADVANTAGED YOUTH OF INDIANA.

ONE OF THE INDIANAPOLIS AGENCY'S STRENGTHS LIES IN ITS BROAD RANGE OF CREATIVE STYLES—FROM THIS WARM AND SOFT PRINT AD FOR PLANO (ABOVE LEFT) TO AN AGGRESSIVE, IN-YOUR-FACE APPROACH FOR THE U.S. SKI TEAM (ABOVE RIGHT).

BENEFIT BALL VI

BLAISING ST. CLAIRE ASSOCIATES PRODUCED THIS SUCCESSFUL "REPOSITIONING" SPOT (BELOW, FROM FAR LEFT) FOR THE *INDIANAPOLIS STAR* AND THE *INDIANAPOLIS NEWS.*

Not just something you read. Something you use.

FORTUNE 1000 COMPANY AND ONE OF THE LARGEST MEDICAL device manufacturers in the world, Guidant Corporation offers minimally invasive products that fall within three areas: vascular intervention, cardiac rhythm management, and minimally invasive systems. The company is strongly focused on developing and producing innovative new technologies, increasing the value of clinical procedures, and lowering health care costs. Above all, Guidant is committed to furthering the well-being of patients worldwide who are faced with some of today's most common life-threatening conditions.

Guidant's three business groups are made up of companies that were formerly part of the Medical Devices Division of Eli Lilly and Company. Advanced Cardiovascular Systems, Inc. and Devices for Vascular Intervention, Inc. now form the Guidant Vascular Intervention Group; Cardiac Pacemakers, Inc. and Heart Rhythm Technologies, Inc. are the Guidant Cardiac Rhythm Management Group; and Origin Medsystems, Inc. and the Compass business development unit form the Guidant Minimally Invasive Systems Group. Guidant was incorporated in September 1994 and had an initial public stock offering in December of that year.

The company is headquartered on the 29th floor of an office tower overlooking downtown Indianapolis, but its market presence and strategic vision reach around the globe. With approximately 4,500 employees worldwide, Guidant serves its customers from sales offices in North America, Latin America, Europe, Asia, and Japan and has manufacturing facilities in Puerto Rico, Europe, and the United States.

A PIONEER IN VASCULAR INTERVENTION

Guidant is a worldwide market leader in percutaneous transluminal coronary angioplasty (PTCA)—also known as balloon angioplasty—systems and a recognized leader in the industry. The company pioneered development of PTCA perfusion systems, rapid exchange systems, guidewires, and atherectomy catheters and is a recognized innovator and global leader in minimally invasive cardiology. Guidant offers interventional cardiologists one of the broadest product lines for PTCA and atherectomy systems. These technologies provide less invasive and less expensive alternatives to coronary artery bypass surgery.

PREVENTING HEARTBEAT IRREGULARITIES

Advanced cardiac rhythm management systems from Guidant are today saving the lives of thousands of patients by helping prevent life-threatening heartbeat irregularities with implantable defibrillators and pacemakers. Guidant developed the world's first implantable defibrillator system and the world's first endocardial single-lead defibrillation system, which doesn't require open-chest surgery for implantation. Placement through a vein significantly reduces perioperative mortality,

GUIDANT CORPORATION IS LED BY PRESIDENT AND CHIEF EXECUTIVE OFFICER RON DOLLENS (LEFT) AND CHAIRMAN JAMES CORNELIUS.

THE COMPANY'S WORLDWIDE HEADQUARTERS IS LOCATED IN DOWNTOWN INDIANAPOLIS.

▼ TOM SOBOLIK / BLACK STAR

◄ MCGUIRE PHOTOGRAPHY

shortens patient recovery times, and reduces the cost of the implant.

Tools for Minimally Invasive Surgery

While much of Guidant's product line is centered around the cardiovascular system, another important focus for the company is development of innovative minimally invasive systems and tools that allow surgeons to perform procedures that historically required standard surgery.

For example, Guidant pioneered GASLESS™ laparoscopy technology, a surgical system that distends the abdominal cavity without the use of carbon dioxide and reduces patient recovery time and postsurgery discomfort. A recent product introduction, the Origin Tacker™, is the world's first 5 mm-diameter endoscopic fixation device. It is used for securing prosthetic mesh to tissues in laparoscopic surgery.

Product Innovation: A Key to Continued Success

Research and development is extremely important to Guidant as it continually strives to find ways to reduce the cost and discomfort of medical procedures. The company invests an average of 15 cents of every sales dollar in research and development.

Chairman James Cornelius and President and Chief Executive Officer Ron Dollens credit new product innovations as the key to the company's continued success. The increases in net sales during Guidant's formative stages give further evidence of a bright future. In 1994 the company had worldwide net sales of $862.4 million, a 9 percent increase over 1993 sales. Results for the first half of 1995 were equally impressive.

Responding rapidly to customer needs and forming strong working relationships with the health care community are also integral elements of Guidant's growth. Guidant is a leading sponsor of clinical studies that enable clinical decision making based on

improved data, and the company provides a range of educational materials to help patients understand the procedures they are undergoing.

As it looks to the future, Guidant will continue to be an innovative leader in the medical devices industry by providing novel products and technologies. In all three of its business groups,

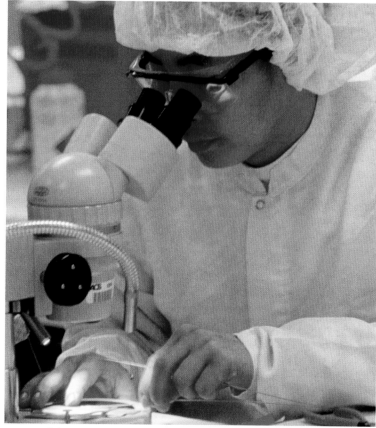

Guidant is at the forefront of the industry movement to help patients, physicians, hospitals, and managed care systems meet the dual goals of improving outcomes and lowering costs. Guidant's ongoing commitment to the medical community and the patients it serves will continue to sustain its innovative spirit well into the next century.

GUIDANT HAS AN IN-HOUSE RESEARCH AND DEVELOPMENT STAFF OF ENGINEERS, TECHNICIANS, AND SCIENTISTS.

GUIDANT'S FIELD FORCE ASSISTS HEALTH CARE PROVIDERS AS THEY UTILIZE THE COMPANY'S TECHNOLOGIES.

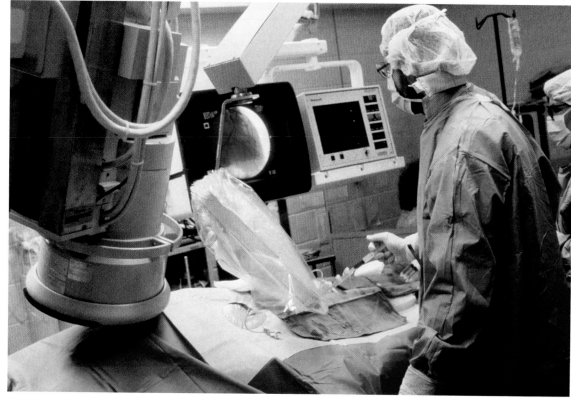

HAUTAUQUA AIRLINES LITERALLY FLEW INTO TOWN OVERNIGHT. When USAir requested that the airline switch routes with one of its fully owned, Ohio-based subsidiaries, Chautauqua obliged. ◆ "It was a turnkey, overnight transition," says Mickey Bowman, Chautauqua's vice president of marketing. "On May 8, 1994, the two airlines literally switched route numbers—airplanes, crew, everything. One carrier moved east, while the other moved west."

According to Aaron Workman, Chautauqua's director of marketing, three other cities courted the company. "We made our decision to move to Indianapolis because of its dynamic economy. It's a growing, regional center," he says.

Operating as a USAir Express carrier, Chautauqua currently flies to 22 cities in 10 states, as well as to Ontario, Canada. With Indianapolis as its regional center, the airline offers nonstop flights to Evansville, South Bend, and Fort Wayne, Indiana; Nashville, Tennessee; Cleveland, Columbus, and Dayton, Ohio; Detroit and Grand Rapids, Michigan; Milwaukee, Wisconsin; Toronto, Canada; and several other cities. In addition to serving the corporate needs of Eli Lilly and Company, Allison Engine Company, and Delco Electronics, Chautauqua offers cargo and passenger charters.

BEGINNINGS OF AN AIRLINE

The company was founded in 1973 by Joel and Gloria Hall

THE AIRLINE'S CUSTOMER SERVICE PROFILE IS OUTSTANDING. IT BOASTS A FLAWLESS SAFETY RECORD, AND ITS COMMITMENT TO PASSENGER COMFORT IS OF UTMOST IMPORTANCE (TOP RIGHT).

OPERATING AS A USAIR EXPRESS CARRIER, CHAUTAUQUA AIRLINES CURRENTLY FLIES TO 22 CITIES IN 10 STATES, AS WELL AS TO ONTARIO, CANADA (BELOW).

when Allegheny Airlines, now USAir, discontinued service to the community of Jamestown, New York. The former Allegheny pilot and his wife reached an agreement with the airline to serve passengers traveling to and from Jamestown, Pittsburgh, and Buffalo. Operating under the name Allegheny Commuter, the company originally had 25 employees and two aircraft.

With a commitment to slow, steady growth, the airline—which now operates 28 aircraft—has chalked up an impeccable record. Its customer service profile is outstanding; it boasts a flawless safety record; and its commitment to passenger comfort is of utmost importance. To date, more than 6 million passengers have flown with Chautauqua.

"Our route network is very different from most commuter airlines," Bowman explains. "We have several routes that exceed 400 miles." Because of these longer flights, the airline offers upgraded cabin services on many of its routes. Complimentary pastries are served on morning flights, while wine, cheese, and fruits are offered at other times.

SUCCESS THROUGH CUSTOMER SERVICE

Excellent customer service has propelled Chautauqua to the height of success and enabled it to become one of the 30 largest scheduled regional airlines in the United States. It also offers benefits frequently found with larger carriers, such as advance seat selection, luggage transfer, and inclusion in USAir's Frequent Flyer program.

To maintain this level of excellence and to better serve customers, Chautauqua began adding Saab 340s to its fleet in 1988. Seating 30 to 34 passengers, these aircraft offer state-of-the-art technology with the conveniences of a jetliner, including comfortable stand-up cabins, ample leg room, wide aisles, overhead storage bins, individual air vents, and reading lights.

"We have a genuine interest in the air-service quality that Indianapolis is going to enjoy over the years to come, and we want to be a large part of that," says Bowman. "We will continue to build service to destinations that have commonality with the city of Indianapolis."

STEVE BAKER, an Indianapolis native, was an Indianapolis 500 staff photographer from 1981 to 1993, when he left that position to work for several corporations involved in the motorsports industry. He currently serves as event photographer for the Circle City Classic and operates his own business, Highlight Photography. Baker is the author of *Racing Is Everything*, a book documenting NASCAR and IndyCar competitions at the Indianapolis Motor Speedway in 1995, for which he also took the photographs. The recipient of a first-place professional photography award from the 1992 Indiana Black Expo Art Exhibition, Baker works with a variety of clients, including Eastman Kodak, Mobil Oil, Budweiser, and the Indiana Sports Corporation.

TIM BICKEL, who holds an associate degree in electrical engineering technology, has attended classes at Winona School of Professional Photography and Indiana University-Purdue University Indianapolis. His work has appeared in *Light and Life, Touring America, Open Wheel, Career World*, and many Indiana newspapers. Previous clients include Indianapolis Mayor Stephen Goldsmith and race car driver Lyn St. James. Bickel is a staff photographer for Eastman Kodak and the codirector of photography for A Diverse Focus, a group that organizes and exhibits its photos in Indianapolis and throughout the state of Indiana.

BRAD W. CROOKS is a photographer working out of Morrison, Colorado.

CHARLENE FARIS, a native of Fleming County, Kentucky, has won numerous awards during her career as a photographer, including several honors from the National League of American Pen Women art shows. Faris was a 1994 Pulitzer Prize nominee for wedding photos of Lyle Lovett and Julia Roberts, which have now been published in 25 different nations. A graduate of Ball State University, she is the owner of Charlene Faris Photos.

MIKE FENDER is a staff photographer for the Indianapolis Zoo.

RICHARD FIELDS, a native of Kokomo, Indiana, specializes in nature, natural history, and editorial photography. Holding a bachelor's degree in natural resources and environmental science, he regularly contributes to such magazines as *Outdoor, Indiana, Audubon, National Wildlife*, and *Nature Conservancy*. A book of Fields' aerial photography, *Indiana from the Air*, will be published in fall 1996. Fields, an active freelance photographer, is currently employed by the Indiana Department of Natural Resources.

AMY HENNING JOBST is a graduate of Chicago's Ray College of Design and has attended Ball State University. Her studio, Henning Jobst Photography, specializes in architectural photography, interiors, exteriors, and landscapes. Jobst produces work for architects inside and outside Indianapolis, and frequently has her photography published in trade journals. She credits her work at Winston Studios in Tucson, Arizona, with sparking her interest in architectural photography.

JOHN KAPKE, a native of Milwaukee, has studied engineering and education at Ripon College, Michigan College of Mining and Technology, and Purdue University. A power equipment service manager for Ace Hardware, he is a freelance photographer within the central Indiana area. Kapke is the current chairperson of the Southport Travel Photo Club, a contributing photographer to the Indiana Department of Natural Resources Shutter Bug program, and an entrant in several photography club contests. Kapke enjoys hiking and outdoor nature photography, and is a member of the Indiana Historical Society, the Conner Prairie Pioneer Settlement, and the Indianapolis Zoo.

HAROLD LEE MILLER, an Arkansas native, specializes in advertising, corporate, and product photography. Holding a bachelor's degree in journalism from the University of Arkansas, his clients include Thomson Consumer Electronics and Conseco, Inc. He has won numerous Addy Awards, as well as many Best of Show awards from the Art Directors Club of Indianapolis. Miller enjoys shooting rural scenes from Arkansas and the Midwest in his spare time.

TERRI QUILLEN, a native of New Orleans, is a self-employed writer, designer, and photo stylist. A registered nurse, she specializes in family celebration and travel photography, though she enjoys many other types of photography. Quillen's photo work has appeared in *Doll World* and *Bridal Crafts*, and she regularly contributes her written work to *Nursing* magazine and other nursing journals. She fondly recalls that her interest in photography was sparked by a dare that her husband made. Quillen owns her own studio, Q.C.C.

DAVID P. SIMS is a photojournalist and portrait photographer who works in a variety of fields. A former stock photographer for Encounter Publications and Charlene Faris Photos, he enjoys wedding, poster, magazine, and custom art photography. Sims has taught darkroom classes at Indiana University-Purdue University Indianapolis and has taken photographs for the Hoosier Lottery. He currently owns and operates Sims Photography, maintaining 10,000 marketable images that can be seen in an array of published works.

STEVE BAKER AT HIS ONE-MAN SHOW AT THE NATIONAL ART MUSEUM OF SPORT ON THE CAMPUS OF INDIANA UNIVERSITY-PURDUE UNIVERSITY INDIANAPOLIS